Access All Eras:
Tribute Bands and
Global Pop Culture

Access All Eras: Tribute Bands and Global Pop Culture

Edited by Shane Homan

Open University Press

Open University Press
McGraw-Hill Education
McGraw-Hill House
Shoppenhangers Road
Maidenhead
Berkshire
England
SL6 2QL

email: enquiries@openup.co.uk
world wide web: www.openup.co.uk

and Two Penn Plaza, New York, NY 10121–2289, USA

First published 2006

A catalogue record of this book is available from the British Library

ISBN 10: 0335 216 900 (PB) 0335 216 919 (HB)
ISBN 13: 978 0335 216 901 (PB) 978 0335 216 918 (HB)

781.63 Hom

Library of Congress Cataloguing-in-Publication Data
CIP data applied for

Typeset by YHT Ltd, London
Printed in Poland by OZGraf S.A.
www.polskabook.pl

Contents

List of contributors

Andy Bennett is Professor in the Department of Communications, Popular Culture and Film at Brock University, Ontario, Canada. He is the author of *Popular Music and Youth Culture: Music, Identity and Place* (2000, Macmillan), *Cultures of Popular Music* (2001, Open University Press), *Culture and Everyday Life* (2005, Sage), editor of *Remembering Woodstock* (2004, Ashgate) and co-editor of *Guitar Cultures* (2001, Berg), *After Subculture* (2004, Palgrave), *Music Scenes* (2004, Vanderbilt University Press) and *Music, Space and Place* (2004, Ashgate). Andy is a member of the International Association for the Study of Popular Music (IASPM) and a former Chair of the UK and Ireland IASPM branch. He is also a member of the British Sociological Association (BSA) and a co-founder of the BSA Youth Study Group. He is a Faculty Associate of the Center for Cultural Sociology at Yale University, an Associate of PopuLUs, the Centre for the Study of the World's Popular Musics at Leeds University, and a member of the Editorial Boards for the journals *Perfect Beat* and *Leisure Studies*. Andy also serves on the International Advisory Board of *The Journal of Sociology*.

Denis Crowdy lectures in guitar studies, Pacific music and music production courses at the Department of Contemporary Music Studies, Macquarie University, Sydney. He has published articles focusing on guitar-based popular music in Papua New Guinea, is involved in various recording projects and currently performs with Torres Strait musician Seaman Dan. He worked at the University of Papua New Guinea's Music Department for eight years in the 1990s.

Shane Homan is a lecturer in media and cultural studies at the University of Newcastle, Australia. He has written widely on Australian popular music, with particular focus upon music industry and cultural policy. He is the author of *The Mayor's a Square: Live Music and Law and Order in Sydney* (2003, Local Consumption Publications, Sydney). He has co-authored commissioned reports on the music and arts industries, notably *Vanishing Acts* for the Australia Council and the New South Wales Ministry of Arts. He is the current General Secretary of IASPM, the International Association for the Study of Popular Music. A rock drummer for over 20 years, he is the co-editor (with Tony Mitchell) of *Popular Music in Australia: Local, National and Transnational*, published by UNSW Press in 2006.

Shuhei Hosokawa, Ph.D., is Associate Professor at the Department of Humanities and Social Sciences, Tokyo Institute of Technology. His publications in English include *Karaoke Around the World: Global Technology, Local Singing* (1998, Routledge, co-edited by Toru Mitsui) and *Salsa no tiene fronteira: Orquesta de la Luz and the Globalization of Popular Music*. He also contributed to two of the books edited by Philip Hayward, *Widening the Horizon* (1999, John Libbey & Co.) and *Off the Planet: Music, Sound and Science Fiction Cinema* (2004, John Libbey & Co.).

Ian Inglis is Senior Lecturer in Sociology at the University of Northumbria, Newcastle upon Tyne. His books include *The Beatles, Popular Music And Society: A Thousand Voices* (2000, Macmillan) and *Popular Music And Film* (2003, Wallflower). His doctoral research considered the significance of sociological social, psychological and cultural theory in explanations of the career of the Beatles. He is a member of the editorial board of *Popular Music and Society*, and his articles have been published in numerous journals, including *Popular Music, Journal of Popular Culture, International Review of the Aesthetics and Sociology of Music, Visual Culture in Britain, American Music, Popular Music and Society* and the *Journal of Popular Music Studies*. He is currently preparing *The Performance of Popular Music: Traditions and Transitions* (forthcoming, Ashgate).

Keiji Maruyama graduated in 2004 from the Tokyo Institute of Technology, and is currently a freelance writer.

Tony Mitchell is a senior lecturer in Cultural Studies at the University of Technology, Sydney. He is the author of *Dario Fo: People's Court Jester* (1999, Methuen), *Popular Music and Local Identity: Rock, Pop and Rap in Europe and Oceania* (1996, University of Leicester Press) and editor of *Global Noise: Rap and Hip Hop outside the USA* (2001, Wesleyan University Press). His is currently editing *Liminal Sounds and Images: Transnational Chinese Popular Music* for Hong Kong University Press.

Guy Morrow is a lecturer with the Department of Contemporary Music Studies at Macquarie University, Sydney. He teaches music production, music theory and arts management and is currently completing a Ph.D. that concerns contemporary music management practices in Australia. He has published articles on a range of topics, including music management, country music in Australia and the music for the opening ceremony of the Sydney 2000 Olympic Games. He is also a drummer and guitarist and has recorded and performed professionally in various contemporary styles. He currently plays in and manages the following bands: Dion Jones & the Filth, Coverdrive and Mood Swing. He previously played drums in the Beach Boys tribute band, the Longboards.

Lutgard Mutsaers is a lecturer, researcher and publicist on popular music and dance culture, and is based at Utrecht University in the Netherlands. Her 1998 thesis, *Beat Crazy*, was a historical study of the impact of the transnational dance crazes the 'twist', 'disco' and 'house' in the Netherlands. She is the author of several books, including *Pop Utrecht* (1987, Matrijs) (30 years of local pop culture in Utrecht); *Rockin' Ramona* (1989, SDU) (the introduction of rock and roll in the Netherlands by Indo-rock bands); *Haring & Hawaii* (1992, SPN) (Hawaiian music and its popular and subcultural manifestations); and *Billie Holiday* (1993, METS) (a personal view on the life and music of a cultural icon). A documentary based on *Rockin' Ramona* (by Hans Heijnen) was nominated Best Documentary Film at the Nederlandse Filmdagen (Dutch Film Festival). She has contributed to academic popular music books and journals both as author, editor and on advisory boards. Her specialist field is Dutch popular music culture of the 20th/21st century. Lutgard worked as a professional musician (bass guitar) in several rock and pop groups in the 1970s and 1980s. In 2002 she worked at Indiana University in Bloomington on a joint project with Professor Dr Portia Maultsby, 'Black American Music in Dutch Culture'.

John Neil is a researcher and lecturer in cultural studies and is currently completing his Ph.D. at the University of Sydney, examining the place of affect in contemporary culture, drawing heavily on the work of the French poststructuralist philosophers Gilles Deleuze and Félix Guattari. He works with both private and public sector organizations and is currently an associate of the Cultural Institutions & Practices Research Centre (CIPS) at the University of Newcastle. He is the author of a broad range of internationally refereed journal articles and co-author (with Stephen Wearing) of an internationally published book: *Ecotourism: Impacts, Potentials and Possibilities* (1999, Butterworth Heineman).

Jason Oakes is a Ph.D. candidate writing about New York City tribute events at Columbia University. In 2004 his article 'Pop music, racial imagination, and the sounds of cheese: notes on loser's lounge' was published in the anthology *Bad Music* (2004, Routledge).

Chris Richards is a senior lecturer in Education Studies at the London Metropolitan University, UK. Previous publications include *Teen Spirits: Music and Identity in Media Education* (1998, UCL Press) and contributions to several edited collections concerned with young people and popular culture. These include *Reading Audiences: Young People and the Media* (1993, Manchester University Press); *In Front of the Children: Screen Entertainment and Young Audiences* (1995, British Film Institute); and *Sound Identities: Popular Music and the Cultural Politics of Education* (1999, Peter Lang). He has also contributed articles to *Screen* and *Screen Education, Changing English, Discourse: Studies in the*

Cultural Politics of Education and *Continuum: Journal of Media and Cultural Studies*.

Holly Tessler is a doctoral candidate and part-time lecturer at the Institute of Popular Music, University of Liverpool. Her Ph.D. research focuses on the concepts of space and place in narrative constructions of the Beatles and Liverpool. Other research interests include music industry studies, media and technology. She is also a part-time lecturer in Media Studies at the Birmingham Institute of Art and Design, University of Central England, Birmingham.

Jesse Samba Wheeler is a Ph.D. candidate in ethnomusicology at the University of California, Los Angeles. His research explores questions of popular music and identity, focusing on Brazilian rock and samba, African pop musics and the zydeco of Louisiana and East Texas. He is also a blues singer, a member of the Los Angeles-based samba band BatUCLAda, where he plays surdo and sings, and a semi-retired DJ. He has been a Portuguese instructor and a teaching assistant for courses in jazz and in the music of South America at UCLA. He has been a visiting scholar at the Universidade de Brasília, Brazil, and the Universidade Federal de Santa Catarina in Florianópolis, Brazil. He has published in the journals *Em Pauta*, *Popular Music* and *Ethnomusicology*.

Acknowledgements

This book derived from earlier work and thoughts about the mixture of media practices and attitudes to nostalgia in many forms, ranging from radio station music formats, to television advertising and the attitudes of various local publicans to live entertainment. I am grateful to Chris Cudmore and Open University Press for allowing this book to air various issues related to the tribute band phenomenon. All the contributors to the book bring different and thoughtful analyses to covers and tributes across a range of sites. Their patience with my endless enquiries, and their enthusiasm for the task was appreciated. This book also provides further evidence of the valuable network that is IASPM, the International Association for the Study of Popular Music.

A note of thanks to Newcastle University colleagues who supported the project, particularly to Michelle Mansfield for her research assistance and Richard Lever for undertaking invaluable work beyond the call of duty. Important research was also undertaken while on study leave in Liverpool, and my thanks to all the staff and students at the Institute of Popular Music who provided their own interesting tales of tribute and cover band experiences. Thanks also to Sarah Baker for her assistance with audience research undertaken in Liverpool, and keeping me sane throughout other research projects.

Finally, as always, I am deeply grateful for the support and wisdom of Justine Lloyd, who has not only been forced to endure a house full of the sounds of drums and guitars, but who has put up with my many discussions of the good, the bad and the ugly tributes that have dominated my thoughts.

Shane Homan

Introduction

Shane Homan

...Well I woke up this morning and dusted my beer
The future is certain
The Australian Doors Show I fear
Jim Morrison IV!
Australian Door!...

Yeah, let me tell you about the New England Highway
And the New South Wales tribute scene
Comes out of an agent's mind!
Cooked!
With a backbeat wide and impossible to get around!
Strange but knowing!
Like some wandering tent show!
Meant to be here!
Way in here!
In the wherever we are...

(Dave Graney, 'Morrison Floorshow' 1995)

Covering and copying

Ten years ago I was struck by my mother's response to a family offer to pay for tickets for her to see Neil Diamond when he was on one of his regular Australian tours. As a long-time admirer, my mother nonetheless wanted to see a local Sydney pub/club Diamond *tribute* performer. She had heard that the approximation of both Diamond's voice and stage mannerisms was uncanny; indeed, 'the next best thing'. A rock fan who had attended many 1970s and 1980s stadium concerts including Rod Stewart, Joe Cocker, Bette Midler *and* Neil Diamond, my mother's changing view about the need to see the original 'Diamond' provoked a range of questions and emotions from me. Given the choice (and the finances), how could my mother possibly prefer the *copy* to the original?

Several years on from my family's discussions of the real Diamond and the local copy, Australian 'indie' performer Dave Graney was confronted by the rise of the tribute act from a very different standpoint. As a performer himself, touring to support the release of his latest album, Graney composed 'Morrison Floorshow' 'in a tour van as we seemed to be following the Australian Doors Show all around Australia' (Graney 1997: 11). The song is a knowing juxtaposition of the tribute phenomenon against local histories, diasporas and geopolitics: 'I imagined singing each line against some classic Doors riffs ... the song uses a lot of Morrisonian stylings ... A poster of the Doors Show outside a venue in the largely Vietnamese Sydney suburb of Cabramatta put my head in a real funk ... Versions of music, versions of Vietnam, versions of Sydney'.

These contrasts between fan and performer perspectives on tribute acts in Sydney raise interesting questions about how tribute acts have evolved, and the varying attitudes towards their success. My mother's desire for the Diamond copy is one small example of the baby boomer rock and roll fan's changing thoughts about and needs from the live music experience, where both the venue and the 'star' are writ small to make for a more comfortable night out. The growth of the tribute band sector signals a significant change in the organization of the live music industries, which in turn reveals broader shifts in the expectations (and ages) of live music audiences. As an original composer who has always existed on the margins of mainstream acceptance, Dave Graney's response to sharing the stage with tributes – part bemusement and part annoyance – reflects a very common reaction within the wider music industry. Yet Graney points to another important aspect of the tribute phenomenon: the interplay of historical imaginings with the contemporary demands of venue managers and audiences, a process which produces very distinct juxtapositions of then and now. In Graney's example, the live tribute performance has the potential to produce a surreal montage of history and performance: a neo-Doors experience relaying the Doors' Vietnam war-era soundtrack in the heart of Sydney's Vietnamese community.[1] The *Australian Doors* show appearing in Cabramatta foregrounds how recorded music and images circulate and reappear in live performance. The tribute band – a remembrance of a remembrance – is therefore one of the most significant examples of the way that live music performance draws on other cultural forms.

The chapters in this book examine both industry and audience perspectives of copying and covering rock and pop stars and genres. In particular, the number of tribute performers has grown markedly in the last decade. While the music cover has been the object of recent study, the tribute act has received little critical attention in popular music or cultural studies. This absence perhaps reveals a scholarly attitude towards tributes similar to that evident within the music industry: neither 'original' or 'authentic', the tribute is not worthy of sustained analysis. The tribute remains in a paradoxical situation, situated at the heart of the suburban live music experience, but remaining 'invisible' within the wider music industry landscape. It is this particular sense of marginality (that is quite different to how the term 'marginal' is understood within popular music and cultural studies) that the writers in this collection wish to examine. Tribute bands occupy a peculiar place within the contemporary music-mediascape. They are the visible Other, omitted from the usual media and publicity machinations: album reviews, performance reviews, television appearances (on mainstream music programmes at least) and press interviews. This invites further examination of the different modes of production and consumption of the tribute that do not correlate with institutionalized (and idealized) discourses that present the contemporary rock and pop star as a package of 'authentic' virtues: self-directed, original and independent of industry standardization.

In different ways and in varying locations, all the chapters address the following key themes:

- *performance:* how the tribute constitutes a 'performance of a performance', and tribute musicians' perspectives towards this construction of rock/pop simulacra;
- *history:* how performers and audiences specifically remember and commemorate stars and eras, and to what extent these texts reinforce or challenge accepted rock/pop historical narratives;
- *audiences:* the role (and role-playing) of fans in the tribute/cover performance, and generational differences in attitudes to the tribute;
- *industry:* the place of covering and copying within wider mediascapes of nostalgia and recycling, and how tributes brand themselves as a distinct product/experience;
- *cultural geography:* the different regional attitudes and legal frameworks to covering and copying, and the role of the western rock/pop canon in non-western music-making;
- *(in)authenticity:* how the tribute challenges the music industry's foundational discourses of the 'authentic' which incorporate specific attitudes to the construction of stardom, stage performances, songwriting and career paths.

As will become clear, copying and covering are not matters of simple imitation, but are practised within more complex cultural systems that govern genres, venues and music history. Live versus recorded reproduction is an important part of industrial, pedagogical and historical discourses within all music genres, both for 'high' and 'low' art music. Classical and pop musicians, for example, are both expected to undertake an 'apprenticeship' that engages them with the iconic examples of their genre. The very different ways this is achieved and emphasized depending upon music genre alerts us to how particular musicians and musics are celebrated and commemorated (or not). For pop and rock musicians, imitation signifies both homage to particular performers, and mastery and deep knowledge of the music genre (and its boundaries). This is manifested within the music industry in a range of ways. For fans, karaoke embodies one form of imitation where the performer's lack of professionalism remains a central part of the 'entertainment'. As observed by Prato (1998: 104, 112), karaoke can be regarded as a 'rock concert where you're the star', with the performance of the person singing standing 'somewhere between games, music, simulation and a community rite'. Karaoke has thus become the public entertainment sphere where enthusiasm for one's rock and pop heroes can unashamedly be displayed.

For those aspiring to even semi-regular employment as a pub/bar cover band musician, however, enthusiasm is not enough. Audiences expect a level of musical competency that enables songs to be recognized; while a bar cover band may bring their own vocal/instrumental inflections to the cover, part of their stock in trade is to enact some form of kinship with the original. Of course, in most cases, not just *any* cover will do: the choice to perform a lesser known Rolling Stones song – 'Continental Drift' from their 1989 *Steel Wheels* album, rather than, say, 'Jumping Jack Flash' (1968) – might not be well received by a Friday night pub audience seeking escape from the workplace. In short, the pub/club/bar cover band, through a variety of repertoires, band line-ups and genres, fulfils a specific commercial function that privileges familiarity over virtuosity.

The cover act can thus be defined as a single musician, or group of musicians that perform a range of others' material, in many instances singling out a particular era or genre for display. These include contemporary top-40 chart performers; blues-boogie acts playing anything from Steppenwolf to ZZ Top; 'the best of' post-war female pop; 1960s 'chart-toppers'; or folk performers ranging across Peter, Paul and Mary and Dylan to Tracey Chapman. Industry – and fans' – understandings of the cover act are in keeping with Griffiths' designation of the main role of the cover to (re)produce 'a straightforwardly faithful version of the original' (2002: 52).

Further, the role of covers has always raised important questions about the discourses of 'art' and 'entertainment' that underline the popular music industry's understandings of itself. By dividing the industry between 'original' composers and copyists, the popular music industry produces a simplistic partition of skills, motives and contexts based on who writes music and who doesn't. Groce (1989), for example, found that the distinction between 'original' and 'cover' was founded upon broader descriptions of the boundaries between 'artist'/'entertainer' by both sets of musicians. While original composers saw themselves as artists *and* entertainers, the same group placed cover musicians distinctly (and disdainfully) in the 'entertainer' box.

These issues continue to circulate in the nightly performance of cover and tribute acts. This book, for the first time, gathers wide-ranging discussions from international scholars on imitation and its role in contemporary music practices from economic, social and cultural perspectives. Underpinning the discussions are the key questions of the commodification of cultural memory, hierarchies of the 'real' and the endurance of the original text. Our main purpose is to lay out a range of theoretical approaches to these questions by investigating specific case studies of performers and scenes. This collection is explorative and hopefully will encourage the reader to reflect on their own enjoyment of and/or distaste towards musical covering and copying. From Bjorn Again to the Illegal Eagles, from Black Stabbath to the Essex Pistols, from the Bootleg Beatles to the Counterfeit Stones, taken together the authors in this book have found that performances of authenticity are implicated in the politics of pleasure and cultural value. There is much at stake in this process, for the careers of musicians, the financial viability of venues and ultimately, the inclusion of iconic performers in the rock/pop pantheon. In their desire to actively participate in a collective remembrance, the tribute fan is deeply implicated in the sense of creative reinterpretation that each individual performance evokes. From the back of the auditorium or pub bar, the fan remains aware of the tensions between the present and past, even as he or she temporarily forgets the layers of reconstruction. Before we can begin to explore the particular ideological and industrial functions of each act in detail, a brief guide to how tributes emerged within the commercial rock/pop live music scenes, and how they are defined, is needed. The next section deals with this history and how circuits of music celebrity work within or against the contemporary range of tribute performers.

The tribute: 'history never repeats'?

The tribute artist or act often plays the same venues as cover bands, particularly at the local bar or pub level, but with a key difference. Tribute acts exclusively perform the recordings of one band or artist, and may even concentrate on a specific period of the artist/group. Many tribute acts operate on a semi-professional basis, with their ability to faithfully recreate songs reflecting their origins as pub and bar cover outfits. Even within the pub circuits, tribute acts are expected to display a sophisticated technical mastery of key guitar/keyboard riffs, drum patterns and vocal delivery. Some may also go to great lengths to recapture the stage appearance and design of the original act, and some bar and club managers (and audiences) prefer those who can also 'look just like' the original. For those tribute acts with an established 'history', the ability to exactly replicate clothes, hairstyles and instruments is mandatory. Their ability to promise venue managers and fans an 'authentic' reproduction (!) has enabled them to bypass the pub circuits and charge premium fees in the larger auditoriums and theatres. Like other live music groups, tribute acts can be found across the range of performance contexts, from those playing for beer in a small local bar, to those engaging in lengthy European and US expeditions, with tour infrastructure akin to multinational bands such as U2.

While now ubiquitous, the tribute concept experienced uncertain beginnings. In Britain, the Counterfeit Stones (established in 1979) and the

Bootleg Beatles (1980) emerged at a very similar time to the Beatnix, who began playing the Perth pub and club circuits in Australia in March 1980. Björn Again was established in 1988 as an Australian pub rock act in Melbourne, with the aim of recreating Abba and the entire 1970s zeitgeist via fashion and sounds; according to one co-founder, 'We were depicting an era' (Leissle interview 2004). British musicians the Bootleg Beatles were created from the US-based musical *Beatle Mania* in 1979:

> We did the stage show ... it wasn't successful at all actually ... at that time, the Beatles could have gotten back together I suppose, so it wasn't really accepted ... and then we [Bootleg Beatles] struggled to get anything going. We started doing student gigs, college balls, men's clubs, and huge tours in quite depressed areas like Newcastle and Scotland ... that was our staple at the start.
>
> (Harrison interview 2004)

Despite international tours, both the Bootleg Beatles and Björn Again transcended the aesthetic and financial limits of the British pub and club circuits where smaller stages and venue capacities resulted in less grand shows and returns. The invitation from Oasis for the Bootleg Beatles to be their support act at Earls Court in 1996 greatly assisted in wider industry approval:

> Because up to that point we weren't taken seriously, certainly not by the rock press and we were also [seen] as a peripheral theatre act, a bit jokey, 'they put wigs on' and all that stuff. Here you get one of the biggest contemporary bands at the time coming up and saying we want you, we've got the choice of anyone ... It was quite a bold move if you think about it because it could have gone terribly wrong ... And then we got the front page of the *NME* [*New Musical Express*], we started getting [the] Glastonbury [festival] ... That Oasis thing was quite nerve-racking; we did Knebworth with nearly 125,000 people, and our little band playing 'She Loves You' on this huge stage.[2]
>
> (Harrison interview 2004)

Nirvana's public endorsement of Björn Again's appearance on the Reading festival main stage in 1992 was equally important to more favourable treatment from within the industry, and grudging acceptance from the 'indie' music press (see Chapter 5).

It is impossible to map the number and range of tribute acts globally. A few examples provide some indication of their popularity. According to the Official International Queen Fan Club, 38 Queen tributes exist in 12 countries, with band titles ranging from the obvious ('We Are Not Queen' in Holland) to the clever ('May Queen' in Germany) (Official International

Queen Fan Club 2004 – www.queenworld.com). The 'world's largest online live music and entertainment booking service', the Alive Network in Britain, lists 64 acts for hire, including 'the New Recruits' (the Village People), 'Lady Madonna' (Madonna), 'Obscure' (the Cure), and 'Once More into the Bleach' (Blondie) (Alive Network 2004 – www.alivenetwork.com). While cover band agencies have been a fixture in rock and pop, booking agencies have emerged that cater exclusively to venues and organizations seeking the imitation, encompassing music eras from the 1940s to the present. A 2004 study of 7000 live music venues in Britain by the publishing body MCPS-PRS Alliance created a 'top ten' list of favoured tribute acts, in highest order: Elvis Presley, Abba, Robbie Williams, Neil Diamond, Queen/Freddie Mercury, Frank Sinatra, the Beatles, Meatloaf, Rod Stewart and the Blues Brothers (Barnes 2004). This list provides a good indication of the tribute as historical project: only four of the original acts are still performing; only one (Williams) did not exist before the late 1990s.

Tributes are rapidly assuming the role of 'proper' entertainment within all sectors of the music industry. Since the early 1990s, some acts have earned more revenue than those in the national charts. In the case of Björn Again, a successful franchise of the original tribute concept now operates, with up to five 'Björn Agains' touring at any one time. Others are regarded as premium entertainment at celebrities' parties and weddings. Tributes have even provided entertainment for the original act: the Australian Pink Floyd Show performed at original guitarist Dave Gilmour's 50th birthday party (Murfett 2004: 8).

With the intentions of tribute ranging from the sincere to the satirical, stylistic differences from and transformations of the original are still important. The main categories can be distinguished by both the object and aim of their reproduction:

- tribute to one band or solo performer (Kisstroyer, Nice Girls, Nowaysis, Gold Zep);
- tribute to a style: Bad Hair Day (80s hair bands from Seal Beach, California); Fabadelic (British invasion, New York); Glambusters (70s Glam rock, Bristol);
- tribute as artistic concept: the Histrionics.

Playfulness with original genres and performers can be invoked without resorting to stage irony, simply by challenging gender formations. 'Gender bender' acts exist that demand spaces for women to imitate their rock heroes: the Iron Maidens (California), AC/DShe (San Francisco), and Exit (U2, Encino, California). Age also brings another mode of performance into play. Using instrumental backing tracks, Li'l G'N'R performs the Guns 'N' Roses repertoire, with the band's ages ranging from 6 to 11 years. A deep engagement with band mythologies and off-stage practices is difficult in this case; as their manager acknowledges, 'It's tricky when you have a six-year-old asking about Slash' (Costa 2004).

Table 1 offers a global snapshot of dominant tribute themes, and similarities according to favoured bands and genres. It also reveals a standardized means of deflecting/anticipating criticism – the use of band title as witticism. Other acts employ satire to more serious ends. The Histrionics bring the tribute sensibility to art, employing a variety of rock standards that heap one simulation upon another:

> The Histrionics' repertoire includes their new single, Drip It, a revision of Devo's Whip It analysing the Abstract Expressionist phenomenon of drip painting identified with Jackson Pollock; AC/DC's classic T.N.T. is reworked as Nam June Paik in celebration of the legendary Korean Fluxus 'grandpa'; The Gridder takes Steve Miller's The Joker as a platform for Carl Andre's response to murdering his wife, artist Ana Mendieta; Pink Floyd's Another Brick in the Wall revisits Richard Serra Tilted Arc controversy in Useless Steel in the Mall; My Sharona by the Knack becomes On Kawara, a meditation upon the methodology of the American/Japanese conceptualist who has devoted his practice to the marking of time. The Histrionics will perform these and other songs from their acclaimed debut album, Never Mind the Pollocks. They will also preview new material from their forthcoming album, Taught to be Mild.
>
> (Artspace 2004)

Tributes are even used to commemorate the spirit of original pop festivals. A variety of Abba, Spice Girls and Queen acts were hired by Lincolnshire Council in 1999 to celebrate the Lincolnshire and Bardney festivals held between 1966 and 1972 that included Joe Cocker, the Faces and Rory Gallagher, and were proud to display new UK acts (Cope-Faulkner and Lane 1999; Heritage Trust of Lincolnshire 2004). As a 'heritage event', the use of tributes seemed distinctly at odds with the earlier festivals' aims. Elvis tributes have been employed to recruit voters (Dean Vegas' 2003 campaign to be Gold Coast Mayor in Queensland, Australia); churchgoers (Reverend Baxter's Anglican services while sporting sideburns in Newmarket, Canada); and tourists (the annual Elvis Revival festival held in the Australian country town of Parkes) (Kornblum 2003; Wilson 2003: 4; Gibson and Connell 2005: 96). For $AUS 7,500 Australian tourists can undertake the 'Tribute to Elvis – USA' tour, a 20-day visit of key sites that culminates in a stop at the annual Tupelo Elvis Festival (Diploma Travel 2004).

Within the tourism industry more broadly the 'need for regular, replicable performances' (Gibson and Connell 2005: 127) often means that tributes are preferred to original acts in providing music entertainment that satisfies global audiences. The Imperial Palace Hotel and Casino in Las Vegas not only

Table 1 The tribute diaspora

Genre	Tribute act	Original act	Tribute location
Jazz	Birdland 55 Yo Miles! (Sky Garden)	Sarah Vaughan Miles Davis	Oakland, US
Post rock	Stereophonies Pirate Radiohead	Stereophonics Radiohead	Essex, UK Chatham, UK
Heavy metal	Paradise City Back Stabbath	Gun 'N' Roses Black Sabbath	Cincinatti, US Austin, US
Country Rock	The Illegal Eagles	The Eagles	UK
Folk rock	Byrds of a Feather 4 Way Street	The Byrds Crosby, Stills, Nash & Young	Woodland Hills, US Los Angeles, US
Country	Shania's Twin Fresh Horses	Shania Twain Garth Brooks	Toronto, Canada Ontario, Canada
Reggae	Australian Bob Marley Show	Bob Marley	Australia
Teen pop	Britney ... One More Time Steps Beyond The J. Lo Show	Britney Spears Steps	Ontario, Canada UK Stoke-on-Trent, UK
Blues	Claptonite Couldn't Stand the Weather	Eric Clapton Stevie Ray Vaughan	Southampton, UK Toronto, Canada
Goth pop	Easy Cure	The Cure	Florence, Italy
Punk	Essex Pistols GGGG	Sex Pistols Green Day	Ibstock, UK New York, US
Prog rock	Emerson, Lake and Palmer Tribute: Fragile Living in the Past Shock the Monkey	Emerson, Lake and Palmer Yes Jethro Tull Peter Gabriel	Mantova, Italy UK Laval, Canada New York, US
Grunge	No Code	Pearl Jam	Ontario, Canada
Alternative	Nimrod's Son Rapid Imitation Movement	The Pixies REM	UK Nottingham, UK
Rap/hip hop	Pop Superstars	P. Diddy	Ontario, Canada
Television bands	Sound Magazine	The Partridge Family	Los Angeles, US
Film bands	Sounds of the Blues Brothers Spinal Pap	Blues Brothers Spinal Tap	Nottingham, UK New York, US

Source: Howard's Tribute Band Heaven and Tribute City websites.

provides nightly 'Legends in Concert' performances; it makes much of its 'Dealertainers Pit' that employs roulette/card dealers who also impersonate Michael Jackson, Cher, Dolly Parton, Ray Charles and Elvis, among others (Imperial Palace 2005). This is perfectly in keeping with the various Las Vegas modes of leisure and cultural production that 'implode artistic periods and forms of entertainment' (Gottdiener *et al.* 1999: 195). The factors examined here – that is the rise of the tribute and its different stylistic forms – point to the ways in which tributes negotiate the structures of the music industry and connect with other cultural industries such as tourism and heritage. It is appropriate to now consider the particular performance spaces and performers that inform this collection. The next section highlights how attitudes towards copying and imitation should be examined through specific and historically contingent pop histories, contexts of local reception and indexes of creativity.

Access all eras: themes and debates

So what are the specific factors that influence the popularity of tributes? As Ian Inglis' chapter points out, given the Beatles' continued presence across all forms of global media, it is not surprising that they remain an extremely popular act of tribute. Inglis reveals how the band's omnipresence in popular culture enables Beatles tributes to be very precise in the construction of individual stage characters, bolstered by audiences well-versed in the Fab Four narrative. Indeed, the level of technical and musical skill displayed by tribute musicians is rarely acknowledged by the wider industry, to the extent that some acts can rightly claim (as some do in this collection) to a more precise rendition of live material than their heroes.

Andy Bennett takes up Inglis' themes of parody and pastiche in Chapter 1 to argue that in an environment of representation, the tribute is a fine example of postmodern spectacle, as audiences place tribute bands within a wide range of music consumption, and where their 'live jukebox' presentation is particularly suited to an ignorance of band member/album chronologies. The resultant simulacrum, argues Bennett, is not only acknowledged as such by audiences, but has become a key referent for emerging fans unfamiliar with the original.

Bennett also raises an obvious and primary rationale for the tribute: its ability to perform in the pubs and clubs that the original act long ago deserted in favour of the stadium experience. The pleasure of the tribute pub night is evident in Chris Richards' analysis of Jimi Hendrix tribute, the Electric Hamsters, in Chapter 6. As the name suggests, the Hamsters satirize some of the foundational discourses of rock: musical virtuosity and flamboyant stage gestures are abandoned in order to seek a proper communal pub experience among predominantly baby boomer fans. The intention of ageing, white pub rockers to concentrate upon the most iconic black blues-rock performer of the 1960s raises interesting questions about the continued circulation of Hendrix mythologies that focus upon heavily stereotyped discourse of black sexuality and masculinity. Stripped of these, Richards shows how bands like the Hamsters can appropriate Hendrix motifs to forge connections with younger blues and heavy metal fans.

Far from the local pub, John Neil investigates Björn Again, the successful troupe of tribute(s) that operate across the festival and theatre circuits of Europe, Australasia and the US.[3] Neil traces the re-emergence of Abba in the early 1990s, in terms of recording sales and media attention, and their belated recognition as innovative pop tunesmiths, that produced the suitable contexts of nostalgia and affectivity for an explosion of tributes. The various Björn Agains provide an excellent example of the franchising of the key textual signifiers of one group for global consumption. As Neil argues, the commercial operations of the band are entirely in keeping with the increasingly themed nostalgic contexts of contemporary cultural production that gain distinct leverage from other packaged reproductions.

Guy Morrow further examines the band-as-brand strategy in the context of the declining number of live music venues in Australia. He provides an interesting insight into the dual role of tribute and original musician, writing as both the drummer of the Longboards, a 1960s Sydney 'beach band', and drummer/manager with Dion Jones and the Filth, an original band seeking national recording success. An increasingly attractive proposition for struggling composers is the strategy of utilizing the success of a tribute/cover act in order to properly finance the marketing, recording and touring costs of an original act. Morrow's chapter raises one of the chief accusations levelled against the tribute musician: that they are 'selling out' their integrity and long-term aims by accepting the wages of the copyist. Instead, Morrow argues from personal experience that the tribute 'apprenticeship' is one means of survival in an industry where the chances of original recording success remain low.

Jesse Samba Wheeler also examines the difficulties live performers face in the context of the tribute and covers scenes of Brazil. His chapter reinforces the nature of the tribute musician as uber-fan, dedicated to precise imitation as the best way to ensure that the 'classic' rock canon endures. The Brazilian musicians in Wheeler's study share the commercial constraints of those in Sydney and elsewhere, where the ability to play in a range of 'authorship' (original), cover and tribute acts is required for commercial survival. Comparisons are made with the 'praise singers' of Africa to argue that contemporary tributes remain important vessels of rock history, mythology and pedagogy.

Keiji Maruyama and Shuhei Hosokawa's chapter examines another important genre of rock history, the 'surf sound' of the 1960s, tracing the impact of the Ventures upon Japanese popular culture memory. They argue that the band was almost single-handedly responsible for the popularity of surf rock in Japan from the late 1960s, and the accompanying explosion of guitar rockers at the time. Some 40 years on, the original teen Ventures fans are again playing 'Wipeout' in collections of amateur tribute groups that assiduously seek the 60s sounds, instruments and techniques of the original. Maruyama and Hosakawa provide an interesting snapshot of how baby boomer audiences and 'Sunday musicians' (to use their term) attempt to reproduce their adolescent music-making for reasons of communal and individual reconciliation with their contemporary place outside rock's obsession with youth.

As I argue in Chapter 4, the tribute fan's reading of the tribute performance involves a layered process of personal music history and media knowledge of the original act within broader knowledge of and attitudes to the entertainment industries. Drawing on interviews with British tribute audiences, the gaps between personal memory and contemporary re-enactment are explored. While audiences may indulge in a shared sense of their distance from the original act, they remain aware of the performative shortcomings of the tribute, and yet see their value as a productive link between different generations of fans and entertainment forms.

Fans also make an important distinction that categorizes bands like Björn Again as *acts of tribute*, as opposed to *tribute acts*. The latter is a derogatory term which has been levelled against ageing rock superstars, such as Pink Floyd's Roger Waters: '... of course with quality musicians, Waters can and does replicate that [Pink Floyd] sound. But then so can any good cover band. And that's what this concert often felt like: note perfect nostalgia rather than an emotional experience for either band or audience' (Zuel 2002: 13).

The denigration of the tribute band phenomenon thus reflects a problem of the demand for constant innovation and eternal youthfulness for original acts as well. As one of their early collaborators and backers, Georgio Gomelsky believed the later, globally-branded Rolling Stones 'had no business going into the [stadium] arena ... [they] Might as well have hired mimes and put records on' (cited in Strausbaugh 2001: 79). For groups with lengthy recording and performance careers, the accusation of becoming tributes to themselves is a constant threat, particularly as they become increasingly distanced from the original contexts of their earlier creative moments. The criticism that copyists 'learn, retain and perform on demand' (Groce 1989: 395) can be equally applied to 'original' composers and performers.

Tributes challenge the traditional music industry discourses of stardom that invoke the unique characteristics of the successful rock/pop composer. Jason Oakes examines how the astounding number of imitators of Elvis Presley ('Elvii') impact upon contemporary constructions of the Elvis iconography, arguing that the multiple readings of impersonation strengthen, rather than weaken, the Presley mythologies.[4] Yet the Elvis copy has been reduced to a handful of signifiers (white jumpsuit, lip curl, finger jewellery etc.) to the extent that many shun the 'impersonator' label in favour of 'tribute artist'. Oakes argues that impersonators such as the 'Mexican Elvis', El Vez, provide meaningful interventions in the Presley narrative. In El Vez's hands, the cycle of repetition and unreflective imitation is broken in favour of an appropriation that directly confronts contemporary class, race and global politics.

Holly Tessler examines how Beatles tribute acts circulate as an integral part of Liverpool's heritage circuits, in a city that has leveraged its Beatles and Merseybeat legacy as a unique form of city branding. Drawing attention to the layered forms of music simulacra at the centre of Liverpool's tourist strategies, Tessler argues that the role of the tribute remains in contestation with city planners' desires to encourage 'high' forms of cultural activity in keeping with its designated 'Capital of Culture' status in 2008. Tessler's chapter echoes the industry tensions depicted in other chapters, where tribute acts thrive while the venues for original bands are lost to other forms of urban redevelopment. In this particular case, the tribute act stands at the intersection of competing economic demands and changing cultural values.

Lutgard Mutsaers explores a very different combination of commercialism and music history in her account of the Marlboro Flashback tours organized in the Netherlands in the mid-1990s. The tours were a mixture of faithful renditions and satire that provided tobacco manufacturer Philip Morris with a useful means to reach youthful audiences. Despite its commercial backing, the enterprise provoked interesting combinations of acts and tribute choices. It also provided the context for one original band to decide to reform after witnessing the success of the tribute. As with the Morrow and Wheeler case studies, the chapter canvasses the Faustian nature of career choices; that is, the extent to which tributes and cover careers should overshadow original songwriting ambitions.

Mutsaers' study also shares the concerns of Maruyama and Hosokawa, about how the dominant canon of western rock and pop performers circulate outside the core industrial centres of the US and the UK. Tony Mitchell analyses the 'Mandapop' and 'Cantopop' phenomenon and its recent history of adapting western pop hits for eastern consumption. This chapter focuses upon the unique career of Faye Wong, and the varying intensity of her collaborations with and copies of various western performers. Wong offers a contemporary model of the Chinese opera tradition of *tian ci* that combines new lyrics with pre-existing melodies. Mitchell outlines how the music cover operates within quite distinct understandings of lyrical and musical appropriation, providing an example where the 'faithful rendition' of the western tribute act is meaningless within an industrial context of deeply individual stylization.

Denis Crowdy offers another environment of distinct adaptation in his examination of the 'kopicat' culture of Papua New Guinea. Here the music cover is highly localized to reflect individual and collective stories and events.

A distinctive set of local subgenres provides a framework for the extent of lyrical and musical revision, with decisions about the retention of English an important choice for local reception. Crowdy argues that western notions of the pop/rock canon are thus all but redundant. The *laissez-faire* copyright environment that exists in Papua New Guinea is founded upon a lack of policing mechanisms and multinational recording company infrastructure, and the view that all songs exist within a broad public domain for local modification.

The contexts of use of tributes and covers are significant within an industry that privileges originality for a variety of cultural and commercial reasons. In Chapter 2, I consider a few of the legal frameworks where the original artist or group has been concerned with aspects of the imitation. Acts can themselves pre-empt/satirize the possibility of a tribute, as Silverchair did, performing as the Australian Silverchair Show in Newcastle, Australia (Apter 2003: 161). As John Neil (Chapter 5) points out, the original act's 'affective imprimatur' bestowed upon the tribute is highly sought by the imitation, not the least because it forestalls any legal objections. Many tributes argue for their marketing value throughout this collection, realized in ongoing album sales of the original. Chapter 2 also considers the views of some well-known tribute musicians. Their often defensive responses can be understood within a wider industrial landscape in which they must continually justify their existence. In some cases, the formation of the tribute has been a response to a shared sense of a general decline in the quality of rock and pop compositions, and a belief that the 'authentic' canon must be preserved. This is both a generational and aesthetic divide that produces 'histories of perfection'. The tribute phenomenon reflects processes of recycling and reinterpretation in which, as Andy Bennett (Chapter 1) argues, both audiences and bands engage in intertextual meaning.

Various postmodernist arguments posit a contemporary era where 'history' and 'authenticity' have disappeared under the weight of instantaneous simulacra. As this collection demonstrates, the imitation exists for many different reasons, and in many music industry environments. At their worst, tributes seem to belong to a new era of musical Fordism, part of an assembly line of unreflective, model-kit acts that flatten pop and rock history to a series of shiny surfaces. At their best, they offer a practical means for audiences and musicians to begin thinking about not only how particular stars and songs are reproduced, but how they are constantly re-engaged and re-interpreted in many media contexts.

This anthology does not therefore privilege either the 'original' or the copy, but seeks to understand contemporary thinking about pop and rock history as it is performed on a nightly, global basis. This involves engaging with the contradictory discourses of authenticity that continue to drive the marketing and consumption of all popular music. The ability of the tribute to ensure that history is endlessly repeated, as 'heritage' acts of a particular kind, must always be set against questions of *why* the tribute is offered, *how* it is performed, and *whose* historical narrative is privileged. The highly localized ways of thinking about stardom, signs and meanings offered here may present new ways to discuss the performance of a 'contemporary past'.

Notes

1   Popular culture since the 1960s has long associated psychedelic rock dirges with the American presence in Vietnam, and even as the soundtrack to battle sequences in many Hollywood films.
2   The Oasis–Bootleg Beatles tour can be considered as commercially and ideologically astute. The support act, aspiring to open celebration of the Beatles, was followed by a group that had been accused of ransacking the entire Beatles 'structure of feeling' for contemporary audiences.
3   The stage photo for the cover of this book is that of the UK version of Björn Again.
4   The 'Elvis' industry predates the new coalition of tribute agencies. There were an estimated 3000 Elvis impersonators in 1992 (Rodman 1996: 6); in 1999, Lott believed that up to 20,000 'Elvii' were in circulation (cited in Doss 1999: 158). A core strength of the Elvis narrative has been his rise from poor origins (Rodman 1996); yet the white rhinestone, jump-suited 'Vegas Elvis' remains the favourite era for most impersonators (Doss 1999).

References

Apter, J. (2003) *Tomorrow Never Knows: The Silverchair Story*. Port Melbourne: Coloumb Communications.

Artspace (2004) Sound and New Media Performance: www.artspace.org.au/2004/06/histrionics.html (accessed 6 October 2004).

Barnes, A. (2004) Start spreading the news: bogus Beatles lose out to fake Frank, the Independent online, http://enjoyment.independent.co.uk, accessed 3 December 2004.

Cope-Faulkner, P. and Lane, T. (1999) *'The Nice People Are Here': Pop Festivals in Lincolnshire*. Heckington: Heritage Trust of Lincolnshire.

Costa, M. (2004) Welcome to the jungle, the *Guardian*: www.guardian.co.uk/arts/features/story/0,11710,1170762,00.html (accessed 8 November 2005).

Diploma Travel (2004) *Tribute to Elvis – USA*. Sydney: Diploma Travel.

Doss, E. (1999) *Elvis Culture: Fans, Faith & Image*. Kansas: University Press of Kansas.

Gibson, C. and Connell, J. (2005) *Music and Tourism: On The Road Again*. Clevedon: Channel View Publications.

Gottdiener, M., Collins, C. and Dickens, D. (1999) *Las Vegas: The Social Production of an All-American City*. Oxford: Blackwell Publishers.

Graney, D. (1997) *It Is Written, Baby*. Milson's Point, Sydney: Random House.

Griffiths, D. (2002) Cover versions and the sound of identity in Motion, in D. Hesmondhalgh and K. Negus (eds) *Popular Music Studies*. London: Arnold.

Groce, S. (1989) Occupational rhetoric and ideology: a comparison of copy and original music performers, *Qualitative Sociology*, 12(4): 391–410.

Heritage Trust of Lincolnshire (2004) *Heritage News – Bardney Festival 1999*: www.lincsheritage.org/news/bardney/festival.html (accessed 24 November 2004).

Imperial Palace (2005) *Dealertainers*: www.imperialpalace.com/entertainment.php?subid=5 (accessed 15 February).

Kornblum, J. (2003) This Elvis says he's doing work of king of kings, *USA Today*: www.usatoday.com/life/2003–01–06-elvis_x.htm (accessed 25 October 2004).

Murfett, A. (2004) Cover stories, *The Age*, www.theage.com.au, accessed 3 December 2004.

Prato, P. (1998) From TV to holidays: karaoke in Italy, in T. Mitsui and S. Hosokawa (eds) *Karaoke Around the World*. London: Routledge.

Rodman, G. (1996) *Elvis After Elvis: The Posthumous Career of a Living Legend*. London: Routledge.

Strausbaugh, J. (2001) *Rock Til You Drop: The Decline from Rebellion to Nostalgia*. London: Verso.

Wilson, A. (2003) It's now or never for King of Coast, *The Australian*, 27 March: 4.

Zuel, B. (2002) Note perfect but non-emotional, *The Sydney Morning Herald*, 8 April: 13.

Discography

Dave Graney and the Coral Snakes (1996) *The Soft 'n' Sexy Sound*. Universal Music.

PART 1
INDUSTRIES AND AUDIENCES

1 Even better than the real thing? Understanding the tribute band phenomenon

Andy Bennett

One of the defining characteristics of popular music performance since the rock 'n' roll explosion of the mid-1950s has been 'imitation'. Throughout ensuing decades, the hits of the day have been slavishly reproduced or 'covered' by local bar and pub bands in cities and towns throughout the world. In more recent years, this desire to imitate has taken on a significant new dimension in the form of the 'tribute band'. Unlike cover bands, tribute bands often go to great lengths to capture the 'authentic' sound and, in many cases, visual image of the tributed band or artist. Tribute bands now cover the spectrum of post-Second World War popular music, with tributed acts ranging from the Beatles, the Rolling Stones and the Doors, through Genesis, Pink Floyd, Abba and the Eagles to more recent acts such as Oasis and Nirvana. There is also a growing trend towards solo tribute acts, both for contemporary popular music artists, such as Elvis Presley, Rod Stewart and Neil Diamond, and those from earlier periods, for example, Frank Sinatra and Dean Martin. While some tribute bands play only in local venues (see e.g. Bennett 2000) others are major touring concerns, their shows featuring lighting rigs, special effects, large PA (public address) systems and all the other trappings that one associates with a headline rock or pop act. Moreover, in a number of cases, a tribute band has received material endorsements from the tributed act. For example, the Montreal-based Genesis tribute band Musical Box, whose stage show comprises purely Peter Gabriel era material, were fortunate enough to receive a donation from Gabriel of original stage props and backdrop effects used by Genesis in their live performances circa 1973.

From a sociological point of view, tribute bands are a highly interesting phenomenon. On the one hand they have a distinctly postmodern character, the ultimate goal of the tribute band being to produce a perfect simulacrum of the tributed act. On the other hand, through their reworking of performances by groups who are either long since defunct, or who tour infrequently and generally perform only in large auditoriums, tribute bands respond to a range of mundane, everyday desires exhibited by audiences: to relive a particular moment in their youth; to experience again their personal icons in a live setting (and perhaps take their children along too); to engage in the rapport between performer and audience deemed integral to the communicative quality of popular music. This chapter considers some of these aspects of tribute bands and, in doing so, attempts to account for the ongoing success and appeal of the tribute band phenomenon.

Tribute bands and postmodernism

At one level, the tribute band phenomenon can be linked to what many theorists have described as the 'postmodern turn' (Best and Kellner 1997). According to a leading exponent of postmodernist social theory, Jean Baudrillard (1983), a centrally defining characteristic of the postmodern era is the dominance of simulacra. The term 'simulacra' refers to the simulation of objects, a process which has been accentuated through the dominance of media representations in contemporary society (Stevenson 1995). Everything, from works of art to significant historical sites and aspects of national culture is now experienced at the everyday level as a series of simulations. Integral to the process of simulation is the loosening of objects from their original meanings, or at the very least the possibility of a more malleable relationship between object and meaning. As MacCannell and MacCannell observe: 'The *simulacrum*, by definition and by contrast, can exist with reference to anything, even other simulations, and therefore has no particular relationship to the real' (1993: 131–2). To put this another way, reality has given way to simulated representation to the extent that representation has become, in itself, a reality for citizens of postmodern society. This argument is supported by Lash (1990: 24) through his observation that: 'We are living in a society in which our *perception* is directed almost as often to representations as it is to "reality". These representations come to constitute a very great proportion of our perceived reality. And/or our perception of reality comes to be increasingly by means of these representations'.

Lash's comments have a distinct resonance with certain qualities associated with the tribute band. The art of the tribute band involves creating as perfect as possible a representation of the tributed act. Many tribute bands go to great lengths to achieve this, both musically and visually. In some cases this involves seeking out vintage guitars, amplifiers and electronic effects, or having them specially built in order to capture the 'authentic' sound of the tributed act. Moreover, in many cases individual members of tribute bands attempt to emulate as closely as possible the image and persona of the musician they are portraying. Where a tributed act has a prominent front-person, the individual assuming this role will work particularly hard to 'be' that person, often perfecting his/her onstage posturing, and in many cases popular onstage phrases, the latter being learned verbatim by repeated listening to live albums and/or viewings of film and documentary footage of the tributed act.

As Jason Oakes suggests, through such emulative techniques, tribute bands 'try to capture [the tributed act's] essence' (1995: 1). This involves studiously identifying those aspects of the tributed act that make it unique and perfecting its re-creation to the extent that a tribute band can pass itself off as 'the real thing'.

The success of the tribute band in achieving this aim is of course also highly dependent upon the willingness of the audience to buy into and go along with the 'trick of illusion' that the tribute band attempts to stage. The issue of audience reception also needs to be set in context. As noted above, tribute bands have assumed their place in a world where the replication and reproduction of objects and images is increasingly taken for granted and largely perceived as 'normal'. This is particularly striking in the case of popular music where, in addition to tribute bands, a range of television shows, such as *Pop Idol* and *Stars In Their Eyes*, feed an apparently inexhaustive desire on the part of audiences for rock and pop impersonators. However, a question might be asked as to why it is specifically popular music that has become the object of tribute acts. Certainly, other aspects of contemporary popular culture, notably sport, are now the focus of a 'lookalike' culture, demonstrated by the growing industry for imitators of sports personalities such as David Beckham at parties, weddings and other social functions. In the case of the tribute band, however, it is not 'just' the individual personality, or rather the latter's representation, that provides the spectacle. Indeed, when seen close up, tribute band artists may not look that much like the artists they portray (and in some cases tribute bands consciously avoid attempting to copy the image of the tributed act altogether). Rather, the key ingredient of the tribute band and its success is the authentic reproduction of the music. Arguably, the appeal of the tribute band formula has everything to do with the way audiences respond to popular music and tribute bands' understanding of this response. As a primary form of 'youth' leisure and entertainment during the 1950s, popular music was initially the most systematically commodified form of mass produced, post-war popular culture. Certainly, with the progression of time, popular music has given rise to its own taste cultures whose canonical discourses are often at least as elaborate, in terms of their justification for consuming particular objects and artefacts, as those used by connoisseurs of 'high' culture (Frith 1996). Indeed, one might go as far as to argue that, in mobilizing such discourses to separate out the good from the bad, the authentic from the inauthentic, certain popular music audiences engage in a process of 'aurification' (Benjamin 1973). One need only think of how, during the 1970s, 'serious' music fans held progressive rock groups, such as Genesis, Yes and Emerson Lake and Palmer in high esteem because of their technical ability and virtuosity, while rejecting top-20 orientated pop groups such as the Bay City Rollers, for their allegedly unashamed commercialism. Progressive rock groups commanded their own particular kind of aura. Fans of these groups engaged in an almost ritualistic form of fanship which involved the 'correct' displays of musical appreciation and a knowledge about the musical backgrounds and technical abilities of the musicians involved.

However, as Frith and Horne (1987) observe, while progressive rock groups were highly revered by their fans, at the same time they were subject to exactly the same processes of commercialization as those regarded as being at the bottom of the artistic ladder. Irrespective of the particular discourses of authenticity that fans may attach to their icons, the latter are ultimately consumed as 'products' (Negus 1992). Moreover, as Frith (1988) notes, fans do not form direct relationships with rock and pop stars, but rather understand and articulate this relationship through the medium of their music and image. It is this quality of post-1950s popular music – the mechanical re-production of its sounds, and the packaging of its stars – that has primed audiences for the tribute band experience. Already used to treating recorded sounds and mediated images as the primary text (Moore 1993), from the point of view of the audience it could be argued that tribute bands are merely another medium for the enjoyment of their favourite music. The audience realizes that the tribute is not the 'real thing', but this is not the point. For decades, records, tapes and videos have had to stand in for the original. Tribute bands follow this pattern of standing in for the original, but with the added novelty of the flesh and blood dimension which they bring to the reproduction of the music. In many ways, tribute bands are, to paraphrase Bob Geldof's definition of his 1985 Live Aid event, a 'live jukebox', showcasing the hits and other old favourites from the tributed act's back catalogue with the added appeal of a concert atmosphere.

All around the world

The global ubiquity of the tribute band phenomenon also lends itself to a postmodern interpretation. Bands tributing a variety of artists from each era of post-Second World War popular music history can now be found in major cities around the world. As previously stated, for Baudrillard (1983) a key manifestation of postmodernism's representational affect is the ever intensifying global flow of images, with the image taking priority over the original artefact. For example, although a minority of people may have visited the Taj Mahal, or the pyramids of Egypt, through their appropriation by the media the images of these buildings have come to be known and instantly recognizable throughout the world. Moreover, the imagery and design of these and other buildings have been endlessly replicated in public spaces such as restaurants, shopping centres and theme parks. Eco (1987) argues that this increasing emphasis upon replication has led to a transformation of reality into 'hyper-reality'. As Smart observes, the hyper-real has effectively dissolved the boundaries between 'true' and 'false', reality and reproduction, creating 'a spatio-temporal haze where virtually everything appears present' (1993: 53).

The tribute band phenomenon fits well with Smart's description of a postmodern landscape in which the real and the hyper-real blur into one. An often cited explanation for the origins of the tribute band phenomenon is that it began as a response to the perpetual 'unavailability' of original acts in particular parts of the world (see Chapters 2 and 5). Many rock and pop acts, although having attained a global audience, may tour infrequently, and a tour of any given country on the international circuit may extend only to a few large venues. Thus, opportunities for fans to see a favourite group or artist are in many cases limited, both due to ticket availability and cost. Tribute bands effectively fill this void by providing an opportunity for fans to see authentic simulations of their favourite artists in a live context. In such instances, a tribute band's replication not only stands in for the 'real thing'; it frequently becomes a primary referent for the audience.

Playing with time

One further aspect of the tribute band phenomenon with a distinctly 'postmodern' edge is the often evident 'disrespect' displayed by tribute bands for chronological continuity. According to Redhead (1990), popular music is, by its very nature, a postmodern form due to its disruption of linear time. Pop time, argues Redhead, is 'circular', a feature that is most readily observed through the continuous re-emergence of music and related styles of clothing in a continuous cycle of pop-revivalism. Tribute bands add a significant new dimension to this process. In the course of tribute band performances, dead rock stars are brought back to life, defunct bands are reassembled, and classic live performances of yesteryear are accurately reproduced again and again. Moreover, in revisiting a tributed group or artist's recording and performing history, tribute bands are in the privileged position of being able to creatively play around with that history and will often do so to present an idealized version of events. The following examples illustrate this point. The world renowned Beatles tribute band the Bootleg Beatles perform a cross-section of material from the entire Beatles' back catalogue. This includes songs from post-*Revolver* albums which were never performed live by the Beatles themselves, the group having retired from live performance following their concert at San Francisco's Candlestick Park in August 1966 (Giuliano 1992). Indeed, some of the later Beatles' songs performed by the Bootleg Beatles, notably material from the 1967 *Sergeant Pepper's Lonely Hearts Club Band* album, were deemed to be irreproducible in a live context at the time of their release (see Martin and Hornsby 1979). Being in a position to reproduce this music, using state of the art digital effects to create the brass and string parts, together with other sound effects heard in later Beatles' songs, the Bootleg Beatles cut through such accepted historical narratives, presenting instead the show that members of the audience 'want to see'.[1] For example, during their national

Figure 1.1 The Bootleg Beatles playing material from the 1967 *Sergeant Pepper's Lonely Hearts Club Band* album, with orchestral backing

UK tour of 2002, the spotlight trained on 'Bootleg John' as he sang 'A Day in the Life' (the closing track from *Sergeant Pepper*), complete with his pastel green Sergeant Pepper bandsman's uniform and seated at the trademark white grand piano.[2]

Three years earlier, the Bootleg Beatles had recreated the Beatles' legendary 'rooftop' concert at 3 Saville Row, formerly the headquarters of the Apple Organisation. Held to mark the 30th anniversary of the original rooftop concert, the Bootleg Beatles played an entire set to the delight of the crowd. The Beatles' original concert, as depicted in the 1970 film *Let It Be*, had to be cut short part way through the song 'Get Back' following an intervention by the police who were concerned about the traffic congestion caused by the large numbers of people that had gathered in the streets below to listen. As with the live rendition of 'A Day in the Life', prior to the Bootleg Beatles' performance, the complete rooftop concert had existed only in the imagination of Beatles' fans. Through the hyper-reality of the Bootleg Beatles' re-creation of the event, however, this particular fan fantasy was brought dramatically to life.

To cite a further example of how tribute bands use their creative licence to rework pop history, the Rolling Stones tribute band the Counterfeit Stones perform a selection of music from the complete Rolling Stones' back catalogue. During the course of their career, the Rolling Stones have had three different lead guitarists: Brian Jones, Mick Taylor and Ronnie Wood.

Although the Counterfeit Stones perform songs originally featuring each of these respective musicians, until quite recently the lead guitar was played throughout by 'Bryon Jones', a band member posing as original Rolling Stones' lead guitarist Brian Jones. At a pragmatic level, the inclusion of 'Bryon Jones' for the whole of the performance helps retain a sense of continuity. Replicating the series of Rolling Stones' line-up changes over the course of a two hour stage performance, with one band member periodically changing identity, would disrupt the flow of the performance both temporally and visually. However, the omnipresence of Bryon Jones also works at an aesthetic level. For many Rolling Stones fans, the line-up featuring Brian Jones marks a time when the group released their best songs, and were at their best musically. Similarly, what are now regarded as the 'classic' Rolling Stones publicity shots, and those which established the group's reputation as rock icons, are the ones taken during the mid-1960s prior to Jones' departure from the group and subsequent untimely death.[3]

Thus far, I have been concerned to address those qualities of the tribute band phenomenon that most closely align with alleged characteristics of postmodern affect. There are, however, a further set of issues that need to be examined in relation to why tribute bands have become such a popular form of entertainment over the last 20 years. I have already noted how part of the appeal of the tribute band phenomenon relates to its feeding the audience's desire to experience again the spectacle of their favourite artists in a live setting and, in some cases, to have particular unfulfilled dreams regarding these artists brought to life. I have also noted how a major part of the tribute band's success rests on the willingness of the audience to go along with the 'trick of illusion' that the tribute band performs. At the same time, however, tribute bands bring their own particular performative conventions to the live concert experience as a means of drawing the audience into the event, which I will now consider.

Small is beautiful

While the level of success achieved by some tribute bands is such that they now attract a considerable audience and thus play primarily in larger venues, many tribute bands continue to play in small clubs and bars. In certain cases, a tribute band performing in a small venue can seem anomalous, particularly when the act they tribute would generally perform in much larger venues. For example, in the course of researching the Benwell Floyd, a Pink Floyd tribute from the city of Newcastle upon Tyne in the North East of England, I attended one of the band's concerts at a workingmen's club in a small village in County Durham. On entering the club, just prior to the band's soundcheck, I was struck by the amount of instruments, sound and lighting equipment and stage props crammed onto the small stage (see Bennett 2000). As the performance got underway, however, it became evident that the compact nature of the venue facilitated a sense of intimacy, and thus an easy interaction, between the band and its audience. In this respect, there are clear comparisons between the tribute band phenomenon and the British pub rock scene of the early 1970s. Central to the pub rock ethos was an emphasis on small-scale, accessible live music performance in contrast to the growing trend towards stadium rock. As Laing (1985: 8) observes: 'The size of the bar-room allowed for, even insisted upon, the intimacy between musicians and audience [that pub rock bands] believed was somehow essential for meaningful music. Pub rock's stance implied that things went wrong for bands when they became superstars and "lost touch" with their original audiences.'

While most tribute bands do not share the reactionary stance of the pub rock scene, the chemistry underpinning tribute band performances is equally reliant on the creation of an intimate relationship between performance and audience. Perhaps the primary difference is that pub rock bands challenged stadium rock, not only ideologically but also musically, and prided themselves on performing simply arranged three-minute songs in contrast to the musically complex, and often elongated, songs of stadium rock bands (see Bennett 2001). In contrast, tribute bands span the whole spectrum of post-1950s popular music, including those stadium rock artists so despised by the pub rock movement. For some rock 'purists', the notion of a tribute band remaking the music of stadium rock giants such as the Eagles, Genesis or Pink Floyd in a local bar may seem repulsive. And yet for many members of the audience, the success of a tribute band in transcending the 'epic' quality of stadium rock appears to form part of the appeal of the tribute band formula. By taking stadium rock and performing it in small, accessible, local venues, tribute bands effectively bring this music 'home' for their audience. Although the gravitation of many rock and pop stars to the stadium (or, to use current parlance, arena circuit) may have suited the commercial incentives of the music industry, it has not uniformly been to the liking of music fans. Having shared in the excitement of early live performances in smaller local venues, fans of the more successful rock and pop artists saw their icons become bigger and more remote, in some cases becoming casualties of rock excess. Thus, for many fans, tribute bands present something of a 'return to form', turning the rock process full circle by bringing the music back into smaller, more intimate and accessible venues. Indeed, as a member of the Benwell Floyd observed on one occasion, people in the band's audience had openly expressed their preference for Benwell Floyd concerts over Pink Floyd concerts because of the intimate atmosphere. The band member continued:

> Wherever we go there's always a core of people there who we know and vice versa. But I also think it's how we're doin' it . . . I mean, I like Pink Floyd a lot, but there's this thing you know, you're shelling out

a load of money to watch four dots on a stage half a mile away. What
we're doing is accessible ... it's there like ... for people to see.

(Bennett 2000: 176)

In addition to lending intimacy to tribute band performances, smaller
venues have the added attraction of charging more affordable ticket prices
and being situated in easy to reach locations. The relatively low-key, affordable and accessible nature of tribute band performances has also made them
highly popular among family groups. Cohen (1991) and Bennett (2000) have
each noted the significance of popular music in parent–children relationships, with children often inheriting tastes in music directly from their parents. Moreover, such shared musical tastes may form the basis for other
aspects of kin relations, with parents and children listening to music together
and collectively discussing the meaning of lyrics, and so on. Such discussions
may in turn lead to parents sharing particular music-related stories with their
children, for example, seeing Jimi Hendrix perform at the 1970 Isle of Wight
Festival, or queuing for hours to buy tickets for a Led Zeppelin concert. In an
age where such conventions of music fandom have been displaced by
breakthroughs in television broadcasting, dedicated music channels and in-
ternet ticketing services, such stories may seem even more magical from the
point of view of children for whom music of all kinds is now available quite
literally at the touch of a button. Tribute bands thus provide an ideal, and in
some cases exclusive, opportunity for parents to take their children along to
experience in a live context the music they share and talk about at home.

Sharing the joke

Another device used by tribute bands as a means of connecting with their
audience is the use of humour. Although the tribute band performance is
ultimately about reproducing the music and onstage persona of the tributed
act, there is often scope for the use of humorous asides. Even among those
tribute bands who have achieved higher levels of success, necessitating that
they play in venues with a capacity of several thousand, a level of rapport
with the audience is maintained through the injection of humour into the
performance. For example, during a Bootleg Beatles performance which I
attended in 1999, part way through the band's set Bootleg John suddenly
broke into the opening bars of 'Imagine' on the piano, before stopping
abruptly and exclaiming, 'oops, I haven't written that one yet!'. Similarly,
during a Counterfeit Stones concert, lead singer Nick Dagger noted on several
occasions how well Bryon Jones had done to learn 'all the new songs'
(meaning those songs written and performed after Brian Jones' departure
from the Rolling Stones). In addition to adding to the entertainment value of
a tribute band's performance, such devices, drawing as they do on elements of

satire, function as important role-breaking moments. Although the primary function of the tribute band is to replicate the object of its tribute as accurately and 'authentically' as possible, it is important that tribute bands do not overstep the mark in this respect. Tribute bands gain the adulation of the audience through the quality of their portrayal of the tributed act, not through actually claiming to 'be' the artists they tribute. It is thus crucial in this respect that tribute bands are seen to not take themselves 'too' seriously. This is achieved by occasionally reminding themselves and the audience that they are not 'the real thing'. The use of humour enables tribute bands to laugh about themselves and invites the audience to share the joke.

Opportunities for the use of humour also exist where both the tribute band and its audience are from a particular place or region and share the same local knowledge and experience. During my research on the Benwell Floyd, I would often note how the group's frontman made use of local dialect and in-jokes common to the North East region of England as a means of generating a rapport with the audience. On one occasion the frontman emerged onto the stage for the group's second set of the evening wearing a Newcastle United football shirt, knowing full well that many members of the audience were Sunderland supporters, the intense local rivalry that exists between Newcastle and the nearby town of Sunderland being echoed in the support for their local football teams. There then followed an ongoing banter between the frontman and the audience regarding the relative merits and shortcomings of each other's team. During an interval between songs a member of the audience jokingly commented 'Your music's great man, no worries. But that top stinks' (Bennett 2000: 190). At the end of the performance the Benwell Floyd's frontman had one last football-related joke with the audience: 'Goodnight, thanks for having us and I hope your team does better next year!' (Bennett 2000: 191).

Although musically very proficient, much of the success generated by the Benwell Floyd undoubtedly revolved around their ability to engage at a local level with their audience in this way. The use of a strong local dialect by the group's frontman, his ability to name-check local places and his knowledge about the region's local culture, were all crucial to the rapport he shared with the audience and made his tongue in cheek references to issues such as the rivalry between Newcastle and Sunderland acceptable; lacking such local knowledge, a person from outside the region would almost certainly have failed to achieve the same level of rapport with the audience.

The use of local imagery is another way in which tribute bands can imbue themselves with a sense of humour and highlight the parodic aspects of their craft. For example, during a mid-1990s tour of the UK, the Australian Pink Floyd Show issued a tour poster and flyer listing concert dates that drew on the design of the 1977 Pink Floyd album *Animals*. On the original album cover, a huge inflatable pig is seen floating above the derelict Battersea Power Station in London. The Australian Pink Floyd Show's poster and flyer replaced the inflatable pig with an inflatable kangaroo. Clearly, at one level, such a branding device adheres to a particular stereotype of Australia. On the other hand, it communicates the Australian tribute's sense of parody and imitation to the audience. Like the Benwell Floyd, they are accepting of the fact that they are 'not' the real thing and draw on a particular local resource as a means of underscoring this fact.

Conclusion

This chapter has examined the tribute band phenomena both as an aspect of postmodern culture and a form of performance that draws on everyday knowledge relating to place, intimacy and humour. It has been argued that from a sociological perspective many of the features of the tribute band phenomenon align closely with particular characteristics associated with postmodernity. In particular, the tribute band's aim of achieving a near perfect simulacrum as possible of the tributed act corresponds with the re-production and simulation often associated with postmodern affect. Similarly, in using their creative licence to recreate aspects of a tributed act's performing history, tribute bands exemplify the process identified by Red-head (1990) whereby popular music, as a quintessentially postmodern cultural form, subverts the linear progression of time associated with modernity and replaces this with 'circular' pop time. Despite these features of the tribute band phenomenon, however, it has also been argued that a great part of its appeal also depends upon the willingness of the audience to buy into the illusion staged by the band. To some extent this can also be attributed to postmodern affect in that we now live in a world where reproduction and simulation are taken increasingly for granted. At the same time, however, tribute bands use a number of other, more mundane, strategies in achieving a rapport with their audience. Thus, the use of small venues creates an intimacy in tribute band performances which in turn ensures a high level of communication between band and audience. Similarly, the use of humour by tribute bands allows them to periodically come out of their role as imitators and helps them retain affinity with the audience. The use of humour also serves to emphasize the point that a tribute band is an elaborate trick of illusion, rather than 'the real thing'.

Notes

1   The Bootleg Beatles' reproduction of later Beatles songs is also sometimes achieved by using real orchestral instruments played by guest musicians. The combination of these instruments with the conventional rock instruments used by the Bootleg Beatles in a live context is reliant on the use of high

quality acoustic pickups capable of accurately reproducing the sounds of orchestral instruments from the piccolo trumpet, featured on 'Penny Lane', to the strings used on 'I Am The Walrus'. Again, this technology was unavailable to the Beatles at the time when this material was originally released.

2   John Lennon is seen playing a white grand piano both during a performance of the song 'I Am The Walrus' in the film *Magical Mystery Tour* (1967) and four years later in the promotion film for his post-Beatles hit 'Imagine' (1971).

3   More recently, the Counterfeit Stones have acquired a new member, Dave Birnie, who does indeed change identity throughout the band's set, beginning as 'Bryon Jones' (Brian Jones), then changing into 'Mick Tailor-Made' (Mick Taylor), and finally becoming Ronnie B. Goode (Ronnie Wood). The band has added a further member in the form of 'Nicky Popkiss' (keyboardist Nicky Hopkins who recorded and performed with the Rolling Stones as a guest musician during the late 1960s and early 1970s). Significantly, however, the pictures on the Counterfeit Stones website continue to feature the original Rolling Stones line-up, including a recreation of the promotional shot for the group's 1968 rockumentary, *Rock and Roll Circus*.

References

Baudrillard, J. (1983) *Simulations*. New York: Semiotext(e).

Benjamin, W. (1973) *Illuminations / Walter Benjamin*, edited with an introduction by H. Arendt, trans. H. Zohn. London: Fontana.

Bennett, A. (2000) *Popular Music and Youth Culture: Music, Identity and Place*. Basingstoke: Macmillan.

Bennett, A. (2001) Plug in and play! UK Indie guitar culture, in A. Bennett and K. Dawe (eds) *Guitar Cultures*. Oxford: Berg.

Best, S. and Kellner, D. (1997) *The Postmodern Turn*. London: The Guildford Press.

Cohen, S. (1991) *Rock Culture in Liverpool: Popular Music in the Making*. Oxford: Clarendon Press.

Eco, U. (1987) *Travels in Hyperreality*. London: Picador.

Frith, S. (1988) *Music for Pleasure: Essays in the Sociology of Pop*. Oxford: Polity Press.

Frith, S. (1996) *Performing Rites: On the Value of Popular Music*. Oxford: Oxford University Press.

Frith, S. and Horne, H. (1987) *Art into Pop*. London: Methuen.

Giuliano, G. (1992) *The Beatles: A Celebration*, 2nd edn. London: Sunburst Books.

Laing, D. (1985) *One Chord Wonders: Power and Meaning in Punk Rock*. Milton Keynes: Open University Press.

Lash, S. (1990) *Sociology of Postmodernism*. London: Routledge.

MacCannell, D. and MacCannell, J. (1993) Social class in postmodernity: *simulacrum* or return of the real? in C. Rojek and B.S. Turner (eds) *Forget Baudrillard?* London: Routledge.

Martin, G. and Hornsby, J. (1979) *All You Need Is Ears*. London: Macmillan.

Moore, A.F. (1993) *Rock: The Primary Text – Developing a Musicology of Rock.* Buckingham: Open University Press.

Negus, K. (1992) *Producing Pop: Culture and Conflict in the Popular Music Industry.* London: Edward Arnold.

Oakes, J. (1995) The song remains the same: tribute bands perform the rock text. Paper presented to the 1995 International Association for the Study of Popular Music International Conference, University of Strathclyde, Glasgow, July.

Redhead, S. (1990) *The End-of-the-Century Party: Youth and Pop Towards 2000.* Manchester: Manchester University Press.

Smart, B. (1993) Europe/America: Baudrillard's fatal comparison, in C. Rojek and B.S. Turner (eds) *Forget Baudrillard?* London: Routledge.

Stevenson, N. (1995) *Understanding Media Cultures.* London: Sage.

2 'You've got to carry that weight': tribute acts in the entertainment supermarket

Shane Homan

Popular music is part of the set of industries and debates about differences between 'art' and 'entertainment' (Dyer 1992; Frith 1996). In this chapter I want to examine tribute performers' thoughts about their location within 'entertainment' discourses. 'Just a tribute' reveals an attitude that such acts are unworthy of any consideration, as apolitical cultural forms that trade on the falsification of both performers' and audiences' desires. As Richard Dyer has argued, entertainment is 'not so much a category of things as an *attitude* towards things' (1992: 12). It is useful, then, to examine the 'professional ideology' (Dyer 1992: 8) of tribute musicians and their own logics of reason about producing the musical copy. Their practices are not just part of changes within the music industry. It is equally important to consider the role of other media forms and economies, and how they represent, recycle and 'sell' the past to particular audiences. Popular music is not alone in its ability to exploit nostalgia to specific economic and representational ends. Successful British and Australian tributes to the Beatles and Abba are examined to reveal case-specific understandings of authenticity and creativity, and how such bands, to borrow from the Beatles' 1970 *Abbey Road* album, 'Carry That Weight' of performing music history.

Media, nostalgia and reinterpretation

As a different niche form to the much longer traditions of cabaret covers and club/casino impersonators, tribute acts are relatively recent imitation forms within the more usual rock and pop circuits. It is no accident that tribute bands emerged in step with other media strategies to expand audiences' desire for nostalgia. Since the 1980s, radio, and particularly film and television, have looked to 'the vault' of archival material that reveals particularly cynical discourses of pop culture history, media markets and contemporary youth. Reconnecting ageing 'baby boomer' audiences with their audio-visual memories has become a key survival strategy for a range of media. Yet the very different contexts, and more significantly, the different audiences granted access to this form of programming means that it offers not just recycling, but *reinterpretations* of the past. As Grainge (2000: 31) has argued, 'the content and meaning of nostalgia is in many respects secondary to strategies of production and consumption'. Popular music remains a central component of the 'contemporary past' derived from changing media and entertainment environments.

Television – a medium that has always been sensitive to its own histories and immediate past – has recycled older programmes in various forms. The Nostalgia Network was established in 1985 as a US cable network drawing on the popularity of shows like *The Love Boat* and *The Rockford Files*; Nickelodeon exploited its parent company Viacom's large library of programmes to present reruns in an ironic and playful way (Grainge 2000: 30). Deprived of an immediate past of their own to plunder, cable and pay television networks have invested heavily in older film, television drama and sitcom stocks to attract viewers.

Music television has been an important part of this process. Both free-to-air and pay networks offer programmes that relive pop and rock's history. This is achieved through the presentation of a 'past-iche' of iconic social/generational/music moments, evident in VH-1 and MTV strategies (Burns 1996: 132). A favourite is the 'instant nostalgia show' (Frith 2002: 227) that compiles endless lists of the 'greatest' bands/songs/decades/videos. The global success of the talent shows *Pop Idol, Popstars, The X-Factor* and their equivalents, purportedly about the airing of new stars, relies heavily on pop and rock's past to achieve this. Aspiring youthful stars unashamedly delve into the past, with unspoken 'rules' about appropriate (and the appropriation of) songs within the MOR (middle of the road) canon: Mariah Carey, Whitney Houston, Rod Stewart, Frank Sinatra and the like. Hoping to reflect their own unique qualities, the contestants must first display their abilities as ciphers of the past. The British programme *Starstruck* eliminates the veneer of individualism, instead explicitly seeking to confer stardom upon the best tribute. Television advertising exploits older hits for a wide variety of products, consumers and televisual contexts. As a medium 'organised around an aesthetic of immediacy (rather than reflection)' (Frith 2002b: 280) the disjuncture between personal memories of hits, and their use on television as contemporary commodity, is more keenly felt.

This sense of historical displacement is also an issue for contemporary film. The success of the *Saturday Night Fever* soundtrack in 1977 produced new connections between sound and image: 'by 1984, all five of the best-selling pop singles came from movies' (Grossberg 2003: 84). The use of past or contemporary hits to facilitate Hollywood interest, financial backing and the marketing process has reached the point where sound can take priority over visual narratives:

I started realising how much I liked pop music and how much I listened to it. I'd hear music and I would imagine a scene for it – this would be a great opening sequence in a movie. One of the things that I do as a film-maker now is if I start to seriously consider the idea of doing a movie, I immediately try to find out what would be the right song to be the opening sequence even before I write the script.

(Director Quentin Tarantino cited in Romney and Wootton 1995: 130)

The use of popular music in this way 'assumes that the music can be separated from its anchor in other media forms' (Grossberg 2003: 83), even as audiences seem momentarily detached from the music's wider contextual baggage. Tarantino's films (particularly *Reservoir Dogs* (1992); *Pulp Fiction* (1994); and *Jackie Brown* (1997), all Miramax films) are good examples of reviving older hits for contemporary use, often resulting in a 'second life' in the charts. To borrow from Frith (2002b: 282), these forms of intergenerational coupling assume a circular marketing rationale: 'because this is your sort of music this must be your sort of [film]; because this is your sort of [film] this must be your sort of music'. The reproduction and reinterpretation of both famous films and television shows is a more recent, but related tactic. The 2004 release of *Starsky & Hutch* (Warner Brothers) serves to illustrate the template as a parody of the US television crime show that aired from 1975 to 1979. The film's central characters remain secondary to smug reminiscing of the 1970s, while appropriating scenes from both *Saturday Night Fever* (Paramount/RSO 1977) and *Easy Rider* (Columbia 1969) (Byrnes 2004: 19).

Radio has also played its part in exploiting rock and pop archives, although by different means. 'Hits and memories' radio, like its televisual equivalents, is effective in capturing older audience groups. MOR stations in the US, for example, derive 86 per cent of their audience from those aged over 55 (Huntemann 2003: 74). Network tendencies to homogenize playlists, to achieve wider national audiences and station identities, were commensurate with the changes brought about by the 1996 Telecommunication Act. Written as a means to increase US industry competition and diversity of ownership, the policy has instead concentrated ownership, with one company, Clear Channel, owning 973 stations by the end of 1999 (Huntemann 2003: 72). For Canadian radio, the shift from local to more explicitly national networks had begun in the 1980s with the emergence of the Gold format (recycling past hits). As Berland (1993) has argued, the two events are not mutually exclusive. The de-localization of radio stations, particularly in smaller markets, is more easily achieved with formats that do not privilege either contemporary sounds or knowledge. The rise of 'Golden Oldies' formats was also evident in European states at this time (Wallis and Malm 1993: 166). With a 'target group [that] would have bought in numbers during the 60s, 70s and 80s', these formats operate on the 'fear ... that sudden confrontation with the unfamiliar, unexpected or difficult will disrupt the easy flow of daytime radio and cause listeners to reach for the dial or off-switch' (Barnard 2000: 130–1).

In Australia, 'heritage rock' (Potts 1992) has also been a staple of commercial music radio since the 1980s, to the extent that 'the audience originally targeted in the 1980s (eighteen to thirty year olds) has largely remained with these stations – they are now in their forties' (Cupitt *et al.* 1996: 21). The popularity of 'Classic Hits'/'Gold' formats stretches to both AOR (album-oriented rock) and 'contemporary hits' stations. Responding to complaints that these stations were fulfilling their 25 per cent local content quota with recycled 'classic' Australian hits, the Australian Broadcasting Authority introduced a new requirement in 1999 – that at least 25 per cent of the quota be Australian music released in the past year. The Australian federal government's National Radio Plan, introduced in 1988, influenced these formats. Public service models of programming diversity (to include youth stations and audiences) and ownership were scrapped to enhance a licensing process that favoured the highest bidder for FM licences (Turner 1993: 148). National networking of advertising, formats and recycled hits in the 1990s became the most effective means of stabilizing profits and recouping large licence fees.

'Hits and memories' radio appeals to both personal ('remember this') and national ('Britain's greatest band') memories. This is partly the product of the deregulation of national networks, tighter profit margins, 'de-localization' of stations and changing ownership patterns. These formats best suit an industrial practice where DJs cannot be located to a particular (local) space or time. They reinforce the 'museum of rock/pop' canon ('the best there was/is') that countenances no argument about the pantheon of great songwriters and songs. This important discursive role is shared by a sector of the music press that privileges popular music history and reflects upon the role of older bands and genres in a way that is 'indicative of its affluent middle-class readership' (Shuker 2001: 94).

The nexus between these forms of retro-music media and audiences is reflected in recording companies' penchant for re-releasing 'classic' albums and, in many cases, an artist's entire recorded output. In Britain, 'back catalogue albums accounted for 31.6 per cent of unit sales in 2003; in expenditure terms this represents 25.5 per cent [of all sales]' (Green 2004: 71). For men, back catalogue purchases represented the highest proportion of all sales (69.1 per cent). Age distinctions are also important: those aged between 30 and 60 accounted for over 70 per cent of back catalogue sales (Green 2004: 7). This is also reflected in the large rise in DVD sales, driven by 'baby boomer' audiences seeking home copies of historic/'classic' events like Elvis' 1968 Comeback televised by the US NBC network. Music DVD sales were valued at $US 1.8 billion in 2003, reflecting a 67 per cent increase in global revenue (IFPI 2004).

These forms of popular music media, then, have an important place in

Table 2.1   The entertainment supermarket

Category	Text/Context	Example
Theatrical reinvention	Theatre-as-film	Saturday Night Fever
	Theatre-as-TV	Jerry Springer Musical
	Theatre-as-film-as-book	Mary Poppins
Fortifying the canon	TV 'greatest' hits	100 Greatest Albums (Channel 4, UK)
	Talent quests	Popstars/Pop Idol
	Music press 'greatest' hits	Mojo/Q/Rolling Stone
	Radio's 'Eternal Top 40'	Hits and Memories/Gold
Song-drives-narrative	Musicals exploiting one band/ artist	Mamma Mia! (Abba)/We Will Rock You (Queen)
Ironical distance	Film parodies of TV	Starsky & Hutch/Pleasantville/ Brady Bunch
	Soundtracks-as-juxtaposition	Muriel's Wedding/Reservoir Dogs

the disjuncture between popular music's foundations as youthful expression, and the continuing commodification of youth memories. Tribute bands fit easily within media markets that perform a careful balancing act between affecting a contemporary superiority about the past, and the reaffirmation of 'unarguably great' performers. The contemporary 'entertainment super-market' offers a rich assortment of intertextual pleasures (see Table 2.1). The steady growth in stage versions of 'classic' (musical, film, television, book) texts such as *Saturday Night Fever*, *Titanic: the Musical* and *Mary Poppins the Musical* has produced a bewildering number of shifts between 'definitive' portrayals and performative moments. For example, *Saturday Night Fever* (the musical) invites audiences to simultaneously incorporate both the film and the Bee Gees/RSO recording as reference points, and the various personal contexts in which they previously heard these songs (radio, television reruns, concert performances). As musical theatre, such shows rarely do justice to the extended performative landscapes available in other modes of performance.[1]

Audiences have not shared the reviewers' criticisms of such multimedia ventures. The musical derived from the Abba back catalogue, *Mamma Mia!*, plays in 11 sites globally, with mid-2004 takings of more than £410 million (Rampton 2004). The interplay between theatre, television, musicals, film, radio and various live venue enterprises has provided a lucrative niche of popular music memory and reinterpretation: entertainment-histories-as-entertainment. Ranging from the respectful (*Pop Idol*; *Mary Poppins the Musical*) to 'camp lite' (Robertson 1996: 120) (*Mamma Mia!*), they ensure the continued circulation of the 'Eternal Top 40' (Burns 1996: 134) within contemporary mediascapes.

Rather than viewing the tribute phenomenon as an aberration, it should instead be seen as a logical part of a series of broader entertainment discourses that have privileged intergenerational and intertextual interpretations of popular music history. The global popularity of Queen tribute bands, for example, cannot be disassociated from Queen's 'eternal presence' in classic hit radio formats; 'Bohemian Rhapsody''s ironic (and iconic) status in the film *Wayne's World* (Paramount 1993); the British televisual moment of lead guitarist Brian May opening the Queen's Jubilee celebrations in 2002 on the roof of Buckingham Palace; or Freddie Mercury songs chosen by contestants in television vehicles such as *Pop Idol* or *Starstruck* in 2005.

Performance contexts

As a further layer of historical and performative interpretation, the tribute raises other questions about how it is produced and consumed within particular performance settings. Where and how tribute acts emerged reveals much about their relations to other sectors within the 'entertainment supermarket'. Further, which specific media texts and histories are highlighted in live tribute performances?

The 'Send in the Clones' article published in *Melody Maker* (see Figure 2.1) captures the 'Australian invasion' of tribute acts in Britain in the early 1990s, with a useful summary of arguments about their popularity, delivered with a distinctive 'indie' press understanding of relationships between core (UK) and marginal (Australian) sites of music production. Within the mixture of musician and booking agency rationales offered for their success, the tribute phenomenon is ultimately dismissed as the product of a range of industrial changes: the lack of innovation from original acts; ageing live music audiences; genre shifts; and a return to 'entertainment' (Joy 1992: 45).

Contemporary tribute forms (encompassing musical theatre like *That'll Be The Day* and tribute acts) remain important for British seaside resorts, accounting for about 8 per cent of all live entertainment; in some cases, tributes subsidize less profitable acts (Hayler 2004). They can be viewed as logical extensions of the seaside theatre traditions of pantomime and the variety show, where these formats are increasingly regarded as outdated. A common argument for the popularity of the tribute act is its ability to offer the famous in venues that the original has outgrown.[2] The intimacy of theatre or pub tributes cannot be matched in stadiums where, in the case of Michael Jackson's 1997 tour, the audience purchased cardboard periscopes in order to see the stage (Cunningham 1999: 221). The stadium experience, as live performance, is ironically flawed, given its dependence on other media forms for representation:

> . . . the use of giant video screens at rock concerts provides a means of creating in a large-scale event the effect of 'intimacy and immediacy'

SEND IN TH[

What the hell's going on? BJORN AGAIN are on at Reading, ABBA are more popular than they have been for years and tribute bands devoted to impersonations of dead or distant megastars are a boom industry. SALLY MARGARET JOY guides us through...

THE WHO'S WHO OF TRIBUTE ROCK:

THE RUTLES – Eric Idle woz 'ere first. Like Spinal Tap, this Beatling bunch were put together in order to make a spoof-ish rockumentary. Fans include Cass of the Senseless Things and your dads.

THE BOOTLEG BEATLES – Started up 12 years ago from the remains of the musical "Beatlemania", they've watched the Australian lead assault with a jaundiced eye. Three astonishing (ish) facts about the band are that they toured extensively before wide-eyed Russians who were keen to experience the Swinging Sixties in 1982, there's a rumour that Macca saw them perform in Margate, and ex-Bootlegger Dave Catfin Birch is now the bassist in World Party.

They have a fanzine which Neil (the John one) says is, "jolly difficult to write because, aside from a couple of alterations in the line-up a few years ago, and the fact we've recently put 'Please Please Me' into the set – which is big news – there's never that much to say, really.

"Of course I'd have liked to have made it in a band with my own original material. I tried, but it never worked out."

Well popular on the college circuit. And at least they don't do Linda.

ABCD – ACDC

DREAD ZEPPELIN – Do a kind of Elvis/dub/Zeppelin thing which provided much amusement for Time Out readers a couple of years back.

THE WHITE – Led Zeppers who neither resemble their heroes nor, come to that, sound like them. Horribly enough, they've made records which share 1 be named in case some readers are divvy enough to want to buy them. I hooked up with two 18-year-olds at a recent White gig. Needless to say they were lying on the floor.

Ian: "I like Nirvana, and I'm here because I like Led Zep. But this lot are crap."

Guy: "That singer is just a fat bastard pretending to be Plant."

THE ZEP BOYS – More? Yes!

JAILBREAK – Thin Lizzy. Bloody brilliant. Shame about the boot polish.

AUSTRALIAN DOORS SHOW – Aussie combo that takes it all seriously. "How many bands do you know who play new material every night?" they argue. Their singer is scared of offending Morrison fans by coming across too Jim-like and says modestly, "If you're half blind and you've been drinking all night and you stand right at the back, then maybe I look like Jim Morrison." A tad creepy and over-reverential. Hey cobber, Mozzer's dead, man!

The first thing their manager asked me is if I'm going to write a positive piece about his boys. *Christ, do they think they're a proper band or something?*

THE COUNTERFEIT STONES – Their only boast is that they're younger than Mick and the boys. Not necessarily a recommendation.

THE ROYAL FAMILY – Queen.

THE AUSTRALIAN CURE – Bunch of wally wombats.

THE JOSHUA TRIO – Laff-mongers U2 style. Were recently seen on TV reading out Bono's lyrics like they were part of the Old Testament.

RANDY HANSEN – Jimi Hendrix-er from The Netherlands. Made tons of albums and has a following. For squares only.

ELTON JACK – Doomed from an early age. He is Elton's double: "If I didn't do Elton, people would compare me to him anyway." But let's not be too sorry for the wee chap, he gets to play to around 700 people a night and he's

coming here next summer!

ROBERT REED – Hero or villain? He is the man responsible for ensuring the Australian Doors and Bjorn Again got work permits in Britain. A shadowy figure, he seems to live and work from his car and his carphone is always engaged.

YOU WAKE UP WONDERING where you are. You haven't been home for months. You look up and see your hair on the bedside table. Your nylon catsuit is scrumpled up on the floor and it needs a dry-clean but you've only got an hour until check-out and then there's an interview before that. How many more Swedish gigs can you wring out of an interview this time? Tonight is your 710th in three years. How many more Swedish gigs can you wring out of a gig this time? It's not as if you're making loads of dosh, or even a name for yourself, for that matter. You are a puppet. You are famous but nobody knows (or gives a toss about) who you really are. You are in **BJORN AGAIN**.

Bjorn Again are the most famous of all the lookylikies. They are very entertaining. Their representation of ABBA is pure burlesque. It is brassy, dumb and undemanding entertainment. If the band were human it would be a bimbo. Everybody loves a bimbo.

I'll never forget seeing Emma Lush's upturned face utterly bedazzled by the glittering spectacle of Bjorn Again at London's Subterania last year. All the normally rather cool London sceneasters laughed insanely at the band's groan-worthy double entendres and sang their lungs out. And bugger me if I didn't join in, too. It was very cosy. And, sickeningly enough, very hip.

After several faxes explaining what this feature is about (Christ! *Do they think they're a real band or something?*) I finally get to meet Bjorn Again. They are wandering around looking lost, pale and gloomy against their dingy London hotel's chocolate, orange and lime

interior. They seem irritated at having to get back in costume so early in the day. We get off to a bad start because (a) they pretend not to grasp my questions because, supposedly, they are Swedish, when in actual fact they don't grasp my questions because they're a bunch of Australian actors who, had ABBA never existed, might be pulling pints in a pub owned by a sadistic landlord who doesn't care a jot about living standards for his staff, and don't have the grace or incl come up with any original preferring instead to give m terrible old Swedish-accent about being "found on an i Australia after a helicopter and when we came to we v this..." Oh, brother.

They may only be people to be a band, but they suffe same things that people in suffer, and without any of t For instance, one senses an unpleasant rivalry betwee (brunette) and "Agnetha" (You see, chaps at their sho into the spirit of the thing or for them like starved dogs. "Agnetha" appears to ignc sex interest, going more for altogether-now-come-on-t

LONES

WHY ARE THESE TROCADERO ROCK CIRCUS BUFFOONS SO POPULAR? WHY ARE MOST OF THEM AUSTRALIAN? AND WHY ARE THEY PISSING SO MANY PEOPLE OFF?

1. THE BABYBOOMERS ARE GOING GREY THEORY

In Australia (where tribute bands are breeding like kangaroos) radio stations play oldies to keep in step with the ageing population. It keeps their advertisers happy, too. They play music by bands who rarely, if ever, tour Australia, so there's a huge audience for imitators playing the rock classics live.

Semi-precious gems: The Counterfeit Stones

2. THE DEATH OF THE TEENAGER THEORY

FACT: The teenage population is dwindling. Teenagers (real, and those in their thirties) are an endangered species and feel threatened by copycat bands on a more profound level than they realise. They sense that the phenomenon marks the beginning of the death of the teenager *as we know it*. Actors and comedians are using the instruments associated with teen rebellion (guitars, bass and drums) for entertainment, for laughs', and without a whiff of sincerity, *and they're making a bloody living out of it*. Meanwhile, thousands of Bens and Tims are creating proper, serious, original music in bedsits in suburbia and rock venues won't give them a gig! That hurts.

Another snobbo gripe is that these Trocadero Rock Circus buffoons are making a quick buck from songs that real artists sweated blood over. But then, one could argue, just how original are artists like Primal Scream or Ms Minogue or anyone that makes records out of joining samples together?

3. THE THERE'S TOO MUCH MUSIC THEORY

It's easy to get left behind when new bands and new types of music seem to spring up overnight replacing bands that haven't been around five minutes. The people who can't keep up (regular gig-going and record-buying is too stressful, boring or expensive for them) turn back to what they recognise – lookalike bands.

4. THE THINGS AIN'T WHAT THEY USED TO BE THEORY

People are bored and alienated by the dull careerist yuppies in the charts and the facelessness of Techno. Who's innovative these days? Taking a peek at the charts, we find Genesis who certainly aren't new, a Whitney Houston revival 20 years too early in the form of Mariah Carey, and Shakespear's Sister, who could be Marc Bolan turned female and split in two.

It's difficult to accuse copycat bands of being an insult to the intelligence when the alternatives seem so nostalgic for rock's glory days themselves. Remember that "Teenage Fanclub sound just the same as Big Star" debate that raged on our letters page last year? Some people are more hung about originality than others.

5. THE PEOPLE JUST WANNA HAVE FUN THEORY

The majority of copycat bands don't make records so gigging is their livelihood. Their shows have to be entertaining, made to keep the Ozzies away from their beach-barbies and inside the pubs. They attempt to recreate the atmosphere of yore, when stars were stars and people shagged Mars bars and nobody took the nightbus home. Nobody's saying they've succeed by any means, but at least you get value for money! The Counterfeit Stones claim that for a mere fiver they'll deliver in-his-prime Jagger in an intimate pub setting which is much better value, they argue, than paying £25 to see a 50-year-old dot bobbing about in the distance at Wembley. Personally, I'd rather spend my fiver on some bad crack.

6. THE PEOPLE ARE STUPID THEORY

Yeah, and?

Bjorn Again play Reading Main Stage on Saturday, the same day as that other great Australian showman, Nick Cave. Wonder if they'll jam?

SCOTTISH SEX PISTOLS – Johnny MacRotten bears a striking resemblance to the real thing (maybe with a little Jah Wobble thrown in there, too). He is the proud owner of a *BJORN AGAIN ARE F***ING SHITE* tee-shirt, and talking to him is eerie. The sneer is haddie-raisingly accurate, the heh-heh-heh's, hideous. "Hello, m'dear... (whines on menacingly, calls me a 'corporate rock tart'!) ... yeah, we got an ugly shit called Malcolm MacMaclaren, and even a Vivian MacWestwood. Why do we do it? Because we think tribute bands like the Australian Doors take themselves too seriously. It's like they're into total fan adulation and we think that's sad and pah-feh-ik. Plus, the charts today are exactly like the charts in 1976 - a lot of crap. Everyone's a poseur nowadays. That Bjorn Again are an out-and-out joke, totally ridiculous."

Is it likely that one of their members will die of a massive overdose in the near future?

"Ha ha ha. Another dull Melody Maker question. I ought to march across the border and beat the crap out of you. Nah (sighs wearily), no one's gonna be committing suicide. Well, at least not until we've found a Nancy MacSpungen, anyway."

He's got Rotten down pat. Doesn't he ever get confused about who he's supposed to be sometimes? And don't the audiences get a little too carried away by their brilliant resurrection of the spirit of punk. All of a sudden, he lapses into his native Scottish brogue. "Look, we're a novelty band with teeth. I don't go round thinking I'm the real Johnny Rotten, spitting on me mum and that. I know I'm playing a character. I study Johnny Rotten like I'm cramming for an exam, getting the accent and his quotes just right. I've got total respect for him. He took me bullshit. "Yeah, people in the audience get into it, you know, pogo and spit – but that's very passe. Some take it too seriously. At St Andrews some guy bit me under my arm.

"We perform nearly all the Pistols songs, but we don't do 'Belsen Was A Gas' for obvious reasons. It's embarrassing watching our video where there's some guy screaming, 'Ye cannae get a hard-on, you wanker!' when me mum's in the room."

---

long-with-me style of ace, "Frida" seems to relish on much more than the part he really goes for it, ottom-skimming skirts long belts really) with h slits.

ne that when Nirvana came in Melbourne, Kurt invited y in their transit van. She's er remarkable for a woman "Frida" how she feels netho"'s rear being voted lum In The World". She se the bait, but later, in an ir cross-dressing fans, is me that she's seen "lots to try to look like Agnetha do succeed". I can just "Agnetha" flinching ever her seat. the chaps. I tell them that

people can't believe there are love affairs within the band because the guys are so hideous. If only "Bjorn" (guitar) and "Benny" (keyboard) did something with their hair. The women aren't exactly great role models but you can understand little girls wanting to look like them, but nobody wants to look like the guys in ABBA... uh, I mean Bjorn Again.

"If you go to Sweden you'll see that all the men look like us," says "Bjorn", a mite huffily. He's noticed that I have the upper hand in the interview and decides to give me a sharp telling off for a Maker editorial last year in which Andrew Mueller wittily called them "a bunch of f***ing c***s". Well, he's a barbarian, I tell them, from Australia.

associated with smaller live events. In order to retain those characteristics, large-scale events must surrender a substantial measure of
their liveness to mediatization. Ironically, intimacy and immediacy
are precisely the qualities attributed to television that enabled it to
displace live performance. In the case of such large-scale events, live
performance survives as television.

(Auslander 1999: 32)

Auslander's thesis is evident in many forms of contemporary live performance – for example, the use of video footage by artists to anchor their
'liveness' in specific historical moments from a televisual vault of memories:
career highlights, marriages, television performances, key videos and so on.
However, Auslander's claim, after Gracyk (1996), that 'rock exists primarily as
recorded music and only secondarily as live performance' (1999: 8) under-
states one of the genre's key discourses: the ability to 'cut it live' has long been
a marker of rock musicians' credibility, and the difference between pop acts
who are not burdened by audience demands of stage virtuosity. Auslander's
'mediatization' thesis is argued to the point where *sound* is obliterated from
analysis.

The emergence of tributes on the pub and university circuits in Australia
and Britain in the 1980s provided (relatively) intimate approximations that
were affordable. The most popular tributes have bypassed the pubs in favour
of theatres, which provide a more comfortable setting, as explained by Björn
Again co-founder, Rod Leissle:

You can't go into a grand scale [in the pubs], but the theatre circuit is
great, it allows for a better show. The other Abba bands can't play at
this level – the costs are massive. Our current theme for this tour is
'Home Swede Home', with a backdrop of a house, fjords in the
background, a grand piano and candelabra.

(Leissle interview 2004)

For the top tier of tribute acts with established credentials like Björn
Again, theatres are their 'natural' home in both an economic and conceptual
sense. The tribute theatre (or pub/bar) performance must overcome the same
problems confronting the large-scale musical discussed above: the construction of a dramatic piece that does not overly simplify either the emotional or
historic authenticity of its characters. Theatre ticket prices provide the means
to think more grandly about stage production, and to realize profits from
fewer performances. For the Bootleg Beatles, it costs £250,000 per year to
produce 100 shows. The band's founder, Neil Harrison, also places the act in
the lineage of 'theatre – the show has a storyline; we're not simply dressing up
and playing' (Harrison interview 2004). The ability to charge around £10,000
per show affords the Bootleg Beatles the opportunity to augment the 'Fab

Four' line-up with cello, violin and trumpet – a source of pride to the band in rejecting synthesized versions of the more complex band arrangements. It also enables more sophisticated televisual prompts: short videos in the Bootleg set provide crucial time for costume changes, and equally, the historic ambience for the subsequent Beatles 'era'.[3]

The significant number of tribute musicians who began their imitations in stage shows reinforces the tributes' claim to theatre as their ideological 'home'. After playing George Harrison in the film *Backbeat* (Channel Four 1994), Chris O'Neill formed the Backbeat Beatles in Britain in the early 1990s. Lance Strauss, the Australian 'Elton Jack', had first performed in *Lennon the Musical* in Sydney in 1986. Before establishing the Bootleg Beatles, Neil Harrison was a cast member of the US show *Beatlemania* in 1979 (Harrison interview 2004).

Creativity and copyright

In the absence of access to the original songs, tributes have also been useful for performing various types of copying. The Bootleg Beatles have provided soundtracks for television and films, ranging from direct copies to Beatleesque sounds and riffs. The Cavern Beatles provided voices and sounds for software company Music Playground, as part of its Beatles content in 2001 (Cavern Beatles 2004). Tributes challenge the music industry's desire to protect artists as both 'original' and brand. Aesthetic and commercial considerations can become inseparable. Consider Björn Again's various phases as an Australian Abba tribute:

> We had a lawyer worried about our dress, [saying] 'You're trading on them, and you're going to get sued'. I thought that would be fantastic, but at that point we weren't making any money . . . our logo, if you see the reflection on our logo, it is 'ABBA', and our lawyer told us that we were using the exact trademark, but we still use that trademark today. In the US with [the musical] *Mamma Mia!*, they didn't want us advertising the 'ABBA' logo just down the road [from them]. But it was OK if our ad was 25 per cent smaller than the theatre one.
> (Leissle interview 2004)

Graceland/Elvis Presley Enterprises have provided a template for zealous protection of the music brand. Sanctioned tourist narratives are 'sterile and predictable', with the Elvis story 'cleaned up for mass consumption' (Rodman 1996: 120). Acts of legal injunction against non-sanctioned 'Elvii' activity, in the name of ensuring 'quality' memorabilia, are rendered hollow by other rights to the Elvis image granted to casinos, restaurants and television commercials. Elvis Presley Enterprises initially sought to prevent impersonators from performing what they considered to be inappropriate imitations (Wall 2003: 41). The Bootleg Beatles experienced similar problems in Britain:

> Once we had an advert out with 'the Beatles' stamped over 'Bootleg', which was very faint, so when you printed in the paper you could hardly see the 'Bootleg'. We got this phone call from a huge legal firm, with a million names on the first page, to say that some people might think that this is our client (the Beatles). Well, you'd hardly think the Beatles are playing St Albans or Watford Coliseum. But you have to kind of salute and say 'Yes, we'll change that immediately' . . . and [lawyers representing Apple] made us change the dropped 't' in the Beatles logo.
>
> (Harrison interview 2004)

National copyright laws make a distinction between recordings of live performance, and attempts to recreate them. As Auslander (1999: 140–1) has explained in the context of US law, while he is prohibited 'from making a video of a Rolling Stones concert without their permission, it would not prohibit me from recreating their concert as a live performance'. Permissions for song use are covered by the payment of performance royalties, while copyright law 'does not protect live performance in and of itself' (Auslander 1999: 141). This remains distinct from the many court disputes about the rights to band names after original members have left (e.g. the Buck's Fizz case in the UK; see BBC 2002); or even accusations that artists have plagiarized or written tributes to their earlier work (e.g. the Fantasy Records/John Fogerty case; see Columbia Law School 2005). 'Passing off' laws, derived from broader trademark law, remain the only legal recourse for original performers, where concerns arise over the exploitation of image and music for commercial gain. This partly explains original bands' meticulous attention to and guardianship of other media representations, such as tribute attempts to replicate band logos and other iconic merchandise.[4] In the US, many states have enacted 'celebrity rights acts' (Wall 2003: 42) to provide some protection of the management and circulation of existing and posthumous celebrity publicity.

Curiously, the rights of tributes to exist have been challenged by other tributes. In 1996 one member of the (Australian) Beatnix, Bruce Coble (John Lennon), left to form the Beatels, to be threatened by a Supreme Court injunction from Beatnix manager/founder Tony Dean. Rather than being seen as a dispute centred upon the (more than ironical) view that the 'original' tribute could not be copied, the Beatnix manager attempted legal redress in the belief that the emerging Beatels leveraged off the existing audience goodwill and brand loyalty developed by the Beatnix. The case was settled out of court.

In some ways, tribute and cover bands invoke Benjamin's (1973) assertion that mechanical reproduction has destroyed the aura of the original (see

Chapter 1). This is a common belief held by many performers and managers; that the 'aura' of the music star – the 'innate' musical and personal qualities of the original – is tarnished by the success of the copy. This has economic consequences:

> It's ok if you want to be a Queen tribute band, playing the songs of a band that no longer exists ... But when they start doing a tribute to a current Australian band in the Australian marketplace where we were making our money, it was a bit off. There would be an element of people going, 'Oh, I've already seen a band play the songs, so I don't really want to see The Angels play'.
>
> (Angels' manager and drummer Brent Eccles cited in Benedictus 2004)

The Angels example brings us back to the harsher economic principle of 'free riding': tributes have the capacity to trade upon the original band and its many years of visibility in the marketplace. It also reveals the band as brand, and how it circulates as a series of signs, where 'controlling the symbol or sign is often more lucrative than manufacturing an actual product with the sign on it' (Negus and Pickering 2004: 67).

Unlike many copies of paintings, where 'it is often difficult to detect whether a work was made with the intention to deceive' (Benhamou and Ginsburgh 2002: 38), the tribute act works from the premise that their performance is an open deception, more obvious when the original act has retired from writing and performance, or has died. Like all 'good forgers' of historic art works, the tribute musicians 'often have an extraordinary knowledge of the work of an artist, and of what [pop] history has to say about him' (Benhamou and Ginsburgh 2002: 39). This forms part of the basis for counter arguments put by tribute musicians: that, done well, the imitation contributes further to the value of the original artist. Björn Again's management believe there are direct economic benefits for Abba in the international success of the tribute:

> I think [Abba] acknowledge the role we've had in their re-emergence. We looked into it, and found that [the greatest hits compilation] *Abba Gold* sells a lot more in towns that we tour, and so we can quantify that our tours promote their CD sales. It's a case of scratching each other's backs – but they don't need us at all. If they wanted to wipe us out, they could – but it comes back to us meeting them early on, and explaining what we were about.
>
> (Leissle interview 2004)

At the same time, the tribute undermines the legal and discursive foundations of the entire music industry: copyright and originality. The industry has functioned on an understanding that financial wealth is derived from original recordings and subsequent performance of those recordings, as the economic incentive for musicians' creativity. As in other cultural industries, 'originality becomes a risk that is rewarded by a copyright, as a patent rewards invention' (Benhamou and Ginsburgh 2002: 48). The industry's use of 'originality' is dubious in many historical and practical contexts. Firstly, all musicians begin their musical life by copying favourite artists, as a crucial means of establishing credibility (Jones 1993; Frith 2002a). From the outset, musicians are embedded in a culture of copying, and have to be attentive to distinctions between genres and artists, whether 'producing an exact copy' or in 'the adaptation of stylistically suitable components from one song or one stylistic context to another' (Green 2002: 29). An environment of imitation is necessary to produce an individual playing style.[5]

Secondly, sampling practices have shattered, or at least questioned, the notion of the 'distinctive' and unique musical work; rather, all pop derives from a combination of reheated riffs, lyrics and themes. While sampling is more brazen in its use of past works, the endless number of plagiarism cases within the courts attests to the industry's sensitivity to copying by stealth. Thirdly, the industry itself has relied upon the copy as a strategic way to reach audiences. Recording companies have 'advised' artists in the early stages of their careers to record a well-known cover version as the best means of 'introducing' them to potential fans.

In short, tributes both challenge and confirm the 'romantic notions of the authentic, misunderstood, creative genius' (Negus and Pickering 2004: 82) upon which the music industries are founded. Tributes highlight the familiar as unique, emulating those who have perfected conventional performance and composition methods (Kylie, Robbie Williams, Frank Sinatra, Status Quo), and those who challenge rock and pop conventions (Hendrix, the Beatles, Queen). Moved by the 'ineffable' creativity of particular instrumental, vocal and studio techniques, they nonetheless seek to demystify technical proficiencies. In some cases, audiences are witnesses to a 'master class' of iconic virtuosity. At the same time, to borrow from Negus and Pickering, tributes 'can only parrot the definitions they have internalised' (2004: 126). Their educational function, the ability to impart knowledge about canonical artists, only works up to a point: tributes rarely privilege the influences upon the original (e.g. the various black artists from the US who provided the template for the Beatles and the Rolling Stones). In this sense, the original artist's reputation as a creative icon is reconfirmed.

'Be here now': the search for authenticity

Discussions of the tribute's sense of historical tradition are, of course, intimately tied to meanings of authenticity, a contentious enough word within the world of original recording artists, music journalists and fans. As Moore (2002: 209) has pointed out, 'authentic' is one of 'the most loaded' terms in popular music. It is arguably the most often used (and abused) term within the tribute band sector and popular music journalism about tributes. It is appropriate, then, to briefly consider how tribute acts contend with band histories, technical expertise and judgements about musical competency.

If 'honesty (truth to cultural experience) becomes the validating criterion of musical value' (Middleton 1990: 127), then the tribute experience is seemingly worthless. The tribute performance, at its centre, is not derived from subjectivity, but objectivity (in search of the perfect copy). The individual tribute musician's own personal and musical history collapses within the broader historical project. The tribute cannot state 'this is what's like to be me' (Moore 2002: 215). Despite its constructed nature, rock performance has always shared this sense of 'unmediated expression' as the essence of truth of feeling. For the management of Björn Again, an effort is made to erase the individual in favour of a faceless franchise; musicians are interviewed 'in character' and do not share their opinions and experiences (see the off-stage acting of the UK troupe in *Abba: Björn Again* 1999). This makes sound commercial sense, with no particular regional variant privileged over the global franchise.[6]

Further, tributes can be seen to represent the worst kind of made-to-order popular culture: 'It is valid to think we're being highly unoriginal and that's the case with many tribute bands today: "let's get some costumes ..." But I see Björn Again as being highly creative, as a pastiche ... I get a lot of offers to manage Beatles tribute bands, and it's like, "start a Beatles band, just add water"' (Leissle interview 2004).

Varying notions of the authentic can be discerned, where the more elaborate tributes view their rivals as inferior, standardized copies. Hierarchies of taste are constructed according to levels of musicianship, stage presentation and motives: 'for a lot of Abba bands, it's about "this is how we make a fast buck", and many have fallen by the wayside' (Leissle interview 2004). With no claim to an authentic subjective experience, testimonials are sought from the original. Björn Again's founders met Benny Andersson and Björn Ulvaeus to explain the band:

> We met them during our 1991–92 tour of Sweden, and they asked us 'Why are you wearing those horrible old costumes?' But they came to realize it was necessary in that time with Glam rock, and the Eurovision [appearances], to have the fashion side ... Björn said 'I used to hate wearing those costumes, I'll never wear them again'. That's how people remember Abba, and he didn't want that. Benny didn't care, but Björn was very image-conscious. Björn was very analytical and businesslike: 'They're our songs, how do we make money out of it?'

I'm not saying [the release of] *Abba Gold* is down to us, but I think we might have been the catalyst.[7]

(Leissle interview 2004)

The tribute takes great pride in technical proficiency and attention to detail. After once observing the Bootleg Beatles from the side of the stage, George Harrison asserted that the group 'probably know the records better than I do' (Harrison interview 2004). This is an astute observation about the tribute's relationship between the live and recorded moment. Such purity of practice in technical terms (exemplified in the ultimate fan compliment, 'If you close your eyes, they sound just like them') also underwrites the tribute's broader ideological premise. It has been argued that the various manifestations of nostalgia in the media economy are not 'in response to the yearning for continuity' (Grainge 2000: 27). Yet a striking similarity can be discerned in the (often defensive) rationales argued by tribute musicians, who stake their own claims in the 'continuous struggle over what is really authentic rock and which groups are really invested in it' (Grossberg 1994: 51). Despite different genres and historical periods, all the tribute musicians I encountered shared the sentiments of Bootleg Beatle Neil Harrison: 'I think a lot of people think the music scene is shit, which I believe it is ... Everything's derivative, so you go back to the Beatles ... I don't think it can ever be repeated because they took some bold moves, incredible leaps. By the middle of the 70s it was done, the best, you know, pop music ever written' (Harrison interview 2004). These kinds of statements are not merely canonical cheerleading. They also reinforce the cultural authority bestowed upon the 'great' rock and pop composers that at the same time reproduces unreflective, romantic notions of music creativity. It is important to remember that tributes play their part in the ideological work that constructs the pop music canon that is often conservative in terms of genre and era.

If there is remembrance, there is also forgetting: the more faithful tributes privilege the most commercially successful songs and band periods, at the expense of less well known material. The messy narratives of band break-ups, court disputes and bad albums are often erased (although as we have seen with the Australian Beatles acts, court battles can be reluctantly re-enacted). These 'histories of perfection' can produce fairly rigid choices:

We can't really evolve too much without not looking like Abba ... [the greatest hits compilation] *ABBA Gold* – we can't escape too much from that, or you're in trouble ... We try hard, but [Abba] couldn't recreate their own sound. I thought they were pretty awful on stage, to be fair ... but we do it better than they did it, than they could.[8]

(Leissle interview 2004)

> While we're doing things like 'Hey Bulldog' this time around, it's difficult to stray from the Beatles' 'Red' [1962–6] and 'Blue' [1967–70] albums [released in 1973]. There is very much a sing-a-long element. You can't be self-indulgent and play 'Cry Baby Cry' [*White* album, 1968].
>
> (Harrison interview 2004)

Such choices help us to understand the search by both audiences and performers for a series of 'just like . . .' moments. As 'entertainment' rather than 'art' (cf. Dyer 1992); as intense copies in vain search of the original; as an embodiment of artificial sincerity; in their open celebration of surface, rather than essence, tributes invite associations with postmodern affectivity. This is most apparent where the sincere is stacked against parody in a jumble of histories and genres. Björn Again have perfected this: their rendition of 'SOS' merges into the Police's 'Message in a Bottle' ('sending out an SOS' . . .); the staccato chorus vocals in '*Take A Chance*' are further extended in a rap from 'Benny'. Halfway through the first set, 'Benny' states to 'Björn': 'You are a guitarist of the highest calibre – open your axe to the darker side', providing the excuse for Björn to perform Steppenwolf's 'Born to be Wild', before Benny reassures the audience that the group will 'now return to our satin-based music'.[9]

> Abba started off with the girls as the backing vocalists. [Manager] Stig Anderson had the masterstroke of highlighting the girls more, and I think that really rankled with Björn, who saw himself as a real guitarist, but went along with it . . . We're portraying how Björn would like to be, he would love to be a rock god, but he ain't! So we allow a costume change for the girls, and the guys do a rock song.
>
> (Leissle interview 2004)

The insertion of a rock anthem into the neo-Abba experience thus provides more than a costume break for 'Agnetha' and 'Frida'; it attempts to reveal something of the interplay between Abba members as historical formation (whether it is accurate or not). Björn's display of 'rock god' stage clichés – heavily distorted guitar, Van Halen-like finger hammering along the length of the fretboard – is a useful parodic counterpoint to the pop sentiments of the rest of the performance. It is a strategy employed by most of the successful tributes: the need to locate and emphasize an interpretation that serves as an internal narrative anchor. For Björn Again, it is Björn's frustrated guitar ambitions, and his battles with 'Benny' for the affections of 'Agnetha' and 'Frida'. For the Bootleg Beatles, it is the tension between 'Paul' and 'John', and jokes at the expense of 'Ringo'. There are particular boundaries to this:

John used to do this thing with his hands and face, this whole re-
tarded thing, considered very un-PC now. So I began doing it on stage,
and the letters I got from people complaining! My daughter and
others told me that they didn't like me doing it. But people have to
realize that Lennon wasn't a nice character a lot of the time, and could
be rather nasty. It wasn't often a spontaneous thing either; Ringo
would often do a bass drum thump [in time with John's foot stomp].
(Harrison interview 2004)

This amounts to an excess of authenticity, with the Fab Four mythology open
to investigation. There are clearly limits in placing tributes within a 'self-
conscious postmodernity' that shows 'honesty in the acceptance of cynical
self-knowledge' (Moore 2002: 214). As a shared ironic gesture, the joke here
confronts both industry and audience memories of Lennon-as-icon. Perversely, too much attention to detail produces a mythic complexity that the
tribute structure cannot endure. Instead, both history and performance-as-
history is applied with a broad brush that privileges more direct assumptions
about the music industry and how bands have managed their stardom.

The following interviews were conducted with various tribute band
musicians: Bootleg Beatles' founder Neil Harrison at Preston Guildhall, England on 26 November, 2004; Björn Again co-founder Rod Leissle on 27 October, 2004 (by phone); and with Beatnix manager/founder Tony Dean on 23
September 2005. My thanks to all for their patience and insights.

Notes

1   The musical is also often misinterpreted. An *Independent* newspaper article
    about *Mamma Mia!* enthuses that the show 'passes the test of any memorable
    musical: you find yourself singing the tunes the following day' (Rampton
    2004). This criterion dismisses the history of the 'tunes' written for very dif-
    ferent motives and consumption contexts, and not as character and plot
    narratives within the musical tradition.
2   Acts with up to 40 years' history continue to reform for global stadium tours,
    with the Eagles, Fleetwood Mac (without keyboardist/songwriter Christie
    McVie), Kiss, Aerosmith and the Rolling Stones the most profitable acts
    (Jinman 2004: 31). Strausbaugh has dubbed such acts 'colostomy rock' who
    'have become their own nostalgia merchandise' (2001: 3).
3   A central video screen was used throughout the Bootleg Beatles' UK tour of
    2004, which displayed 'snapshots' of iconic 1960s people and events – British
    Prime Minister James Callaghan; Mohammed Ali; the Thunderbirds – ac-
    companied by the hits of the Ronettes and Tom Jones.
4   Popular music legal histories abound with musicians seeking to prevent band
    reformations as hollow tributes to former line-ups. In 2003, the Cult vocalist

Ian Astbury assumed the role of Jim Morrison, touring with two of the three remaining members of the Doors, Ray Manzarek and Robbie Krieger (Cooper 2003). Drummer John Densmore sought legal action to prevent the band touring, claiming that the band were not the Doors without Morrison; this was resolved through the new band's use of the title 'the Doors of the 21st Century' (Cooper 2003).

5   An often-cited example is the influences upon Eric Clapton's development as a blues guitarist/'God'. Clapton has stated that 'at first I played exactly like Chuck Berry for 6 or 7 months' (cited in Bradley 1992: 89).

6   The cover photograph for this book is symptomatic of Björn Again's attitude, favouring a stage shot that eliminates specific individual/regional contexts of the band.

7   Asked whether he had witnessed an Abba tribute act, Björn stated: 'I wouldn't dream of it. Life's too short. It would be so weird. We lend ourselves to tributes because there is no danger of us coming back and spoiling their act' (Rampton 2004).

8   To their credit, the British 'version' of Björn Again I witnessed performed a string of minor ballads that reminded the audience of Benny and Björn's Swedish folk lineage, who politely listened in anticipation of the more commercial pop offerings.

9   Liverpool Philharmonic Hall, 5 December, 2004. The aura of innocence attempted by 'Agnetha' and 'Frida' in their discussions with the audience was consistently broken by theatre staff's strict policing of the front of the stage and aisles to prevent dancing.

References

Auslander, P. (1999) *Liveness: Performance in a Mediatized Culture*. London: Routledge.

Barnard, S. (2000) *Studying Radio*. London: Hodder Headline.

Barnes, A. (2004) Start spreading the news: bogus Beatles lose out to fake Frank, the *Independent* online, http://enjoyment.independent.co.uk, accessed 3 December 2004.

BBC (British Broadcasting Corporation) (2002) Buck's Fizz: making your mind up, *Trouble At The Top*, episode 4(6).

Benedictus, L. (2004) Beneath the covers, *The Age*, 28 November.

Benhamou, F. and Ginsburgh, V. (2002) Is there a market for copies? *The Journal of Arts Management, Law, and Society*, 32(1): 37–55.

Benjamin, W. (1973) *Illuminations/Walter Benjamin*, edited with an introduction by H. Arendt, trans. H. Zohn. London: Fontana.

Berland, J. (1993) Radio space and industrial time: the case of music formats, in T. Bennett, S. Frith, L. Grossberg, J. Shepherd, and G. Turner (eds) *Rock and Popular Music: Politics, Policies, Institutions*. London: Routledge.

Bradley, D. (1992) *Understanding Rock 'n' Roll: Popular Music in Britain 1955–1964*. Buckingham: Open University Press.

Burns, G. (1996) Popular music, television and generational identity, *Journal of Popular Culture*, 30(3): 129–41.

Byrnes, P. (2004) Same names, but not the right moves, *The Sydney Morning Herald*, 8 April: 19.

Cavern Beatles (2004) www.cavernbeatles.com/profile.htm (accessed 8 November 2004).

Columbia Law School (2005) *Fantasy v Fogerty*. www.ccnmtl.columbia.edu/projects/law/library/cases/case_fantfogerty.html (accessed 29 August 2005).

Cooper, T. (2003) Ian Astbury: one door shuts ... another door opens, the *Independent* online, www.enjoyment.independent.co.uk, accessed 3 December 2004.

Cunningham, M. (1999) *Live & Kicking: The Rock Concert Industry in the Nineties*. London: Sanctuary Publishing.

Cuppitt, M., Ramsay, G. and Sheldon, L. (1996) *Music, New Music and All That: Teenage Radio in the 90s*. Sydney: Australian Broadcasting Authority.

Dyer, R. (1992) *Only Entertainment*. London: Routledge.

Frith, S. (1996) *Performing Rites: On the Value of Popular Music*. Oxford: Oxford University Press.

Frith, S. (2002a) Illegality and the music industry, in M. Talbot (ed.) *The Business of Music*. Liverpool: Liverpool University Press.

Frith, S. (2002b) Look! Hear! The uneasy relationship of music and television, *Popular Music*, 21(3): 277–90.

Gracyk, T. (1996) *Rhythm and Noise: An Aesthetics of Rock*. London: Duke University Press.

Grainge, P. (2000) Nostalgia and style in retro America: moods, modes, and media recycling, *Journal of American & Comparative Cultures*, 23(1): 27–34.

Green, C. (2004) *BPI Statistical Handbook 2004*. London: British Phonogram Industry.

Green, L. (2002) *How Popular Musicians Learn: A Way Ahead for Music Education*. Aldershot: Ashgate.

Grossberg, L. (1994) Is anybody listening? Does anybody care? On the state of rock, in A. Ross and T. Rose (eds) *Microphone Fiends: Youth Music & Youth Culture*. New York: Routledge.

Grossberg, L. (2003) Cinema, postmodernity and authenticity, in K. Dickinson (ed.) *Movie Music: The Film Reader*. London: Routledge.

Hayler, S. (2004) Live entertainment at the seaside: a benchmarking exercise for local authority theatres, *Cultural Trends*, 13(51): 41–75.

Huntemann, N. (2003) The effects of telecommunication reform on US commercial radio, in J. Lewis and T. Miller (eds) *Critical Cultural Policy Studies: A Reader*. Malden, MA: Blackwell Publishing.

IFPI (International Federation of the Phonographic Industry) (2004) Global music sales fall by 7.6% in 2003 – some positive signs in 2004. www.ifpi.org/sitecontent/statistics/worldsales.html (accessed 7 April 2005).

Jinman, R. (2004) Can't stop their music, *The Sydney Morning Herald*, 31 January: 31.

Jones, S. (1993) Critical legal studies and popular music studies, *Stanford Humanities Review*, (3): 77–89.

Joy, S. (1992) Send in the clones, *Melody Maker*, 29 August: 44–5.

Middleton, R. (1990) *Studying Popular Music*. Buckingham: Open University Press.

Moore, A. (2002) Authenticity as authentication, *Popular Music*, 21(2): 209–22.

Negus, K. and Pickering, M. (2004) *Creativity, Communication and Cultural Value*. London: Sage.

Potts, J. (1992) Heritage rock: pop music on Australian radio, in P. Hayward (ed.) *From Pop to Punk to Postmodernism: Popular Music and Australian Culture from the 1960s to the 1990s*. Sydney: Allen & Unwin.

Rampton, J. (2004) Björn Ulvaeus: the winner rakes it in, *The Independent*, 2 April.

Robertson, P. (1996) *Guilty Pleasures: Feminist Camp from Mae West to Madonna*. London: Duke University Press.

Rodman, G. (1996) *Elvis After Elvis: The Posthumous Career of a Living Legend*. London: Routledge.

Romney, J. and Wootton, A. (eds) (1995) *Celluloid Jukebox: Popular Music and the Movies Since the 50s*. London: BFI Publishing.

Shuker, R. (2001) *Understanding Popular Music*. New York: Routledge.

Strausbaugh, J. (2001) *Rock Til You Drop: The Decline from Rebellion to Nostalgia*. London: Verso.

Turner, G. (1993) Who killed the radio star? The death of teen radio in Australia, in T. Bennett, S. Frith, L. Grossberg, J. Shepherd and G. Turner (eds) *Rock and Popular Music: Politics, Policies, Institutions*. London: Routledge.

Wall, D.S. (2003) Policing Elvis: legal action and the shaping of post-mortem celebrity culture as contested space, *Entertainment Law*, 2(3): 35–70.

Wallis, R. and Malm, K. (1993) From state monopoly to commercial oligopoly: European broadcasting policies and popular music output over the airwaves, in T. Bennett, S. Frith, L. Grossberg, J. Shepherd and G. Turner (eds) *Rock and Popular Music: Politics, Policies, Institutions*. London: Routledge.

3 Roses and rotten tomatoes: a case study of Liverpool's Mathew Street festival and the contested spaces of cultural redevelopment

Holly Tessler

This chapter evaluates the varied roles and functions of tribute bands in Liverpool's past and contemporary cultural regeneration strategies. I seek to first place the argument in historical context, focusing primarily on contested and conflicted views of Beatles-oriented, vernacular heritage-based tourism schemes. Secondly, I aim to establish a 'cultural framework' (Waterman 1998) for tribute bands through a detailed case study of the city's annual Mathew Street festival (MSF), particularly in relation to the current redevelopment and rebranding plans leading up to the city's designation as the 2008 European Capital of Culture.[1]

Introduction

In the 1960s, Liverpool, once the most venerated of Britain's Victorian port towns, had seen its waning maritime fortunes eclipsed by an industry of an entirely different sort – Beat music. In a city better known for its gritty shipyards and seamy docklands, this new Liverpool – the Beatles' Liverpool – found itself transformed by an unexpected yet not entirely welcome cultural renaissance. In a city so regularly caricaturized by the national media as scruffy, lazy, and aimless, prone to violence, crime and alcoholism, native Liverpudlians, or *Scousers*, as they are known across England, suddenly found themselves in the midst of a celebrated and frenzied Beatle-band production line.

But where countless bands could echo the Beatles' early look and sound, the Fab Four ultimately proved to be a commodity that was not so easily reproducible. When John, Paul, George and Ringo left their hometown in 1964, they took with them a rich amalgam of Liverpool's music scene, as well as its Scouse sensibilities. Moving beyond the Merseybeat cornerstone, the Beatles soon wearied of their matching suits and haircuts, opting instead for a radically new image drawn from a wellspring of worldly influences – Dylan's folk music, San Francisco's psychedelia, Indian mysticism – to create an entirely new pop music paradigm. They were now exploring transcendental meditation, mind-expanding drugs and the *Tibetan Book of the Dead*. Musically, intellectually, and spiritually, by 1967, Liverpool and the Liverpool Beat music scene were being passed by. As Paul Du Noyer (2002: 90) wrote: 'It was a good place to have come from, but not a groovy place to be.'

When the Beatles disbanded in 1970, Liverpool's hope to endure as a creative-commercial hub seemed equally bleak, as city leaders were forced to confront the grim local repercussions of a national economic crisis. Inner cities with a heavy industrial base were hardest hit by a country-wide recession, few worse than Liverpool. Job losses in the docks and ports, the manufacturing plants and railways, led to an unemployment rate of 50 per cent in some of the city's most blue-collar areas (Wilson and Womersley 1976). With Liverpool's population declining by a third (Connell and Gibson 2003), the first years of the post-Beatle era infected the city with an economic, cultural and social malaise:

> Liverpool's inner area then is a combination of three characteristics of urban stress: an extensive area of poor housing and environment with concentrations of those at the economic and social margins of urban society. The inner area of Liverpool contains one half of the city's population and the areas with the worst concentration of economic and social stress alone have a population of 70,000 or about 11% of the total.
>
> (Wilson and Womersley 1976: 17)

Without its industrial lifeblood of the docks or the cultural core of the Beatles and Merseybeat, Liverpool seemed mired in its own depression, both economic and spiritual. The effects of the deindustrialization of Liverpool reverberated all the way to Downing Street, as attempts at generating local initiatives appeared to be diametrically in opposition to the ideas of the Conservative Prime Minister, Margaret Thatcher, who had 'less sympathy for people employed in the public sector, avoid[ed] visits to the depressed north, and on one famous occasion castigated those who "drool and drivel" about caring for those in need' (Jones 1989: 3).

With little more than token national support for investment or redevelopment programmes, the well-worn social fabric of Merseyside unravelled even further. Throughout these troubled circumstances, Liverpool's prospects still seemed synchronistically intertwined with the Beatles. On the very day the world was waking to the news of the murder of Beatle John Lennon, on 9 December 1980, the Policy and Finance Committee of the

Liverpool City Council was passing a resolution to adopt an equal opportunities policy in the hope of cauterizing the racial animosity festering in the toughest quarters of the city (Gifford *et al.* 1989).

Yet in an area never entirely free from upheaval, heightening friction between the unemployed and the working class, and between the poor, the minorities and the *Scallies*,[2] ignited in the city's Toxteth neighbourhood in 1981:

> For two sensational TV nights, this inner city slum enacted England's oldest nightmare: the rabble of masterless men, roaming in fire and ruin. Liverpool's sky glowed red across the Mersey ... Across the main streets, police lined up in medieval battle rank, with helmets, sticks and shields. There was charge and counter-charge, petrol-bombing, looting and the first CS gas used outside of Ulster ... In the avalanche of explanations that followed, unemployment was the favourite culprit, followed by police harassment.
>
> (Du Noyer 2002: 163)

Lennon's death at the hands of a deranged fan seemed to presage and parallel the violence in Liverpool itself. Both Lennon's murder and the Toxteth riots drew a line under the largely unacknowledged, unspoken sentiment that Liverpool could conjure up at will its 1960s self-image as a kind of cultural anaesthesia for its current and substantial social problems. No band member had lived in the city for years; and with Lennon's death, the Beatles were truly never returning to Liverpool. Moreover, the Cavern Club, the venue that catapulted the Beatles to stardom, where they played nearly 300 gigs, was demolished in 1973.

Following the 1981 riots, Mrs Thatcher appointed Conservative politician Michael Heseltine as Minister of the Inner Cities to oversee the rebuilding of Liverpool. He reflected on the post-riot state of Merseyside as one that 'lacked leadership, there was no communal pride; it was imbued with the psychology of failure' (cited in Baxter 2001).

Perhaps unsurprisingly then, in their *Merseyside Structure Plan*, county planners shifted focus from Liverpool itself, concluding instead that Southport – a sleepy coastal village popular with old-age pensioners – was Merseyside's most valuable arts, cultural and tourist resource, where 'trade must be encouraged to grow to keep up with the increasing competition amongst sea-side resorts' (Merseyside County Council 1980: 133). The specific arts and cultural industries to be promoted in Southport were defined as those 'covering independent and subsidised provision of museums, galleries, the performed arts, heritage houses, film and cinema, the arts in the media including television and radio and community and ethnic arts programmes' (Liverpool City Council 1987a: 3). These cultural forms were considered 'crucial to the future of the tourism industry because of the nature of the arts customers from outside the region. Such "tourists", unlike many other visitors, continue to come to Merseyside in winter and are relatively high spenders' (1987a: 5).

Nevertheless, Heseltine remained unconvinced by vernacular strategies like these, and instead utilized the worldwide attention Lennon's death brought to Liverpool as a catalyst for promoting his own, more broadly-based regeneration and redevelopment plans. Conveniently, his ideas fed directly into the national government's growing interest in exploiting sites of cultural heritage as a base for tourism. So at the same time that grieving Beatles fans from all global corners were beginning to make 'pilgrimages' to Liverpool, the definition of UK national heritage landmarks was being broadened to include key popular music sites like the London home of 1960s guitarist Jimi Hendrix (Cohen 2003). Long-time Merseybeat locals like club owner Allan Williams (an early Beatles manager) and former Cavern compere Bob Wooler seized on this perceived opportunity and lobbied stridently for a Beatle-specific development plan, but Merseyside officials were far less enthusiastic. Pam Wilsher, director of the Merseyside Tourism and Conference Bureau, observed that two different 'camps' existed in Liverpool: 'those who feel that the Beatles were local lads who made good and then turned their backs on the city'; and those who feel 'that Liverpool shouldn't have to rely on four lads – there's more to it than that' (cited in Cohen 2004: 8).

The coexistence of two such divergent views regarding the role the Beatles should play in the regeneration of Liverpool underscored the long-standing ambivalence local residents felt towards the group and their legacy. When asked how Liverpool should remember the Beatles, Mike McCartney, Paul's younger brother, suggested the council could 'Erect two separate statues. Rotten tomatoes could be thrown at one, and bunches of roses at the other' (cited in Du Noyer 2002: 15).

Accordingly the city's official *Tourism Strategy for Liverpool*, published in 1987, acknowledged the need to include the Beatles in development plans for Merseyside tourism, but did so with a decidedly understated tone:

> The Cavern Quarter has obvious musical associations, particularly with the Beatles, and has therefore been of tourism interest for some time. This role has considerably expanded in recent years with the development of Cavern Walks as a speciality shopping centre, and the future of the area as a retailing/tourism and music area is becoming established.
>
> (Liverpool City Council 1987b: 9)

Despite the tepid support for a Beatle-based tourism industry, private interests persisted, catering not to the broad-based cultural tourist market in general, but rather to the niche market of Beatle enthusiasts, encouraged by local fan-based, grass-roots organizations:

In 1977 a couple of local Beatle fans established the Liverpool Beatles Appreciation Society ... with the help of a couple of associates of the Beatles and other local fans such as Ron Jones, Public Relations Officer at Merseyside County Council. Ron knew that Beatle fans visiting Liverpool would like more information on the city and its Beatles connections ... Eventually the County Council took over the running of the fan convention, but when the council was abolished by Thatcher's Conservative government a year later, Cavern City Tours (CCT), a private company which had been set up by a couple of official Beatles guides, took over.

(Cohen 2004: 7)

When the city finally began culturally-based revitalization efforts along the Albert Dock and in the central business district, there were designs for likening 'the connection between Liverpool and the Beatles to that between Shakespeare and Stratford, thus suggesting a parallel with high culture' (Cohen 2004: 8).

From this historical basis, Liverpool brought its troubled economy, its ambivalence toward the Beatle legacy, but also its indefatigable entrepreneurial bent, into the 1990s, with mixed results: 'No other urban area in the UK can lay claim to having been host to every major urban policy experiment introduced over the past 35 years, including a Community Development Project, Inner Area Study, Urban Development Corporation, Enterprise Zone, and City Challenge programme' (Couch 2003: 344).

Despite its notoriety for the guzzling of regeneration monies, Liverpool was, gradually, beginning to see signs of improvement: from 1995–9, total employment in the city grew by 10.4 per cent and tourist spending also grew sharply, reaching £604 million in 2000 (Jones and Wilks-Heeg 2004: 345). In a significant shift from policies formulated just a decade earlier, Liverpool leaders had come to realize the economic potential of activities rooted in the leisure, arts and tourism industries, making activities based in these areas the central focus in the city's successful bid to become Europe's 2008 Capital of Culture (Jones and Wilks-Heeg 2004: 347).

Using Liverpool's annual MSF as a case study, the remainder of this chapter will seek to explore the role of and implications for festivals and tribute bands in this new cultural regeneration paradigm for the city.

The MSF

The first MSF was held in 1992, as an adjunct event to the annual Liverpool Beatles convention started by Ron Jones and Cavern City Tours (CCT) in 1977. The one-day convention, then wholly self-contained in the city's Adelphi Hotel, attracted an array of Beatle memorabilia merchants, fans and

Figure 3.1 The 'Mona Lennon', St George's Hall, Liverpool. The work is the creation of Alex Corina (Art Works agency), Liverpool. Photograph courtesy of Holly Tessler

various Beatle-related guest speakers such as Allan Williams and Sam Leach (an early Liverpool Beat music promoter). As the day ended, many convention attendees would informally gather at sites that were of importance to the Beatle legacy, especially the pubs and clubs of Mathew Street, the home of the Cavern Club, reconstructed in 1984 and integrated into the surrounding upmarket shopping centre now called Cavern Walks. As both the owners of the Cavern Club and the organizers of the Beatle convention, CCT saw a natural link between tribute bands and the reconstituted Cavern, and sought to exploit the economic potential inherent in having a captive and Beatle-friendly audience already present in Liverpool. For Beatle fans, many of whom had never been able to see the Beatles perform, watching a tribute band performing the group's music onstage at (a version of) the Cavern Club would fulfil a large part of the 'pilgrimage' and celebratory experiences of coming to Liverpool for specific Beatle-related events.

From this beginning, the festival gradually evolved into 'Beatle Week', an annual celebration of the Beatles in Liverpool, spanning the days around the UK Bank Holiday at the end of August. In ensuing years, Beatle Week was incorporated into the more broadly-based MSF. In 2005, approximately 300,000 people participated in the festival, with another estimated 50,000 accessing live feeds of the event through the official website (Tinniswood

2001: 3). It is a significant contributor to the estimated £200 million Liverpool reaps each year from Beatles- and Merseybeat-related tourism (*Liverpool Echo* 2005). Groups with names like the Aussie Beatles, Ringer, the Repeatles, and Tripper travel from places as remote as Tokyo, Argentina and Australia to provide Beatle music to festival-goers in venues across the city.

That the MSF has become such a successful and iconic element of Liverpool's cultural regeneration strategies is worthy of investigation in several ways. Firstly, it can be argued that the MSF serves a transformational function for both fans and entrepreneurs, temporarily altering 21st-century Liverpool into a re-creation of its 1960s image. Secondly, this 'transformed' Liverpool has become a key site for heritage-based tourism, or 'pilgrimages', not only generating significant amounts of revenue, but also, more significantly, working as a cultural bridging mechanism, linking 'high' and 'low' cultural forms (Waterman 1998). Finally, this melding of high and low culture legitimates the involvement of public-private enterprise and investment in popular music and Beatle-related events in the city. On a pragmatic level, implications of this paradigm shift are visible in the Liverpool Culture Company's involvement in and extension of the MSF as part of the re-branding of Liverpool.[3] In assuming control of the MSF in 2004, the Culture Company broadened the scope of the festival to include a wider array of tribute bands as well as recruiting well-known acts for the first time in the event's history. This administrative and aesthetic shift in spirit also underscores the importance, although perhaps obliquely, of the economic and social benefits of tribute bands in a cultural industries-based economy.

Waterman (1998) writes that festivals transform landscape and place into temporary environments, but ones that are imbued with meaningful cultural status by a particular group or segment of the population. More critically, however, he argues that 'a festival's designers use it to (re)construct the place at which it is held' (p. 58). This seems especially true of the MSF, where the reconstruction is both literal and metaphorical. There is an inherent resonance, or perhaps even irony, in that the MSF's central focus is on Beatle *tribute* bands performing in a *replica* of the Cavern Club.

This emphasis on simulated experience and artificiality seems to underscore the city's historical ambivalence about the relevance of the Beatles to the long-term plans of the city. That is to say, there is a clear peculiarity in 300,000 people making a trip to Liverpool each year, a kind of popular music pilgrimage, when the Beatles as a group ceased to exist in 1970, and left Liverpool even earlier still. The function of the festival, then, is plainly not to fete the Beatles themselves but in the words of CCT Director Bill Heckle, to 'celebrate the music of the Beatles by listening to great musicians play their songs' (cited in Shaughnessy 2005: 20).

So it may be argued that the Beatles or their music actually have very little to do with the motivation and expectations of the festival-goers. Fans of the group are not directly supporting the Beatles through their participation in the MSF, but celebrating their Beatle *fandom*. The reconstituted Cavern Club and the scores of Beatle tribute acts are not the central focus of the festival after all, but simply the backdrop and the mechanism that enables attendees to reaffirm their fan status through the adaptation/imitation/re-creation of 1960s audience behaviour in approximations of the places where the original musical events took place decades earlier. In a broader sense, Waterman views this aspect of festival-going as 'a group celebration of shared mythologies and values through managed interaction' (1998: 59). Indeed, in personal observations made during the last four MSFs, many attendees arrive in Liverpool in fancy dress. A walk down any city centre street during festival time will produce sightings of dozens of people dressed as the Beatles, with appropriate props: 'John Lennon'-styled round glasses, Sergeant Pepper-era jackets, or mop-top wigs. Others will arrive in Mod- or other 1960s-styled outfits, with Beatle boots and caps, or mini-dresses and 'retro' hairstyles. Some demonstrate their fandom in less noticeable ways, through the wearing of Beatles T-shirts, jackets or by carrying rucksacks with Beatles patches or de-signs. These highly visible and distinctive 'badges' of Beatle fandom are de-signed not only to attract the attention of other like-minded people, but also to publicly display a high degree of devotion to the group. During perfor-mances by Beatle tribute acts, I have witnessed some festival-goers who will also re-enact 1960s audience behaviour by rushing to the front of the stage, performing dances of the era, or yelling 'I love you, Paul!' to performers.

Liverpool as a site of musical pilgrimage

By distinguishing themselves from the crowd through such visible and memorable displays of fancy dress or mimicked 1960s behaviour, it may be suggested that many of the fans attending the MSF are at least partially motivated to do so through a desire to experience the full festival environ-ment. By extension then, it could be argued that MSF attendees are looking to experience Liverpool as a *place* – perhaps firstly as a festival spot, but also, more critically, as a social, historical and symbolic site (Waterman 1998) of personal significance. Drawing attention to how music comes to embody particular generational experiences, Connell and Gibson cite Wheeler to suggest that 'Music has the ability to evoke personal memory, to place something in one's life in a personalised period context' (2003: 222). The MSF may serve as a catalyst for fans to reminisce about events from their youth, to relive through the tribute band experience how it was to be in Liverpool, in the Cavern Club, listening and dancing to the music of the Beatles. It may also give these original supporters a kind of 'cultural capital' (Bourdieu 1986) in the form of 'bragging rights' around younger or inter-national fans who had never had the opportunity to see the group perform, particularly in Liverpool.

The MSF can also be seen to serve a fetishistic function that embodies something more than nostalgia. For collectors and trivia buffs, a trip to Liverpool, to participate in the largest celebration of Beatles music, particularly in the group's hometown, represents the ultimate souvenir – another kind of intangible, invaluable piece of cultural capital, of one-upmanship among fellow enthusiasts. Connell and Gibson (2003: 223) argue this kind of commodity fetishism can segue into *place* fetishization. For fans who live either far away from Liverpool or are simply too young to have participated in the first wave of Beatlemania, a trip to Liverpool very much serves two purposes of pilgrimage: first, like a true religious pilgrimage, fans may seek to make a journey of reverent homage. Particularly in the years following Lennon's murder, musical pilgrims came to Liverpool to honour Lennon (and increasingly also George Harrison following his 2001 death from cancer) as a musical or social martyr in the same way religious pilgrims may journey to sacred places like Israel or Mecca. It is an everyday sight in Liverpool to see visitors laying flowers and cards, taking photos and listening to music on headphones while standing in front of Beatle-related local sites. While this behaviour may be marginalized or even mocked by non-fans, the MSF then becomes almost a quasi-religious holiday, gathering like-minded people in a celebration of a shared and collective understanding of the Beatles' influence on their lives but also on contemporary society.

A second type of pilgrimage served by visits to the city of Liverpool, and specifically the MSF, is a pilgrimage of self-introspection, perhaps even of 'retro-introspection', in what Herbert suggests is a 'merging of the real and the imagined, which gives ... places a special meaning' (cited in Kruse 2003: 158). Music can be understood to imbue its listeners with an 'affective investment' (Connell and Gibson 2003: 222), creating multi-layered emotional and/or personal meaning. For Beatles fans removed either geographically or temporally from Liverpool and/or the 1960s, music can generate representational notions of place as mediated through personal constructs of lyrical references. Kruse (2003) argues that this is a kind of discursive practice, with fans seeking to reconcile and contextualize their own meanings of the Beatles, of their music and of Liverpool with their own imagined and perceived notions of them. In other words, MSF-goers come to Liverpool to experience the 'real' Liverpool, to understand the essence of the city as embodied and made meaningful through their own consumption and understanding of the music of the Beatles. By allowing festival attendees to stand where the Beatles stood, to see what the Beatles saw, to be where the Beatles were, the MSF serves as a medium for the transmission of social and personal knowledge.

Bridging high and low cultural forms

There are many potential (and overlapping) motivations for audience members attending the MSF. I would now like to turn my attention to some of the implications of the MSF for city leaders and local entrepreneurs. Within the context of the city's designation as the 2008 European Capital of Culture, cultural and vernacular celebrations, including the MSF, have come under close scrutiny as Liverpool seeks to rebrand itself under the literal and metaphorical banner of 'The World in One City'. My aim in this section is to illuminate several reasons why the MSF should be considered as a kind of 'cultural bridge' in this transitional period in Liverpool's redevelopment history.

Firstly, as Chapple (2005) suggests, there is an underlying but significant change in the perception of tribute bands within Liverpool's larger popular music economy. He argues that 'nostalgia fuelled by the realisation of the impossibility of seeing bands such as the Beatles performing live again' (p. 22) may be generating heightened interest in the tribute band experience. He makes a second point in stating that escalating and exorbitant ticket prices for concerts by chart acts like Robbie Williams, Madonna or U2 make a night out to see a tribute band in a small local venue an increasingly attractive proposition. Finally, he suggests that tribute bands serve a postmodern, ironic niche-market appeal, 'being so unhip they [are] hip among the cognoscenti' looking for an alternative to the usual local musical offerings (p. 22).

Tribute bands are increasingly becoming a very specific micro-market in Liverpool, operating under a unique set of cultural and economic practices. For instance, The Word is Love website is an e-zine 'featuring reviews, articles, and the latest news about Beatles tribute bands all over the world' (2005). Similarly, Fab Productions is a Liverpool-based booking agency involved with the organization of the MSF. Its website heralds the company's involvement in the 1999 MSF, specifically its role in bringing together '6 top tribute bands providing the most amazing recreation of a late 60s pop festival' (Fab Productions 2005). A 2000 newspaper article estimated the number of Liverpool-based Beatle tribute bands to be around 250, including acts such as the Bootleg Beatles, Help, Revolver, the Apple Pies, the Roaches, the Scarabs and the Nowhere Men (Moyes 2000: 9).

Perhaps the most compelling evidence to date for the importance of the tribute band subculture to Liverpool's music and local economies is the announcement of a series of 'tribute conventions' organized for 2006 by CCT and From Me To You, a Beatles memorabilia and souvenir shop inside Cavern Walks, adjacent to the Cavern Club itself. Billed as '12-hour rock extravaganzas' (Cavern City Tours 2005), promoters have, to date, booked 34 events to be held from January to November 2006. Beginning at noon and ending at midnight, each convention is expected to have a 'headline tribute act, support act, rare and vintage film footage, guest speakers and forums, and memorabilia'. Featuring 'classic' rock line-ups, the weekly events have conventions celebrating acts such as Bon Jovi, Kiss, the Rolling Stones, Status Quo, Queen and the Jam.

Significantly, this growing tribute band micro-economy and the MSF have clear ties to the more formalized and 'high culture' regeneration efforts ongoing in the city. In its *Strategic Business Plan* for 2005–9, the Liverpool Culture Company lists the MSF alongside other local events like the Arabic Arts festival, the Merseyside Dance Initiative's annual LEAP festival and the Children's Theatre festival in a bid to foster 'a creative communities programme that forms an integral part of the arts programme linking through content, subject matter, audience development and participation opportunities, with artists that work across participation boundaries' (Liverpool Culture Company 2005b: 14).

This type of vague and loosely-phrased hyperbole certainly gives the dubious impression that 'Liverpool's cultural identity is in the process of being actively created rather than simply being revealed' (Jones and Wilks-Heeg 2004: 352). Along with the Liverpool Culture Company's involvement with the festival in 2005, an added £350,000 was found for a radical makeover of the MSF's more homespun, DIY aesthetic (Riley 2005: 15). In a press release issued on 12 August 2005, the Liverpool Culture Company stated that it: 'has sought to revolutionise the festival ... by signing named bands for the first time in the event's 13-year history. The aim is to reflect the fact that Mathew Street did not just create the Merseybeat sound via the Cavern in the 60s but was hugely influential in the 70s, 80s, and 90s' (Liverpool Culture Company 2005a).

The added investment and publicity increased the viability of the MSF to the extent that it is now promoted as Europe's biggest free annual music festival (Chapple 2005). What the 2005 festival lost in focus it certainly gained in breadth, as the two headlining bands, the Buzzcocks and the Stranglers, played alongside acts as diverse as Tony Christie, McFly, Lemar and a variety of local acts including Amsterdam, Zombina and the Skeletones, and Tramp Attack.

The 2005 event unfolded at six main outdoor stages dotted around the city centre and Pier Head, including one across the River Mersey at Woodside, Wirral. Tribute acts, while no longer the featured element of the overall festival, were still the star attraction in the designated 'Mathew Street Music Zone' during the three-day Bank Holiday between 27 and 29 August, with just over 150 acts playing in 15 participating clubs and pubs in the Mathew Street area.

In a sense, then, Jones and Wilks-Heeg's (2004) argument that the Capital of Culture redevelopment plans are privileging tourism and 'branded' culture is self-evident. They cite the recent closure of the Picket (a live music venue and recording studio constructed within the Merseyside Trade Union building) for a proposed conversion to loft apartments as a particularly austere example of the commodification and politicization of vernacular culture (and cultural spaces). Indeed, their position could be extended to include the MSF. Once the exclusive space of Beatles fans, the symbolic and celebratory act of making a pilgrimage to the 'place where it all began' has been eradicated by a louder, bigger and more generic music festival in which Beatles music and tribute bands play only a supporting role. From a historical perspective, it would appear that local leaders were slow to draft any formal Beatles-based tourism and regenerations plans, but quick to adapt and enhance them when the promise of Capital of Culture beckoned. Jones and Wilks-Heeg ultimately conclude that the Capital of Culture process 'is in danger of simply using "diversity" and the discourse of social inclusion to legitimate an economically motivated regeneration strategy' (2004: 357). While this may be true, I feel it is perhaps an unduly cynical view. By contrast, Waterman takes a more moderate and pragmatic theoretical stance, one that I feel ultimately has more resonance for the MSF, the Capital of Culture plan, and Liverpool in general. In referring to the 'bridging' function of festivals Waterman suggests they serve as vital links between the global and the local; between elite and popular culture; and between public and private enterprise (1998: 67). He argues that festivals, like any kind of arts development, are part of the inevitability of the fusion between the commercial and the creative.

Conclusion

In a strange way it stands to reason that in the birthplace of the Beatles, the city's most popular tourism and music venture, is a week-long festival of tribute bands housed in a re-created Cavern Club. Liverpool has always been a city slow to appreciate its own worth; a place determined to pave over its history only to re-create it decades later. It is the city that bulldozed the Cavern Club only to excavate it not ten years afterwards. The Beatles Story museum at the Albert Dock features mock-up displays from Brian Epstein's NEMS department store,[4] as the store itself has since become an Ann Summers lingerie shop. The city is presently razing Ringo Starr's childhood home on Madryn Street in Liverpool's Dingle neighbourhood, only to reassemble it, brick by brick, in a more tourist-friendly part of the city.

This behaviour suggests the city has always been uncertain of the worth of its cultural assets: whether to throw roses or rotten tomatoes at the legacy of the Beatles and Merseybeat. The MSF and its emphasis on tribute bands and artificiality may suggest city leaders are indeed attempting to 'normalize' or even obliterate vernacular culture to make way for tourist-friendly, 'destination' or pilgrimage experiences of Liverpool. But I would argue this view is only a superficial reading of the MSF and its full cultural worth. While it is not the most readily evident, or perhaps even the most desired, form of vernacular culture, the tribute band experience, via the MSF, has nevertheless had an undeniable impact on the city. Critics of Liverpool's impending Capital of Culture status argue that events like Beatle Week and the MSF contribute to the quashing of 'alternative' or 'authentic' local music and culture in the city. To an extent, this is true. A walk through the city centre is all that is necessary to plainly understand that Liverpool is being figuratively and physically transformed through and because of its Capital of Culture status.

Yet to adopt a bifurcated, 'us and them'/'visitors and locals' stance is perhaps unnecessarily defensive. The MSF and tribute band culture can more optimistically be perceived as a kind of 'cultural bridge' (Waterman 1998) serving the pragmatic function of linking economics and infrastructural dynamics to this idea of 'capital-c' Culture. Through their very definition, tribute bands may not be producing original creative material, but they nevertheless need musical instruments, rehearsal spaces, performance venues, promoters, agents and outfitters. The festival-goers that come to Liverpool for a week each August patronize pubs, hotels, restaurants and shops. They take tours, they buy souvenirs, they dine out. The local music industry infrastructure required to support the MSF each summer is utilized by 'authentic' local music acts and fans year-round. Instead of heightening the tensions between high and low, authentic and inauthentic, and vernacular and globalized culture, detractors should instead consider embracing the multifarious perceived ideas of Liverpool that the MSF encourages, and the linkages between art and place, and celebration and enterprise.

Notes

1   The introductory section of this chapter was originally presented in an earlier draft version at the EU Postgraduate Conference sponsored by the Centre de Recherches Interculturelles Sur Les Domaines Anglophones et Francophones/ SOCRATES, Universidado do Algarve, Faro, Portugal, April 2004.
2   *Scally*, deriving from *scallywag*, is derogatory British slang for a Liverpudlian, stereotypically classed as an unemployed, uneducated thug, often with a criminal record and a penchant for wearing tracksuits and baseball caps.
3   Formed on 10 July 2000, the Liverpool Culture Company is the administrative body originally formed 'to prepare and submit the bid to become the UK nomination for European Capital of Culture ... Following the announcement of Liverpool as the winner of the competition ... the transition of Liverpool Culture Company from a bidding to delivery organisation began' (Liverpool Culture Company 2005b: 5–6).
4   NEMS, an acronym for North End Music Stores, was a department store owned by the Epstein family and managed by Brian Epstein, the future manager of the Beatles. The NEMS shop in Whitechapel, Liverpool city centre, was only several hundred yards away from the Cavern Club in Mathew Street.

References

Baxter, L. (2001) The scars that time can't heal. http:icliverpool.icnetwork.co.uk/printable_version.cfm?objectid=11133820 (accessed 8 March 2004).

Bourdieu, P. (1986) *Distinction: A Social Critique of the Judgement of Taste*. London: Routledge.

Cavern City Tours (2005) www.cavern-liverpool.co.uk/12hourrock/main.htm (accessed 19 November 2005).

Chapple, M. (2005) The sincerest form of flattery, *Liverpool Daily Post*, 23 August: 22–3.

Cohen, S. (2003) Heritage, in J. Shepherd, D. Horn, D. Laing, P. Oliver and P. Wicke (eds) *Continuum Encyclopedia of Popular Music of the World. Volume 1: Media, Industry and Society*. London: Continuum International Publishing Group.

Cohen, S. (2004) Screaming at the moptops: convergences between tourism and popular music, in D. Crouch, R. Jackson and F. Thompson (eds) *Convergent Cultures: the Media and the Tourist Imagination*. London: Routledge.

Connell, J. and Gibson, C. (2003) *Sound Tracks: Popular Music, Identity and Place*. London: Routledge.

Couch, C. (2003) *City of Change and Challenge – Urban Planning and Regeneration in Liverpool*. Aldershot: Ashgate.

Du Noyer, P. (2002) *Liverpool: Wondrous Place: Music From Cavern to Cream*. London: Virgin Books.

Fab Productions (2005) www.fabproductions.co.uk (accessed 19 November 2005).

Gifford, A.M., Brown, W. and Bundy, R. (1989) *Loosen the Shackles: First Report of the Liverpool 8 Inquiry into Race Relations in Liverpool*. London: Karia Press.

Jones, B. (1989) *Political Issues in Britain Today*. Manchester: Manchester University Press.

Jones, P. and Wilks-Heeg, S. (2004) Capitalising culture: Liverpool 2008, Local Economy 19(3): 341–60.

Kruse, R.J. (2003) Imagining Strawberry Fields as a place of pilgrimage, *Area*, 35(2): 154–62.

Liverpool City Council (1987a) *An Arts and Cultural Industries Strategy for Liverpool: A Framework*. Liverpool: Liverpool City Council.

Liverpool City Council (1987b) *A Tourism Strategy For Liverpool: A Framework*. Liverpool: Liverpool City Council.

Liverpool Culture Company (2005a) *Is This the Way . . . to Mathew Street?* Liverpool: City of Liverpool, 12 August.

Liverpool Culture Company (2005b) *Strategic Business Plan, 2005–2009*. Liverpool: City of Liverpool.

Liverpool Echo (2005) Our debt to Fab Four: region now reaps £200m annually from its Merseybeat heritage, 30 August: 10.

Merseyside County Council (1980) *Merseyside Structure Plan: Written Statement.* Liverpool: Merseyside County Council.

Moyes, J. (2000) How 2,000 people are employed by the Beatles, *The Independent,* 14 November: 9.

Riley, J. (2005) Big names in festival makeover, *Liverpool Daily Post,* 2 July: 15.

Shaughnessy, J. (2005) 200 bands tune up for a musical double act, *Liverpool Daily Post,* 25 August: 20–1.

The Word is Love (2005) www.thewordislove.co.uk (accessed 19 November 2005).

Tinniswood, R. (2001) Why we're top of the pops all year round, *Liverpool Echo,* 24 August: 3.

Waterman, S. (1998) Carnivals for elites, *Progress in Human Geography,* 22(1): 54–74.

Wilson, H. and Womersley, L. (1976) *Liverpool Inner Area Study: Study Review.* London: Department of the Environment.

4 The Beatles live in Moscow, 1982: tribute audiences, music history and memory

Shane Homan

On study leave from my university in Australia, a visit to Liverpool in the summer of 2004 assumed heightened significance for my family for a number of reasons. I was raised in Australian suburbia by parents well versed in the Beatles. This became clear to me throughout my childhood: being woken at midnight to watch the first television screening of *Help!*; the occasional reminiscences of my mother that she was unable to attend the Beatles' arrival at Sydney airport in 1964 due to my impending arrival. My father had worked as a drummer (with the obligatory black pearl Ludwig drum kit just like Ringo's) in the mid-1960s with a Sydney covers band that owed at least part of its popularity to the number of Beatles songs in the set list.

In terms of my ongoing Beatles education, in the eyes of some of my family, the extent of personal investment demanded that I experience *all* the Fab Four tourist sites on offer. Two memories stand out from my professional and personal tour(ist) of duty. The City Council-sanctioned 'Magical Mystery' bus tour of Beatle childhood homes and song landmarks that ends with a visit to the reconstructed (and slightly re-sited) Cavern Club, was memorable for the guide's refrain 'and the rest is history!' that collapsed tasteless jokes about manager Brian Epstein's sexuality and individual suburban aspirations into a simplistic narrative of supposedly self-evident destiny. Persisting, a visit to the Liverpool Beatles Museum provided one flash of insight among the array of stage costumes, anodyne timelines and Ringo pencil cases. Entering the 'audience room', the visitor is confronted with a wall of television screens/ screams of emotional teens at various Beatles concerts, airport arrivals and television programme appearances. The combination of high volume and multiple screens is effective in conveying the heightened sense of fan emotions.

Continuing my own mapping of the city's 'Beatlescape', I met Tony (36) and Karen (37)[1] at a Beatles charity concert staged at the Jacaranda pub in Liverpool in December 2004. As part of the famous circuit of Beatles tourist pubs, the Jacaranda continues to host Beatles tribute and cover acts and discussion nights in its small cellar performance space. 1960s photos of

Beatles managers, school friends and local music industry figures adorn the pub walls. On the night I met Tony and Karen, several well-known Liverpool Beatles acts played short sets, while the crowd was populated with tribute band musicians and older Beatles fans. While aged under 40, both Tony and Karen provided interesting accounts of how the Beatles have always been present in their lives:

> K: When John Lennon died we were still in middle school, about 11 ... you used to go and buy cheap tapes from Woolworths and they were, like, £1.99 at the time. [I] bought *Rock and Roll Years One and Two* ... My dad used to play Elvis and the Beatles, it was something he encouraged. Jonathon's mum and dad were similar, and [his] mum had seen the Beatles ... it was just a case of we carried on with the Beatles thing until you start to go out with boys who don't like the Beatles. Life changes and you grow out of things like that, but the common denominator is that you're always a Beatles fan.
>
> SH: So if 'you're into my music, I don't want to go out with you'? Was that ever a problem?
>
> K: No, 'cause I always thought I'd educate them ... my dad was always into rock and roll, Elvis, the Searchers, [Herman's] Hermits, Gerry and the Pacemakers ...
>
> SH: Was it the same for you Tony?
>
> T: Very much so actually. My mum and dad used to [pretend to] be Jimmy Saville on a Saturday afternoon and play old songs. And so I'd say, 'What's that song?' and they'd say, 'Oh, it's the Beatles'. The first album I ever bought was called *Beatles Love Songs* and I just played it and played it, the songs I thought were brilliant ... I remember one Christmas I got a radio cassette player and I could record off the radio. I used to wait of an evening, wait for a Beatles song ... I remember coming home early from school just to watch them on telly ... I mean, we tried to buy every single Beatles CD.
>
> K: I've got a *Beatles in Adelaide* on vinyl and that was so special to get ... it's not even their concerts, it's just interviews they did, and I remember thinking 'no one else has got this' and feeling, you felt like you were part of their little world.

The Beatles' impact upon different regions, fans and music industries tells us much about how rock and pop has been associated with youth leisure in specifically historical ways. The adolescent attachment to rock and roll was not simply about their configuration as new music/entertainment consumers; it also codified new forms of social and emotional investment in music's place in their lives. As Grossberg asserts, 'rock emerged as a way of mapping the specific structures of youth's affective alienation on the geographies of everyday life'; youth is thus an 'affective identity stitched onto a generational

history' (1992a: 179, 183). The importance of youth as both social and economic category in popular music has been at least partly eroded by the pur-
chasing power of older music consumers. As I've outlined in Chapter 2 in this
book, a global range of retro-music media exists to cater to the 'youthful'
audiences of the 1960s, 70s and 80s.

In this chapter, I want to briefly reflect upon the interesting position of
the tribute band fan, located between personal and generational histories,
identities and contemporary music experiences. All the tribute bands I've
interviewed stressed the wide age range of their audiences. Young children are
introduced to the Beatles, for example, through their parents taking them to a
Beatles tribute performance; many of the more successful tributes gained their
popularity with university student audiences. However, for most tributes,
those aged over 30 remain a core demographic group. For older tribute audiences, this involves a 'triple reading' of the tribute band experience. Firstly,
their own personal music narrative – why and how particular popular music
stars and genres mattered to them at particular times – must be taken into
account. This identifies the fan's own 'mattering maps' (Grossberg 1992a: 59)
about music within broader generational histories and spaces. Secondly, the
tribute fan engages with the historical narrative of the imitated, recalling
their own hierarchies of career highlights, key recordings and live performances, videos and television moments. Thirdly, the tribute fan must engage
with the contemporary performative moment, the tribute band's staging of
the imitation. We can add to these three layers of interpretation a further
consideration: understandings of how music celebrity circulates at the level of
everyday life, and that of the music industry.

Tribute bands employ a range of music and media texts, and historical
moments, in their representation of the original. The intertextual nature of
the performances obviously calls upon audiences to similarly acknowledge
the tribute as the height of textual mobility that incorporates texts from
different spaces and times. Taking into account the various forms of the en-
coding/decoding (Hall 1981) of particular eras and acts helps in better understanding the contemporary moment of tribute consumption.

As I aim to show, attitudes toward the tribute are informed by fans
making historically specific connections between their earlier music memories and their categorization as youth audiences; and their later understandings of genre, performer and social histories. All of these factors are
important in fan assessments about whether they have received 'value for
their money', that range from the deeply personal to the coolly rational. In
this chapter, I draw upon interviews with tribute musicians and tribute audience members, conducted in Britain in 2004, to provide a snapshot of the
interweaving of history, industry and personal memory in fan interpretations
of the tribute.

The tribute–audience relationship

An obvious, but important, difference between tribute and original acts is the displaced sense of adulation: both tribute performer and tribute fan share their passion for the original. Tribute performers openly position themselves first as fans, stating a case every night for the musical and social innovation of the original. Asked about some fans' obsessive scrutiny of the band's technical competency (did George really play an SG Gibson guitar on 'Revolution'?), the Bootleg Beatles' Neil Harrison stated that 'we're the real train spotters, we pick that stuff up straightaway anyway' (Harrison interview 2004). The tribute musician, like the fan, is an 'excessive reader' (Fiske 1992: 46), requiring an intimate knowledge of the songs to satisfy their own and audiences' satisfaction about the fidelity of the copy. Their function always remains secondary to the 'primary' text of the original star(s): 'I always loved [U2] as a child, but in January of 97, Affa let me borrow *Boy*, *October* and *War*, in that order and by the first notes of "I Will Follow" something in me stirred and I knew I'd never be the same. Being at the LA Popmart show six months later (at age 15) completely changed my life' ('Captive' (Courtney Lavender), guitarist in U2 tribute Exit, cited in Egolf 2003).

I should stress that I'm examining the tribute fan within a specific moment in pop and rock history, where tributes have been commonplace in many live music sectors for at least a decade, with fans able to place the historical deceit. The early experiences of the Bootleg Beatles in Russia in 1982 remind us of the importance of regional and historical contexts of reception:

> Suddenly from playing in these really small clubs [in Britain] we were in Russia playing ice hockey stadiums to 10,000 people. Funnily enough, it did cause a riot because they'd only seen us play 'She Loves You' and we hadn't got into the heavy rock. We were doing 'Back in the USSR' which is a quite heavy song, and then 'Revolution', and you've got these ten rows of Communist Party people all wearing their uniforms with their medals ... and at the back, all the kids and armed guards keeping everyone in their place. The moment we got into the late period stuff, they all got up and they couldn't contain them ... I got the impression that some people thought it was the Beatles. Despite the fact that John [Lennon] was actually dead, I don't think the news had carried to some places. And because my name was Harrison, I'm sure a lot of people thought the Beatles had finally made it to Russia.
>
> (Harrison interview 2004)

Turning pop music history on its head, the impression that Russian fans (and the government) believed they were seeing the Beatles in 1982 is plausible when one considers the absence of international tours and music media networks. Fans' access to stars, taken for granted in western markets, was withheld in the Soviet Union, a nation unfamiliar with rock concert 'rules' of conduct, 'because there hadn't really been anything like that before'. In contrast, Harrison found it particularly 'nerve-racking' in early performances at Liverpool's Everyman Theatre, given the audiences' collective knowledge of the Beatles songs and the city's 'ownership' of their early career narrative.

As with other aspects of popular music, the most intense relationships between tribute and fan are located in the ever-expanding Elvis tribute industry. As Rodman (1996) argues, Elvis fans in general seem more likely to advertise their feelings than other music fans. This is reflected in the circulation of Elvis tributes: marriages between male and female impersonators; fans having sex with impersonators in the belief that they will be closer to the King; fan clubs bestowing credibility upon particular acts as appropriately sincere tributes (Doss 1999). These kinds of relationship are located in 'fandom as pathology' discourses that characterize the fan as obsessive/fanatical, incapable of bringing reason to the intensity of their emotions (Jenson 1992). As Jenson (1992) and Jenkins (1992) have shown, such discourses are predicated upon particular structures of class, race and gender. Fans' enthusiasm for, and knowledge of, popular music is similarly judged (criticized) as a display of 'popular cultural capital' (Frith 1996: 9) at odds with 'rational' high culture. I am interested here in the processes of discrimination employed by fans in assessments of the tribute-as-representation: what kinds of (band, celebrity, industry) knowledge do tribute audiences bring to bear upon liking or disliking the performance?

For Björn Again, the different types of audience reaction supported initial music press assumptions that the fan base of Abba was young and female, according to its co-founder, Rod Leissle: 'I had no difficulty when starting the band asking for an Abba album; girls had them, but they would be down the back of the lounge somewhere ... Girls and gay guys would be into the band. Guys who came to the early shows would stand up the back, arms crossed and saying, "We're not into this"' (Leissle interview 2004). These early reactions say as much about gender distinctions between rock and pop consumption as they do about Björn Again performances within the masculine 'Oz Rock' Melbourne pub circuits of the late 1980s. The Bootleg Beatles were similarly aware of the tribute's attractions:

> When you start off there are many doubting Thomases out there who haven't seen the band and are a bit dubious ... they always think it can't sound as good and it will destroy the image of the band and the memories, that in some way this is a sort of blasphemous, sacrilegious act. We're not saying we're the fucking Beatles. But we're saying come and see it and we think you'll get a buzz out of it. We think

we can make you believe that some of the time *it is* the Beatles. It's a good laugh, it's fun and actually it's great to block out the world for a moment, for a couple of hours and remember those times because those times were so good and optimistic.

(Harrison interview 2004)

As stand-ins for the original band, fans I interviewed seemed to share the musicians' views about the potentially negative effects of tributes for other types of working musician. Asked about the potential for tributes to erode the performance opportunities for original acts, many made the distinction between older and contemporary acts:

It's bands you're not going to see again. It's not taking away from the original performance. It's the only chance you'll get. That's people of a certain generation. I mean, I never got to see Led Zeppelin, and it's a chance to see someone who sounds like them ... it's the closest I'll ever get.

(Michael, 53)

The thing with the tribute band is if the people they are taking off are still going, well, that's a bit rough isn't it? If they're not still with us...

(Dave, 25)

This argument – that most tributes fill a vacuum left by retired or dead stars – was made by different tribute audience members, and for different genres. Many factored in financial considerations, and believed original acts, re-formed or otherwise, had become too expensive: '[even] if they reform it would be like 80 quid a ticket' (Lucy, 26). Acts that reformed were viewed with particular scepticism, as poor tributes to their former selves:

We've seen the Bay City Rollers [10 years ago], absolutely atrocious, there were two or three original members, Les, Eric and the blonde-haired guitarist, I don't know his name, they were just really disappointing. They were the biggest, fattest blokes you've ever seen. They were original, but old. That says a lot about tribute bands, doesn't it? Tribute bands keep it fresh and young.

(Tony, 36)

For acts that remain viable touring and recording concerns, the tribute appeals in the knowledge that the original is less accessible:

I can't imagine you'd get Kylie Minogue playing in Preston [in northern England]. So for a lot of people who I suppose don't have the motivation or the finances perhaps to travel to London, it's the nearest they're ever going to get to see something that's *almost* real.

(Clare, 32)

The current spectacle of multiple 'Kylie Minogues' performing across Britain in theatres and pubs underlines the tribute's suburban roots. In providing a certain form of 'Kylie-ness', they are at the same time reminding audiences of the lack of access to the original, who is connected to global, rather than suburban, spaces and ambitions. If tribute audiences disagree about their favourite original bands and imitations, they share a sense of such events as entertainment. Where tribute musicians often went to great lengths to justify their work, most audience members unhesitatingly regarded the tribute concert as a pleasurable spectacle:

> Well, they're a bit of fun aren't they, really? ... They're good, because they don't take it so seriously ... I first discovered Björn Again at university ... it was just great fun because you know they're a tribute band, but it's just time to have a bit of a laugh.
>
> (Lucy, 26)

The comment that it was 'a bit of fun' was made many times by those interviewed. This was reinforced by groups of people who viewed the tribute concert as the 'fun night out', as a semi-regular event where all individual tastes can be accommodated:

> It's an opportunity for us to meet up and do something and have a bit of fun as well. So we'll get tickets to do this or that. It's the type of event where you can meet up and no one's going to be offended by seeing the Beatles. I would say most people would enjoy it or find some things that are good are about it.
>
> (Clare, 32)

Clearly, some audience members do not regard themselves as fans with a deep knowledge of the original act. For these people, the tribute competes more keenly with the cinema, theatre musical and the pub cover band in terms of defining a 'fun night out'.

At the same time, other fans clearly showed a greater investment in both the original act and the tribute-as-event. For example, girls aged between 10 and 16 arrived dressed in 'Dancing Queen' costumes for the Björn Again performance at the Liverpool Philharmonic on 5 December 2004. The girls' elaborate costumes are personal statements about their knowledge and appreciation of Abba, constructed at some remove from Abba's original performance and media contexts. At the same time, they emphasize such performances as audience events dominated by dancing and crowd singing.

Yet the notion that tributes offer fans the opportunity to indulge in pure pleasures of the past is misleading. In the final sections of the chapter, I wish to examine the ways in which tribute audiences actively judge performances against their own well-defined personal histories and understandings about what is at stake, both for the tribute act and the fan.

Moments of perfection

Some fans strive for the same commitment as the tribute, with careful attention to detail in costumes, make-up and knowledge of the original band's material. If the stage act is regarded as a performance, so too is the audience's role 'performed'. As 'Bono' in the Australian U2 Show, Gary Morris is regularly asked for autographs: '... earlier this year, Morris was mobbed at Dubai airport by fans convinced he was the genuine Bono. For years, he refused to sign autographs for people who mistook his identity. "Now I just do", he admits. "Because people get so disappointed when I say I'm not him"' (Benedictus 2004).

However, the ability to 'believe' in the performance is tempered by audiences' realistic assumptions. Gary, a man in his 'early fifties' who attended the Bootleg Beatles concert in Preston, believed it was important to 'play the music technically correct, yeah. I'll be looking for the guitar patterns, not so much [at] the voices, because anyone can shout. No one's got a voice like John's anyway; it's like trying to match Elvis. I look for the guitar, you know, rhythm and lead guitar and the bass'. Similarly, another audience member at the Preston gig had a series of interesting observations about the tribute:

> I think [the Bootleg Beatles] will be too good. I think they will be better than what the Beatles were in their early days, because I think they've probably practised more, or they've been going longer than the Beatles ... and they're going to be too good, because I imagine that the Beatles in their day when they came down here and played at Guildford Hall, they would have been rattling away with whatever they had. They probably only had some good amps. So you'd never get anywhere near the sound that these guys are going to get tonight.
> (Chris, 54)

Those I interviewed who were interested in the technical staging of the tribute circled around this supposed performative impasse: while individual performances cannot hope to match the original, studied virtuosity and contemporary stage technology offers the collective potential to be 'too good'. The tributes' attention to detail, perversely, can work against them, in producing a performance that is too polished, and in which the earlier limitations of amplification and sound clarity are neatly erased.

Talking about their expectations and knowledge of the tribute, many of the fans I interviewed, when pressed, were able to proceed beyond the 'bit of fun' discourses. As the comments cited above show, in reading the performance, tribute fans' starting point does not derive from a claim to the 'real', but from an acknowledgement that various layers of construction are always in play. This is summarized in one fan's belief that 'I suppose with tribute bands really, they're not lying, are they?' (Karen, 37). This remains the tribute's chief defence against their detractors – both audience and performer share, to borrow from cinema, in the 'referential illusion' (Moores 1992: 141) of the tribute-as-original. The articulation of an 'honest fakery' leaves a discursive space for enjoyment by fans. Here, the tribute can be seen as part of a much longer entertainment tradition; for the fan, its manufactured nature is not isolated from its other qualities.

Greatest hits and memories

Several studies of very different fan cultures and media forms have concluded that fans possess 'already-constituted knowledges and competencies which are drawn on at the moment of interpretation' (Morley 1980: 171). This final section begins to map the types of personal and historical knowledge that fans bring to interpretations of the tribute performance. Pop consumption is socially constructed (Shuker 1994), requiring attention to how audiences are located within specific times and spaces of music consumption. The audiences I interviewed and observed at several tribute concerts in Britain in late 2004 were dominated by groups of men and women, and couples, aged over 35 years. For the Bootleg Beatles performance in Preston, a higher proportion was aged over 40 years; at the Björn Again performances, the audiences were slightly younger as a whole.

While fans bring a range of (often deep) knowledge to the tribute, it is worth noting the many ways that the tribute act frames such performances through the use of elaborate stage props: Union Jack flags as an almost-standard backdrop for tributes to the Who, for example. The Bootleg Beatles' video screen on stage employs a variety of images to depict changing Beatle periods: James Callaghan and the Thunderbirds (early 60s), Batman/Carnaby Street fashions (mid-60s recordings), the Apple record logo (*Abbey Road* period). If not already 'nostalgic' for their youth, fans are confronted with various encouragements to associate the 1960s with excitement and fondness. These symbolic parameters attempt to encode the performance as a series of taken-for-granted moments; some of the interpretation, in a fairly loose historical sense, has been performed for them.

So how do fans reconcile their own 'configurations ... of pleasure and desires ... and emotion' (Grossberg 1992b: 49) of the tribute performance, which offers such acute connections between personal history, national memory and popular music? In keeping with changes to stage settings and visual/historical prompts, most tributes favour a straightforward narrative of song performances, remaining chronologically faithful to the original's history. For those under 40 years of age, the tribute proved to be an inter-generational link:

> I mean, my parents played the Beatles. Yeah, my parents were in their teens in the 60s, so I grew up listening to their record collection. I never really had any records of my own but I listened to theirs. So you grew up listening to the songs and it's like a collective con-sciousness, everybody singing along.
>
> (Clare, 32)

The tribute provoked debates about the 'best' or 'most creative' Beatles period. For Chris, the early Beatles recording period has particular memories:

> Well, I grew up with that, like 'She Loves You', 'From Me To You', 'Please, Please, Please', the very early stuff. You know I listened to that first album when they were in the cellar, I used to play drums to that, week in, week out, 'Roll Over Beethoven' ... I used to play drums as a kid. I weren't only the drummer; I were everything, lead guitar, drummer, singer, the lot.
>
> (Chris, 54)

At the Bootleg Beatles performance, many fans seemed willing to place themselves within the montage of memories presented to them. This was evident in the repetition of phrases put to me that emphasized the pleasures of personal memory over the contemporary performative moment. The Bootleg Beatles provided an opportunity to 'relive my youth' (Trish, 57); to 'remember what it was like and remember what you were doing at the time' (Jean, 61). One woman liked the band because it brought back 'waves of nostalgia' where she 'can be a teenager again; when they bring up the newsprint and everything it really recreates the atmosphere for you' (Anne, 63).

Unlike other attendees of the Beatles charity concert staged at the Ja-caranda pub in Liverpool in December 2004, Tony and Karen were unable to draw upon their own memories of attending a Beatles performance in the 1960s. However, they articulated similar roles of the tribute as a narrative of nostalgia:

> It takes you back to being 13 or 14 again; when you're in the little school disco and you haven't got a care in the world. You know all the words, you know all the [Beatles'] birthdays, you have no worries, and it takes you back to that, for me ... it is getting to be more fun,

you know, not such a shriney-type thing, like a bit of a god experience when you were younger. You go to the Bootleg Beatles and you think, 'Oh my god, this is the nearest thing I am ever going to get to the real thing' ... It's a good laugh, it takes you back.

(Karen, 37)

Both regarded a Paul McCartney concert they had attended in 2003 as 'the ultimate' experience:

Going to a Paul McCartney concert was just like going to a big sing-a-long. There were some songs where his voice wobbled and you thought – you didn't care ... I just couldn't believe I were there. All you wanted him to do was sing; it was fantastic.

(Karen, 37)

The couple shared other audience members' views on how to assess Beatles output, with clear divisions made between early and later recordings. Earlier Beatles recordings were favoured, due to the:

energy and the beat, and you just get carried away with it, you can lose yourself in it and there's no hidden message ... it's just pure energy and music. They didn't actually know what they were doing, they were just enjoying themselves and you can hear that.

(Karen, 37)

Karen pointed out that she made a particular effort to educate her daughter about the Beatles' influence in contemporary British rock and pop:

When you listen to music, you listen for the Beatles riffs, and it's interesting. Even Helen, we've got a 19-year-old daughter and we listen to her music, and we can't fail to hear it ... you'll just say yeah, 'That's Franz Ferdinand!' and it's really funny dissecting the music and saying, 'Oh, I hear so and so' ... when you hear the material so well you can hear it. And you just think you're slightly superior. It's great knowing how you've developed.

(Karen, 37)

Conclusion

It is not surprising that tributes to well-known acts thrive, when industry icons remain so visible. As Neil Harrison pointed out, 'you walk into Woolworths and there'll be a Beatles calendar alongside a Robbie Williams diary, alongside Mariah Carey' (Harrison interview 2004). For Rod Leissle, the co-founder of Björn Again, Abba retains a similar profile: 'you hear "Dancing Queen" when you're buying jeans at the shops' (Leissle interview 2004). These forms of consumption, still lucrative for the original act, are not deemed appropriate for the tribute. As one fan pointed out, 'the last thing you want to do is go and buy vinyl of a tribute band, it just wouldn't make any sense, a bit like listening to Rolf Harris's version of "Stairway to Heaven"' (Andy, 46).

Older tribute fans' sense of distance (from both their own period as adolescents, and their engagement with the original act) is revealed in their awareness of the technical and image limitations of the tribute, and the ability to accept them on such 'honest fakery' terms. They share the tribute musicians' assessment of the night as 'a laugh', though I suspect this is deceptive, masking the extent to which fans bring other expectations and knowledge as part of their judgements. They also share the musicians' judgements about selection of stage material. The tribute performance is exceptional in having fans on both sides of the stage. This extends to mutual consent about an act's most creative songs, and songs which must be played to depict significant moments.

For many, the tribute offers the chance to articulate the role of their favourite acts in their own personal development. For others, the tribute is simply another live entertainment form, comparable to its rivals (those interviewed at the Björn Again concerts, for example, judged the band against earlier attendances at the musical theatre show, *Mamma Mia!*). Fans are less likely to scrutinize how particular eras are packaged for their consumption, preferring to accept the tribute's invitation to invest the performance with an uncritical nostalgia for more 'carefree' times. Displaced from the original locus of affection and desire, fans employ the tribute as a filter for reviewing a complex of memories, generational assumptions and personal narratives. Rather than acting as uncritical fans wanting a quick 'music history fix', tribute audiences remain wary of what is offered:

> *Gary:* Um, I shut my eyes and think 'John [Lennon] wouldn't like this'.
> *SH:* So you think he'd look twice at being imitated like this?
> *Gary:* He'd sneer at them, definitely.

Interviews were conducted with tribute fans at the Liverpool Philharmonic Theatre, Preston Guildhall and the Jacaranda pub, Liverpool, in November and December 2004. My thanks to all the interviewees, and to Justine Lloyd and Sarah Baker and the managers of each venue for allowing interviews to be conducted.

Notes

1   Pseudonyms are used in relation to the names of people I interviewed throughout this chapter.

References

Benedictus, L. (2004) Beneath the covers, *The Age*, 28 November.

Doss, E. (1999) *Elvis Culture: Fans, Faith Image*. Kansas: University Press of Kansas.

Egolf, K. (2003) Tribute band Exit – the exclusive interview, Interference.Com. http://forum.interference.com/+77185.html (accessed 17 May 2004).

Fiske, J. (1992) The cultural economy of fandom, in L. Lewis (ed.) *The Adoring Audience: Fan Culture and Popular Media*. London: Routledge.

Frith, S. (1996) *Performing Rites: On The Value of Popular Music*. Oxford: Oxford University Press.

Grossberg, L. (1992a) *We Gotta Get Out of This Place: Popular Conservatism and Postmodern Culture*. New York: Routledge.

Grossberg, L. (1992b) Is there a fan in the house? The affective sensibility of fandom, in L. Lewis (ed.) *The Adoring Audience: Fan Culture and Popular Media*. London: Routledge.

Hall, S. (1981) Encoding and decoding in the TV discourse, in S. Hall, I. Connell and L. Curti (eds) *Culture, Media, Language*. London: Hutchison.

Jenkins, H. (1992) *Textual Poachers: Television Fans and Participatory Culture*. New York: Routledge.

Jenson, J. (1992) Fandom as pathology: the consequences of characterization, in L. Lewis (ed.) *The Adoring Audience: Fan Culture and Popular Media*. London: Routledge.

Moores, S. (1992) Texts, readers and contexts of reading, in P. Scannell, P. Schlesinger and C. Sparks (eds) *Culture and Power: A Media, Culture & Society Reader*. London: Sage.

Morley, D. (1980) *The Nationwide Audience*. London: British Film Institute.

Rodman, G. (1996) *Elvis After Elvis: The Posthumous Career of a Living Legend*. London: Routledge.

Shuker, R. (1994) *Understanding Popular Music*. London: Routledge.

PART 2
TRIBUTE CASE STUDIES

5 The music goes on and on and on ... and on – popular music's affective franchise

John Neil

> The question was crystallised for me by Ricky Gervais, who used to hire tribute bands for student gigs. Gervais was going to re-book Abba copyists Björn Again when he noticed that the line-up had changed. It was then that he decided to get out of music and into comedy. You know you are in a rut when you start complaining that the wrong person is pretending to be the man who pretends to be the man who co-wrote Chess.
>
> (Dessau 2004)

Repetition has a primacy in the ontology of popular music (Redhead 1990; Frith 1996; Potter 1997). The history of jazz is in many ways variations on a theme with standards, motifs, melodies and phrases (Carr 1999) providing a lineage and a continuity from the present to the past. Rock music in particular has an abiding resonance and reverence for its 'songbook' with its succession of canonical hits neatly packaged into particular eras (Straw 1993), with the cover song serving as an 'ever' present index of popular music's foundational moment(s). Both aspiring musicians and established recording artists have long paid tribute to the previous influences and formative musical experiences through the tribute album.

For Griffiths (2002: 51), cover versions can resonate across time 'as a form of public debate, of critique and empowerments, with the cover offering to us, as listeners in the present, forums for debate' resonating across 'historical contexts'. Clearly, as Potter (1997: 32) notes, this repetition is 'repetition *with a difference*'. It is this repetition-as-difference that has caused much difficulty for cultural criticism. The 'problem' repetition poses, on an ontological level, is its reduction to a repetition of the same (Deleuze 1994).

The cover song in contemporary popular music operates according to a different logic than its function in the 1950s and 60s, when iconic artists such as the Beatles and the Rolling Stones established their early musical credentials with close reference to the styles, sounds and literally the songs of early rhythm and blues[1] in a period where 'writing original material was considered a poor substitute for finding a "real" song to cover' (Sweeting 2004).[2] A range of complex changes militated against this aesthetic of authenticity. As Weinstein (1988: 142) notes: 'the modern romantic notion of authenticity – creating out of one's own resources – became dominant over the idea that authenticity constituted a relationship, through creative repetition, to an authentic source'. In this contemporary aesthetic, the tribute band, with the cover song as its stock-in-trade, occupies an ambiguous position in the popular music and entertainment landscape. The abiding discursive formation of the tribute band is found in its relation to a measure of authenticity, and in this respect the tribute band speaks of a redolent postmodernism, at best parodic, at worst a spectral simulacrum that permeates contemporary culture. In such an ontology the tribute band's existence is a marginal one; it is derivative, a byproduct of an increasingly globalized and commodified cultural landscape – a second-order functionary whose value lies in its efficacy as a supplement for an original and its originary moment(s). If the song is the 'fundamental unit of musical currency' (Sweeting 2004: 3) the tribute band exists as a userer, reviled as an illegitimate profiteer of other's labour and creativity. With no recourse to 'original' authenticity, the tribute act can only be regarded as 'bad' music.[3]

This chapter will argue, however, that the tribute band is only partially explained by its veracity (or otherwise) to an original. The song itself is the *sine qua non* of the tribute act, yet specific tributes cannot be reduced to the veracity of their reproduction of particular songs. Tribute bands occupy a complex set of positions and are constituted within interrelated vectors across a complex 'cultural formation' (Grossberg 1993) and are increasingly inserted in a 'global cultural economy' (Appadurai 1990). In this globalized cultural economy 'notions of originality and authenticity have been problematized in a climate where cultural production has become ever more hybrid, intertextual and digitally reproduced' (Grainge 1999: 625). Indeed, changes in the technics within a given cultural assemblage, such as the impact of digital technology in the production of popular music and entertainment, place significant questions over the status of the 'original' song as the irreducible unit of popular music. Similarly, image, style and marketability are as primary a consideration for major label talent identification as the substantial core of original prerecorded material (Shuker 2001).

The contemporary tribute band is in many ways indicative of broader shifts in the configuration of the aural and visual in contemporary culture 'in which visual media and images are competing with, if not displacing, music and aural images as the site of salvation and transcendence in rock culture' (Grossberg 1993: 186). The tribute act is itself immanent to these shifting configurations across the popular music and entertainment industries. It throws into relief specific indexes of change in production and consumption logics in the cultural industries, which in themselves cannot be reduced to a representational economy, where the tribute's value is circumscribed by its efficacy in reproducing an original.

Through a focus on the Australian Abba tribute Björn Again, this chapter will examine the immanence of tribute bands to the circuits of production and consumption in the contemporary cultural industries through an identification of operative contexts of 'affective production'. These circuits of affective production, or what could also be called visual-aural sensibilities, are increasingly deployed in the production (and consumption) of cultural products. A primary mode of affective production is the contexts and circuits of nostalgia, which are themselves determinant productions within and alongside particular cultural formations such as the tribute band. Through an analysis of a specific tribute band's emergence and operational contexts in recorded music–live entertainment assemblages, we can begin to make connections across and between these contexts of affective production, and their deployment in specific circuits of cultural production and consumption.

The Australian tribute scene

The only tribute you'll remember . . . FOREVER!!

(Abba Forever: 2005)

Tribute acts in various forms have been constant features in live entertainment contexts, evident in cabaret and lounge acts, impersonators, or in the enduring popularity of the Butlin's entertainer ('redcoats') at British holiday resorts. The tribute band seems to emerge 'fully formed' from both the performance and recording contexts of popular music and live entertainment and their embedded histories. One estimate is that almost 10,000 tribute acts exist in the UK (Cox 2005). Rod Leissle, co-founder of Björn Again, puts the number of Abba-specific tribute bands at over 100 in the UK alone (Leissle interview 2005).

The false chronology that positions Australia as the origin of the tribute industry (see Introduction and Chapter 2) has been related to arguments of geography and cost. Australia has been off the path of major touring acts; the associated logistics and cost involved have dissuaded major artists from touring the country (Pearlman and Moses 2002). Prohibitive ticket prices of major acts when they do tour significantly limit the ability of individuals to experience the 'real thing'.

A casual glance across even a small sample of tribute bands operating in Australia would seem to support the supplementary nature of the tribute band, based on the simple fact that for at least half of the tribute acts listed in Table 5.1, the original artists or acts are defunct. As Homan notes in Chapter 2 of this volume, this indicates an important dimension of 'tribute-as-historical-project'. Rod Leissle supports this in his recollections of the motivations behind forming Björn Again: 'When I started, I thought the band had to be Elvis, the Beatles or Abba, because you know they would not reform'

Table 5.1 Sample of Australian tribute acts (2005)

Australian Madonna Show	Australian Blues Brothers Show	Wazzo Clash: The Clash Tribute	Australian Pink Floyd Show	Australian Doors
Australian Robbie Williams Show	Australian U2 Show	Australian Van Morrison Show (Melbourne)	Australian Van Morrison Show (Sydney)	Bob Dylan Show
Cher Tribute Show	Elvis Tribute Show	Frank Sinatra & Judy Garland Show	James Brown Tribute Band	John Lennon Show
Kisstroyer	Let It Be Beatles	Neil Diamond – Acoustic Tribute	Soul Diva's Abba Tribute	Van Halen Tribute – In Halen
From Engelbert with Love	Elton Experience	Creedwater Revival	The Oz ZZ Top Show	Fabba – The Abba Show
John Denver Tribute	Judy Garland – Story in Song	The Elvis Experience	Al Jolson Tribute	The Crooners/ Rat Pack Show
Mannilow Magic	The Deep Purple Experience	The Dancing Queens	A Tribute to Vera Lynn	Imagine That Band – John Lennon
A tribute to Roy Orbison	Cajun Country Revival (International Creedence Clearwater Revival Show)	The Joshua Tree	Achtung Baby	Zed Lepplin
Michael Jackson Tribute	Salute to Boyz from Oz	Blues Brothers Revue	Beach Boys Show	The Eagles Experience
Bob Marley Show	Kissteria	Rumours: Fleetwood Mac	Quo Vadis – Status Quo	The Australian Meatloaf Show

(Leissle interview 2004). Increasingly, the historical remit of tribute bands is being brought forward to include an expanding range of contemporary tributes: from Anastasia to U2; from Coldplay, Jamiroquai, REM and Robbie Williams, to Atomic Kitten and the Foo Fighters.

The line between the tribute as historical project and the contemporary artist as heritage act is increasingly blurring. Veteran rockers Status Quo, for example, embarked upon their '40th Anniversary UK Winter Tour 2005' following a long line of foundational acts, such as the Rolling Stones and Neil Diamond, in putting on the heritage rock slippers. This somewhat problematizes the view that the tribute functions as a supplement, or as a stand-in. Such a situation is captured in a much cited (and most likely apocryphal) story about former Australian Crawl frontman James Reyne and the Australian Crawl tribute Sons of Beaches playing competing venues in the same country town with the tribute attracting twice the audience of the original artist (Baker 1990; Murfett 2004). Similarly, Shuker (2001: 113–14) cites the case of ex-Cold Chisel guitarist Ian Moss 'performing to a handful of people in a Sydney suburban hotel ... [while] Swing Shift, a Chisel clone featuring Moss' music, played to a crowd of a thousand at a nearby venue'.

Same as it ever was – Abba (a) re-vival

Simon Frith (1996: 211) argues that just as 'a sense of "now" is particularly important in music' it also 'has a particularly strong ability to shift, freeze, or alter our experience of time, and in some way intensify it'. In this particular ontology of contemporary music, a sense of time being 'frozen' is all too evident in the case of tribute bands. The nostalgic *raison d'être* of tributes marks them as popular music's illegitimate bastard that is for many critics symptomatic of postmodernity's nostalgic condition:

> Given that modernity is usually described in terms of change, rest-lessness, fragmentation, differentiation and de-differentiation, it is hardly surprising that a common psychological response to these conditions is the idealization of the past and the concomitant longing for stability and security.
>
> (Rojek 1995: 119)

Frederic Jameson (1991: 18) notably finds the prevalence of con-temporary nostalgia symptomatic of 'the waning of our historicity' in which we find ourselves circulating among a 'vast collection of images, a multi-tudinous photographic simulacrum' that constitutes a contemporary 'cultural museum'. The evacuation of history and its aesthetic of pastiche and ironic distance produces 'a lifeless entity which is incapable of supporting any viable motivation for the future. Nostalgia, as it were, immobilizes development because it is only concerned with providing an attractive and unchallenging view of the past' (Rojek 1995: 119). Underpinning these accounts is an over-determined semiotic overlay of the social. Lash and Urry (1994: 15), for ex-ample, argue that postmodernity is a condition where 'objects are emptied out both of meaning (and are postmodern) and of material content (and are thus post-industrial). The subjects in turn are increasingly emptied out, flat, deficient in affect'. The corollary signifying subject is characterized by loss, deficiency and a substantive 'waning of affect' (Jameson 1991: 10).

Traditionally, the humanities have approached the question of affect as culturally constructed 'feelings' and 'emotions' which are 'substantially divorced from the materiality of the body' (Gibbs 2002: 337). Unlike emotion, however, affect is the modality of sensation, or intensity proper. Its registers are the somatic, the biophysical and the energetic in the first instance, and only *ex post facto* psychological. It is in this sense that Brian Massumi (1996) argues that the social, far from being deficient in affect, is in fact 'awash' with it. Indeed, affect is increasingly taking 'centre stage' in economic and cultural life. Shifting the focus from significatory, and therefore textualist, readings of popular culture may allow us to look beyond the often repeated questions over postmodern authenticity, as signifying veracity, which have often stultified the investigation of affect's place in the circuits of cultural production and consumption.

Nostalgia, while not reducible to affect, is a mode of sensation, or more precisely 'a structure of feeling' into which the virtual relations of affect enter. The contexts of nostalgia and of emergent affect are increasingly utilized within cultural formations and these contexts of affective production are increasingly primary contexts of the production of cultural products.

With high levels of operative risk, the 'cultural industries' (Garnham 1990; Hesmondhalgh 2002), and the music industries in particular (Hesmondhalgh 1998, 1999) employ complex strategies of risk mitigation including product formatting (Neuman 1991; Ryan 1992; Frith 1996; Wolf 1999; Hesmondhalgh 2002) along with the utilization of techniques of 'mainstreaming' (Toynbee 2002) and the creation (and capitalization on) a 'star system' (Frith 1996; Negus 1996; Hesmondhalgh 2002). While all of these strategies are interrelated and often extremely variable in terms of their deployment, each attempts 'to order demand and stabilize sales patterns' (Ryan 1992: 185). Nostalgia, as a context of affective production, is utilized as one such risk mitigation strategy. These contexts of affective significance are a domain that is certainly interrelated with symbolic and discursive sets of significance (Ewen 1988; Ryan 1992) but not reducible to them. This chapter examines the place of tribute bands in these specific contexts of production and the construction of contexts of affect that in part constitute these circuits. I will not be examining particular consumption (audience) contexts that are examined elsewhere in this volume. Instead, by examining a specific top-tier tribute, its contexts of emergence and status in live entertainment and recorded music, I hope to provide an examination of the specific contexts of affective production.

Indeed, I would argue that these circuits of affective nostalgia across the complex cultural assemblage are indicative of broader changes in the cultural economy. For example, the introduction of the CD format had a particularly significant impact on the 'consistency' of the heritage assemblage. In 1985 CD sales began their 'long boom' with global sales approaching 260 million in 1987 (Burnett 1992: 750).[4] By 1995, CD sales accounted for 60 per cent of world units of albums and singles and 70 per cent of market value (Strobl and

Tucker 2000). The CD enabled a burgeoning archive of 'present histories' to be available for the increasingly lucrative baby boomer market segment (Savage 1988; Redhead 1990). The 'greatest hits' and 'best of' compilation CDs emerged as a significant source of revenue with the major labels, due to their lower production costs and as packages containing well-known material (Strobl and Tucker 2000: 115, 130).

The 1992 release of the Abba greatest hits compilation *Abba Gold* highlights the centrality of the 'greatest hits' and 'best of' compilation CDs in facilitating the resale of back-catalogue material, in contributing to the generation of nostalgia contexts. In the first 12 months of its release *Abba Gold* sold more than 5.1 million copies outside the US, topping the charts in 13 countries including the UK and Australia (Duffy 1993). Indeed *Abba Gold* has achieved global sales of more than 22 million as Abba's most successful release. The CD was compiled and released by Polygram after the company acquired the rights to the Abba repertoire in 1990 with the purchase of Abba manager Stig Anderson's record label, Polar Music (Duffy 1993). Containing ten of the band's top-20 US singles, the 19-track album is a key reference for both existing and newer Abba fans, and in many respects acts as a primer for Abba tribute acts:

> *Abba Gold* is the kind of benchmark ... it is a reflection of what the biggest hits of Abba are. So basically we fundamentally do the songs that are on that album as a given, as a starting point to any show we do. It's fairly evident. But the selection of back-catalogue songs, depending on the show, part of the machinations of putting a theatre show together, are the ones that lend themselves to a particular theme.
>
> (Leissle interview 2005)

Not surprisingly, the majority of Abba tribute bands emerged after the release of *Abba Gold* with only four bands existing prior to its release (see Table 5.2). Tribute bands such as Abba Gold, Real Abba Gold, and Abba Gold (New Zealand) explicitly reference the CD title.[5]

Two greatest hits albums, *Greatest Hits* (1975) and *Greatest Hits Vol. 2* (1979), had been packaged during the band's career, the latter released to coincide with the band's North American and European tours. Rick Dobbis, President of the Polygram Label Group at the time of the release, stated: 'With ABBA, the timing really is excellent because of the building interest in this music and this era. Enough time has passed that it's no longer "uncool"' (Duffy 1993: 8). A 'critical mass' of Abba-related interest was culminating in the years immediately prior to the CD being considered. The UK band Erasure's 1992 four-track Abba tribute EP,[6] *Abba-esque*, released in July 1992, peaked at number one in the UK charts. In that same month during U2's *Zoo TV* world tour, Benny Andersson and Björn Ulvaeus joined the band on stage

Table 5.2   Sample of Abba tributes by country and date of formation

Tribute name	Location	Date
Björn Again	Australia, UK, Europe, North America	1988
Abba UK	UK	1990
Abba Alive	Germany	1991
Voulez Vous	UK	1992
Abba Gold	UK	1993
Real Abba Gold	UK	1993
Babba	Australia	1994
Abba Arrival	UK	1995
Abba Arrival	Sweden	1995
Abba Girls	UK	1995
Fabba	Australia/UK	1996
The Abba Experience	Scotland	1996
Waterloo	Sweden	1996
ABBAsalutely/Johhnnie be goode	Ireland	1997
Appa	Finland	1997
Bootleg Abba	UK	1997
Platinum Abba	UK	1997
Swede Dreams	UK	1997
Abba Forever	UK	1998
Abba Gold NZ	New Zealand	1998
Abba Mania	UK	1998
Abbamania	UK	1998
Abba Reborn	UK	1999
Abba Singers Show	Hungary	1999
Dancing Abba	Switzerland	1999
Fabbagirls, The	UK	1999
Abba Dabba Doo	UK	2000
Abbababes	UK	2000
Abba AllStars	UK	2001
Abba Dayz	UK	2001
Abba Gold	Canada	2002
Abba 2: Björn Belief	Wales	2003
Abba Party Girls	UK	2003
Abba World Revival	Czech Republic	2003
Abba-Cadabra	Scotland	2003
Abba Stars	Czech Republic	2004

in Stockholm for a cover of 'Dancing Queen' which had been added to the band's song list for the tour.

Björn Again were no small influence in contributing to the Abba nostalgia wave before and during *ABBA Gold*'s immediate pre-release period. In 1990 the band attracted increasing interest in their Melbourne pub shows and began a series of tours to Sydney. In 1991–2 Björn Again began a limited tour of Europe after a Swedish promoter saw the band perform in Melbourne. From that time, the band began to split their time between Australia and Europe. The band's European performances led to their invitation to perform on Swedish television: 'They invited us back to do another TV show, a national Swedish TV show, fundamentally to launch ... the CD [*Abba Gold*]. We came on and sang five or six songs, but it was to launch *Abba Gold* and this was their thinking, "let's try it in Sweden as a test market"' (Leissle interview 2005). Indeed, Leissle attributes the CD's success to the influence of Björn Again in directly generating interest in Abba: 'I think the band has acknowledged the role we've had in their re-emergence. We looked into it, and found that *Abba Gold* sells a lot more in towns that we tour, and so we can quantify that our tours promote their CD sales' (Leissle interview 2004).

The *ABBA Gold* CD was remastered and reissued in 1999 with new liner notes to coincide with the 25th anniversary of Abba's 1973 Eurovision Song Contest performance. It was again reissued with a revised booklet and updated liner notes in 2002 to mark the tenth anniversary of the original release, and reissued again as a two-CD 'special edition' with a bonus CD in 2003. It was also released on VHS format in 1992 and DVD in 2003 (including two bonus tracks) and was included with a further CD and DVD anniversary edition, released in the UK in 2004 as *ABBA Gold – Greatest Hits Sound + Vision Deluxe*.

Alongside a range of single and album boxed sets, CD and DVD boxed sets and compilations including *More ABBA Gold* (1993) (see Table 5.3), the Abba heritage is re-marked and re-inscribed into the popular entertainment marketplace, both capitalizing on and sustaining the popularity of Abba nostalgia. This popularity is clearly an effect in part of the tribute band phenomenon and the widespread 'perpetual present' (see Chapter 2) that Abba tributes maintain along with the 'present market' they contribute to forming.

Similarly, music frequently features in televisual contexts as moments of nostalgia. Tribute band appearances on television initially were limited to curios for news stories but this changed significantly as they became integrated as content into numerous televisual contexts. In May 2001, to coincide with the Melbourne opening of the musical *Mamma Mia!* in Australia, the Australian Nine Network screened a three-hour 'Ultimate Abbathon' special, featuring a performance by Abba tribute Babba among a multimedia tribute of archival original band performances and videos, along with an audience participation 'talent quest' concluding with a screening of *Abba: The Movie* (2001) (Abba fever hits 2001). The tribute band here fulfils its proper televisual supplementary function: providing 'live' or descriptive verisimilitude and as visual-aural anchor of the past in the present.

Table 5.3   Producing the Abba heritage

Boxed sets	*Thank You For The Music*	1994	Polydor
	Singles Collection 1972–1982	1999	Polydor
	Abba – The Collection	1999	Polydor
	30th Anniversary Original Album Box	2004	Polar Music
	Abba Gold	1992	Polydor
	More Abba Gold – More Abba Hits	1993	Polydor
Compilations	*The Abba Collection*	1993	Polydor
	The Music Still Goes On	1996	Karussel
	Abba (Master Series)	1996	Polydor
	Forever Gold	1996	Polydor
	Abba – The Collection	1998	Polydor
	Love Stories	1998	Polygram
	The Complete Singles Collection	1999	Polydor
	Classic Abba – The Universal Masters Collection	1999	Polydor
	The Best Of Abba – The Millennium Collection	2000	Polydor
	The Complete Gold Collection	2000	Polydor
	S.O.S. – The Best Of Abba	2001	Universal
	The Definitive Collection	2001	Universal
	The Name Of The Game	2002	Spectrum
	On And On	2003	Universal
	The Ultimate Collection	2004	Reader's Digest
	The Abba Story	2004	Universal
	The Best Of Abba	2005	Universal
	18 Hits	2005	Universal

Source: compiled from a range of Abba-related websites, including the Official Abba website (2005), Abba World (2005) and Abba Forever (2005).

An affective imprimatur

The hierarchy of value inherent in popular music places important, but often ineffable criteria of judgement upon particular artists and genres. The value of 'cultural capital'[7] and forms of distinction bestowed upon cover and tribute bands has traditionally been low (Shuker 2001: 126). The forms of direct and indirect legitimacy not reducible to representational or explicitly legal sanction are becoming increasingly important within cultural industries. These types of legitimacy are granted across interrelated and often informal sets of sanction in what may be referred to as an affective imprimatur. The common usage of 'imprimatur' denotes a sense of acceptance and approval, however its Latin etymology also denotes an explicit sense of official licence and authorization.[8] Both uses of the term capture the tension inherent in the contested nature of the tribute and its multiple deployment in the music and cultural industries. Informal forms of legitimation range from specific tribute bands being invited to play special events at the request of original band members, using equipment donated from the original band to their tribute or as a literal substitute for promotional or formal functions.[9] Alternatively, the imprimatur may be granted through the direct participation by members of the original act in the tribute.[10]

Another form of affective imprimatur occurs through the supporting roles tributes play to major label recording artists. Björn Again have been deployed in support of a diverse range of major label artists such as Shania Twain (2003 UK and 2004 European tour), Foo Fighters (2003 Lowland Festival in Holland), Cher (2004 European Farewell Tour), and Green Day (2005 Ireland's Oxegen Festival). The imprimatur of original acts was critical to the success of both Björn Again and the Bootleg Beatles. In February 1992 the members of Nirvana, who were in the country on the Australian leg of the *Nevermind* tour, attended Björn Again's performance at the Central Club in Richmond, Melbourne: 'We had no idea they were there until someone told us that they'd bought all our T-shirts' (Leissle interview 2005).

A request was then made through Nirvana's agent for Björn Again to play at the Reading festival in August of that year. For the first time a tribute band appeared alongside some of the major original recording acts at the time in a festival setting. This move was paralleled four years later when Oasis requested the Bootleg Beatles to be their support act at Earls Court in 1996. The appearances of Björn Again and the Bootleg Beatles in support of two of the major recording artists of each respective period marked the formal integration of tribute bands into the live entertainment circuit. In the case of Björn Again, the imprimatur elevated the band into the mainstream circuit and served to bestow cultural legitimacy:

> That was a turning point in a sense. That same year, Björn Again was voted 'best band on university circuit', which included all the original UK bands ... [our] audiences now come from younger people who saw us in the 1990s on the college and uni circuits. People say 'I remember seeing you at Oxford in 1991'.
>
> (Leissle interview 2004)

The imprimatur granted by Nirvana was immediately followed by endorsement from the music press:

> Which brings us to Björn Again who are a total contrivance. A straw poll halfway down the field reveals several irked souls who feel like this is a party to which they haven't been invited. 'They're a fucking disgrace' says Dan from Windsor. A few yards away though, a girl who can only have caught some of the original Abba in the womb, is kicking up mud and singing every word of 'SOS'. Gradually the crowd's collective cool is discarded. By the time they launch into a

snatch of 'Smells Like Teen Spirit' Björn Again have the majority on their side. The roar which goes up is one of the loudest of the day. It was a brilliant piece of crowd warming. (Pause while Reviews Ed inserts snidey aside). (You're fired, baldy – Ed).

(Melody Maker 1992: 31)

Simon Frith notes that rock critics and their readers bestow significant distinctions on the categories of judgement and taste, acting as 'opinion leaders' (Frith 1983). Combined with Nirvana's approval, the *Melody Maker* review underlines the broader sense of the imprimatur as a formal licence with 'official sanction'.

Weddings, parties ... anything ...

Björn Again was formed in 1988 by Rod Leissle and John Tyrell, who were working as chemical engineers in Melbourne. Their first gig took place in 1989 at inner-city Melbourne pub the Tote, and the band's early years were spent at various pub residencies around Melbourne.

> There was an organic growth about the band, there was no grand scheme to it, or to forge a career. It was all about having fun on a Friday night at a pub in Melbourne. People could sense it was just good fun ... For the first five to six years we were a pub/club band [in Australia]; the audiences can be much harsher, so you have to play that much harder and involve the audience, give them dance steps to do or whatever. We're very big on that.

(Leissle interview 2004)

The Australian live entertainment circuit began to experience fundamental structural changes throughout the 1980s, and the trajectory of Björn Again's financial success is in part emblematic of those changes. Alongside an increasingly homogenized radio playlist centred upon canonical recordings of 'greatest hits and memories', a corollary 'live nostalgia' circuit was established through a rationalization of the number of venues available for live performance. The tribute band offers a ready-made audience and mitigates some of the risk associated with untried or emerging original bands along with the cost savings of booking established acts. Fees in Australia for tribute bands range anywhere from $2,000 to $6,500 depending on the type of venue; at the smaller pub/club level, UK tribute bands charge between £200 and £800. This is reflected in the premium fees the more popular cover bands can receive, with nightly wages in the UK of £800 to £2,000, depending on a band's experience and the quality of their equipment. The corporate events market is a particularly lucrative one for tribute bands with premium fees able to be

Figure 5.1   Björn Again promotional shot, with a referential nod to the ABBA album cover photograph of *Arrival* (1977)

charged for corporate theme events. In Australia, fees of $5,000 to $10,000 are not uncommon.

The reduction in live venue contexts through the 1980s and 1990s was accompanied by a broader shift to themed performance contexts, reflected in the emergence of tribute-specific venues. Bourbon Street in Glasgow, for example, began as a jazz venue in the 1990s before repositioning itself as a tribute-specific venue after a series of successful tribute band bookings, with an Abba tribute band notably being the first (Brown 2000).The transition from smaller pub venues to larger theatre[11] and arena shows marked a significant commercial shift for specific acts, and also indicates a further integration of the tribute into the mainstream live entertainment market.

In 1991–2 Björn Again began a limited tour of Europe after a Swedish promoter saw the band perform in Melbourne. During this time co-founders Rod Leissle and John Tyrell took up roles as backing band musicians, allowing them to focus on the managerial and promotional operation of the band. The reception of the European shows led to the band's migration, primarily from 1992–4, to larger-capacity venues. For Rod Leissle, the change in venues was a natural progression: 'Bands weren't trying hard. I was a big fan of the [New Zealand] band Split Enz and they had an amazing stage show with great sets and big costumes. I loved that crossover with theatre' (cited in Chamberlain 2000). The broad appeal of particular tributes is not only reflected in their ability to fill larger venues; they are also common features, often with headline billing, in special events. In 2004 Robbie Williams impersonator Mathew Hollbrook 'performed in front of 65,000 rugby fans at the Super League grand final at Old Trafford' (Mugan 2005). Tributes are increasingly utilized as feature billing for national tours such as the June 2005 'Tribute to Music's Legends' concert at Cardiff's Millenium Stadium. More recently, tribute bands have appeared in their own dedicated festival setting. Billed as a low cost alternative to the Glastonbury festival, the *Glastonbudget* festival (April/May 2005) featured tributes to Meatloaf, the Jam, U2, AC/DC, Tom Jones and the Stereophonics.

Do you want platforms with that? The tribute as cultural franchise

By most measures, Björn Again have been the singularly most successful of the Abba tributes. In 2002 they recorded their highest annual earnings of $8.8 million (The Top 50 Entertainers 2005), placing them in the top seven Australian entertainers by earnings behind Nicole Kidman ($25 million), John Farnham ($24 million), AC/DC ($20 million), Russell Crowe ($20 million), the Wiggles ($14.2 million), and Peter Weir ($10 million). By 2004, however, gross earnings had dropped by almost half ($4.5 million). For Rod Leissle, 2002 was the band's 'golden period':

> We had some extraordinary years in 1999, 2000 and 2002. It's basically got a lot to do with a range of things. *Mamma Mia!* the musical would be one. People would go and see that musical and love it, it's a great musical, but realize that they've heard all the Abba songs but not really seen what Abba is on stage. I think there was a direct spin-

Figure 5.2 2005 'Glastonbudget' promotional poster

off for us that people were saying 'Right, seen the musical *Mamma
Mia!*, let's go and see Björn Again' ... we started going up that level
and doing some arenas.

(Leissle interview 2005)

While not strictly a franchise in the formal sense (see Litz and Stewart 1988;
Stanworth and Curran 1999), Björn Again utilizes a sophisticated *de facto*
franchise model that capitalizes on its strong brand across all modes of live
performance, from smaller venues to feature performances in large theatres
and arenas. This is a particularly effective strategy in an increasingly competitive local and global market, not only in the Abba-specific tribute niche,
but the increasingly global tribute market.

Under the Björn Again brand, Rod Leissle and John Tyrell operate five
troupes across the UK, Australasia and the Pacific, Europe and North America,
with a further troupe focusing on corporate gigs. The Björn Again 'franchise'
has completed 3300 shows in 17 years in 50 countries. On average 150 shows
would be performed in the UK; 150 in Europe; 100 in North America and 50
in Australasia annually (Leissle interview 2005). This illustrates the ability of
top-tier tribute acts to use their premium position in the tribute market to
expand into the international live entertainment market, and points to a
further structural homology with the culture industries. The cultural industries are characterized by their high degree of risk and central strategies for
risk mitigation, in an increasingly globalized and competitive market that
often experiences a fast moving turnover of product, and the contingencies of
evanescent taste preferences. In such a climate this *de facto* franchise model is
becoming an increasingly common operational strategy for cultural producers. The Guggenheim Museum, for example, now operates museums in
Bilbao, Venice, Berlin and Las Vegas along with its original New York location. In August 2004, a local version of Liverpool's Cavern nightclub, made
famous by the Beatles in the 1960s, opened in Adelaide, Australia. Branded
'the most famous club in the world', the Cavern franchise clubs, themed
extensively with a range of Beatles memorabilia, now operate in Rio de Janeiro, Moscow and Tokyo, along with the 'original'[12] club in Liverpool.

Branding strategies provide a key mode of differentiation in an increasingly saturated niche. Branding and the widespread theming (Gottdiener
2001) of entertainment venues are key indexes of significant changes in the
cultural industries. Contexts of nostalgia as emergent 'structures of feeling'
are increasingly becoming modes of extracting immaterial value and it is in
the deployment of such contexts that cultural industries should be understood. In this sense tribute bands, rather than being supplemental to the 'real
business' of music-making, recording and performing, are themselves immanent to the industry and have been important indexes of change in the
production of popular music in the contemporary era.

Research undertaken for this chapter included telephone (18 May 2005) and email interviews (24 May 2005 and 26 May 2005) with Björn Again's co-founder Rod Leissle, and access to interview transcripts of a phone interview between Shane Homan and Rod Leissle conducted on 27 October 2004. Personal communication between several bands and band members was also used, including Karen Graham from Abba Gold on 14 May 2005.

Notes

1   The Rolling Stones' first UK charting entry (as high as 21) was with a cover version of Chuck Berry's 'Come On' in 1963 (Sweeting 2004).

2   As Paul McCartney stated: 'none of the other groups did it ... it was actually a bit of a joke to dare to try your own songs' (Sweeting 2004: 35).

3   As Frith has argued: 'Good music is the authentic expression of something – a person, an idea, a feeling, a shared experience, a Zeitgeist. Bad music is inauthentic; it expresses nothing' (1987: 136).

4   The 660 million units sold in 1990 represented six CDs for every album sold (Burnett 1992).

5   Although Karen Graham from Abba Gold insists that 'the band wasn't named after the CD, we just really liked the name' (Graham interview 2005).

6   Track listing: 1. 'Lay All Your Love On Me'; 2. 'S.O.S'; 3. 'Take A Chance On Me'; 4. 'Voulez-Vous'.

7   For Bourdieu, 'nothing more clearly affirms one's class, nothing more infallibly classifies, than tastes in music' (1984: 18).

8   The *Shorter Oxford Dictionary* (1993) defines imprimatur as 'The formula (= "let it be printed"), signed by an official licenser of the press, authorizing the printing of a book; hence as n. an official license to print'.

9   As was the case with Oasis cover band Nowaysis who, along with playing at several parties thrown by Oasis' record company, also accepted an award for Oasis at a function in Norway that the original band was unable to attend (Brown 2000).

10 In the case of Swedish Abba tribute band *Waterloo*, original Abba backing band members that have taken part in their show include saxophonist Uffe Andersson (who joined the band on stage in their debut performance in 1996) along with Rutger Gunnarsson (bass), Ola Brunkert (drums) and Mats Ronnander (guitar and vocals). Similarly, in 2001 former Stone Roses bass player Mani joined the Complete Stone Roses tribute for a Dublin show. In some cases, original bands have directly recruited members from their tribute. The Australian band the Angels, for example, reportedly hired a bass player from one of their at least five tributes (Scott 1997) while in 1996 Judas Priest, following the resignation of singer Rob Halford, recruited Tim Owens as his replacement, plucking him from British Steel, the tribute band he formed to pay tribute to them.

11   The Bootleg Beatles are credited with being the first tribute band to make the step up to theatres in 1990 (Mugan 2005).
12   Reference to an 'original' Cavern nightclub is problematic. Following the club's closure in 1973, it was extensively rebuilt and remodelled prior to its reopening in 1984; it did not operate as a nightclub until the 1990s. The current Cavern is only partially sited on the original club location, a further problem for its authenticity as a tourist location (Cohen 1995).

References

Abba fever hits (2001) *Sunday Herald-Sun*, 27 May.
Abba (2005) Official website, http://www.abbasite.com (accessed 24 November 2005).
Abba Forever (2005) Promotional material emailed to author, 17 August, www.abbamail.com (accessed 28 November 2005).
Abba World (2005) Abba World, http://www.abba-world.net (accessed 28 November 2005).
Appadurai, A. (1990) Disjuncture and difference in the global cultural economy, *Theory, Culture and Society*, (7): 295–310.
Baker, G. A. (1990) Tribute-band movement swells in Australia, *Billboard*, 102, 7 April.
Bourdieu, P. (1984) *Distinction: A Social Critique of the Judgement of Taste*, trans. Richard Nice. London: Routledge & Kegan Paul.
Brown, A. (2000) Wish upon the stars: festive season special, *Sunday Times*, 10 December.
Burnett, R. (1992) The implications of ownership changes on concentration and diversity in the phonogram industry, *Communication Research*, 19(6): 749–69.
Carr, I. (1999) *Miles Davis: the definitive biography*. New York: Thunder's Mouth Press.
Chamberlain, D. (2000) Tribute bands: the next best thing – Björn Again Björn Again: not just an Abba tribute act, http://news.bbc.co.uk/2/hi/in_depth/entertainment/2000/brit_awards/657042.stm (accessed 16 November 2004).
Cohen, E. (1995) Contemporary tourism – trends and challenges: sustainable authenticity or contrived post-modernity?, in R. Butler and D. Pearce (eds) *Change in Tourism: People, Places, Processes*. London: Routledge.
Cox, T. (2005) Clonin' Jack flash, the *Guardian*, 3 April, www.guardian.co.uk/arts/features/story/0,11710,1450925,00.html (accessed 5 May 2005).
Deleuze, G. (1994) *Difference and Repetition*. New York: Columbia University Press.
Dessau, B. (2004) Should the band play on? the *Guardian*, 8 July.
Duffy, T. (1993) PLG finds 'Gold' in Abba's vault, *Billboard*, 105(40): 8.
Ewen, S. (1988) *All Consuming Images: The Politics of Style in Contemporary Culture*. New York: Basic Books.

Frith, S. (1983) *Sound Effects: Youth, Leisure and the Politics of Rock*. London: Constable.

Frith, S. (1987) Towards an aesthetic of popular music, in R. Leppert and S. McClary (eds) *Music and Society*. Cambridge: Cambridge University Press.

Frith, S. (1996) *Performing Rites: On the Value of Popular Music*. Cambridge, MA: Harvard University Press.

Garnham, N. (1990) *Capitalism and Communication: Global Culture and the Economics of Information*. London: Sage.

Gibbs, A. (2002) Disaffected, *Continuum: Journal of Media & Cultural Studies*, 16(3): 335–41.

Gottdiener, M. (2001) *The Theming of America: Dreams, Media Fantasies, and Themed Environments*. Boulder, Co: Westview Press.

Grainge, P. (1999) Reclaiming heritage: colourization, culture wars and the politics of nostalgia, *Cultural Studies*, 13(4): 621–38.

Griffiths, D. (2002) Cover versions and the sound of identity in motion, in D. Hesmondhalgh and K. Negus (eds) *Popular Music Studies*. London: Arnold.

Grossberg, L. (1993) The media economy of rock culture: cinema, post-modernity and authenticity, in L. Grossberg and A. Goodwin (eds) *Sound and Vision: The Music Video Reader*. London: Routledge.

Hesmondhalgh, D. (1998) The British dance music industry: a case study in independent cultural production, *British Journal of Sociology*, 49(2): 234–61.

Hesmondhalgh, D. (1999) Indie: the institutional politics and aesthetics of a popular music genre, *Cultural Studies*, 13(1): 34–61.

Hesmondhalgh, D. (2002) *The Cultural Industries*. London: Sage.

Jameson, F. (1991) *Postmodernism, or, the Cultural Logic of Late Capitalism*. London: Verso.

Lash, S. and Urry, J. (1994) *Economies of Signs and Space*. London: Sage.

Litz, R.A. and Stewart, A.C. (1988) Franchising for sustainable advantage? Comparing the performance of independent retailers and trade-name franchisees, *Journal of Business Venturing*, 13(2): 131–50.

Massumi, B. (1996) The autonomy of affect, in P. Patton (ed.) *Deleuze: A Critical Reader*. London: Blackwell.

Melody Maker (1992) Reading festival review, 12 September: 31, 34.

Mugan, C. (2005) Rock & pop: gonna live for ever, the *Independent*, 8 April.

Murfett, A. (2004) Play it again, *The Sydney Morning Herald*, 26 June.

Negus, K. (1996) *Popular Music in Theory: An Introduction*. Middletown, CT: Wesleyan University Press.

Neuman, W.R. (1991) *The Future of the Mass Audience*. Cambridge, MA: Cambridge University Press.

Pearlman, J. and Moses, A. (2002) Attack of the clones, *The Sydney Morning Herald*, 2 August.

Potter, R.A. (1997) Not the same: race, repetition and difference in hip-hop and dance music, in T. Swiss, J. Sloop and A. Herman (eds) *Mapping the Beat: Popular Music and Contemporary Theory*. Malden, MA: Blackwell.

Redhead, S. (1990) *The End-of-the-century Party: Youth and Pop Towards 2000*. Manchester: Manchester University Press.

Rojek, C. (1995) *Decentring Leisure: Rethinking Leisure Theory*. Thousand Oaks, CA: Sage.

Ryan, B. (1992) *Making Capital from Culture: The Corporate Form of Capitalist Cultural Production*. Berlin: Walter de Gruyter.

Savage, J. (1988) The enemy within: sex, rock and identity, in S. Frith (ed.) *Facing the Music*. New York: Pantheon Books.

Scott, J. (1997) Profit in among the covers, *The Australian*, 11 March.

Shuker, R. (2001) *Understanding Popular Music*. London: Routledge.

Stanworth, J. and Curran, C. (1999) Colas, burgers, shakes and shirkers: towards a sociological model of franchising in the market economy, *Journal of Business Venturing*, 14(4): 323–44.

Straw, W. (1993) Popular music and postmodernism in the 1980s, in L. Grossberg and A. Goodwin (eds) *Sound and Vision: The Music Video Reader*. London: Routledge.

Strobl, E.A. and Tucker, C. (2000) The dynamics of chart success in the UK pre-recorded popular music industry, *Journal of Cultural Economics*, 24(2): 113–34.

Sweeting, A. (2004) *Cover Versions: Singing Other People's Songs*. London: Pimlico.

The Top 50 Entertainers (2005) *Business Review Weekly*, 7–13 April.

Toynbee, J. (2002) Mainstreaming, from hegemonic centre to global networks, in D. Hesmondhalgh and K. Negus (eds) *Popular Music Studies*. London: Arnold.

Weinstein, D. (1998) The history of rock's pasts through rock covers, in T. Swiss, J. Sloop and A. Herman (eds) *Mapping the Beat: Popular Music and Contemporary Theory*. Malden, MA: Blackwell.

Wolf, M. (1999) *The Entertainment Economy*. London: Penguin Books.

6   In the wake of Hendrix: reflections on a life after death

Chris Richards

Prologue

I was never a fan of Jimi Hendrix. I was the right age at the right time; but I bought none of his records (Richards 1998). Perhaps Hendrix was just too much on show. The sort of exotic piratical bricolage of his first TV appearances, with the success of 'Hey Joe', certainly tore into the banality of pop. But the accumulation of subsequent images seemed to flip over, in their excess, from cool to uncool, productive more of embarrassment than identification.[1] Kneeling in feigned orgasm over the body of his guitar or lecherously waving his tongue (more phallic display than an offer of oral sex; see Dyer 1985) did not provide a space for a sexuality with which I could be at ease. On the contrary, this was a masculinity I couldn't emulate, couldn't inhabit.[2] In 1968, *Electric Ladyland*'s display of naked women ended the lingering possibility that I might actually buy one of his LPs. It must have been a close thing, with the inclusion of 'All Along the Watchtower'. I wasn't articulating some kind of proto-feminism. I just couldn't 'do' this apparently predatory masculinity, not so much because it oppressed women, but because it oppressed me. Following *Are You Experienced?*, the cover of *Electric Ladyland* looked like a boast, showing off Hendrix's groupies. But somewhat contradictorily, I also didn't like the photograph; too many of these women didn't look good enough (see Perry 2004: 62). Because I neither went to see Hendrix, nor bought his records, I heard only the most widely-played tracks on TV and radio. His musical innovations, and his subsequent influence, were thus unknown to me.[3]

Beverley Skeggs (2004: 100) provides one way of rethinking the grounds of this rejection:

> To ... read the site of projection as the 'truth' of the person or object is to mis-recognize and mis-read one's self. To read something (a body or object) as excess is to render it beyond the bounds of propriety, to locate it within the inappropriate, the matter out of place, the tasteless. A reading of a body as excessive is therefore to display the investment the reader has in maintaining propriety in

> themselves ... Excessive sexuality, as Mercer and Julien (1988) detail,
> is the thing which, *par excellence*, is a threat to the moral order of
> Western civilization.

Perhaps disowning and denying material taken to be 'embarrassing' or 'vulgar' was integral to the production of a particular, and especially white, middle-class self, almost austerely remote from the risk of bodily contamination (Dyer 1997). Maybe this was also about the production of a self-identity, defined against the 'common', undiscriminating consumption of trash. In the later 1960s, 'excessively' commercial black music and the 'show business' stylized choreography and stage dress associated with it, or the 'vulgarity' of sexual display in some musical performances, including those of black performers, certainly provoked the kind of response Skeggs suggests. And even Hendrix, though apparently playing 'innovative' rock, was perhaps not cool (or cold) enough and not white enough (Dyer 1997). By contrast, as John Perry notes, 'English blues guitarists of that era generally stood still looking *extremely* serious' (2004: 40).

This brief sketch of my own response to Hendrix, during his life, illustrates a problem: the construction of Hendrix, then and since, as a fetishized and racialized body, the extraordinary locus of, simultaneously, sexual and musical virtuosity. To disassemble such a construction, even to open space for some irony in its performance, has seemed a long time coming. In reading many of those who have written about Hendrix since his death, I have found plenty of expressions of reverence, awe and admiration. Many of these writers, both black and white, also implicitly sustain aspects of the sexual mythology of the black male body in paying their often lavish tributes to Hendrix. This mythology is central to the posthumous debate around Hendrix examined in the following pages of this chapter. My own early rejection of Hendrix, tentatively reconsidered above through Skeggs' analysis of 'propriety', informs the standpoint from which I now write, though I do not intend simply to confirm my rejection in the argument I pursue here. The issue is one of clarification – of the terms on which to re-engage with Hendrix so long after his death.

'Jimi Hendrix' has been contested, constructed and reconstructed, in a wide array of biographies and other more passing tributes to his short but spectacular career. In these writings, the sexual and racial politics of his legacy are inextricably interwoven with accounts of his musical 'virtuosity'. To begin with I want to examine the comments of several prominent black commentators on popular music, particularly Nelson George and Greg Tate. I turn then to a variety of white authors, some specialists in popular music studies, others offering memories of Hendrix in the context of more general autobiographical reflections. The mapping of these debates in this section provides a basis for the subsequent reading of the Hamsters, a white band paying musical tribute to Hendrix while refusing to become a Hendrix tribute band.

The Hamsters, declining to 're-embody' Hendrix, and thus avoiding charges of mimicry, of 'black-face' minstrelsy, play with considerable musical conviction but as ageing white men at some ironic distance from the hypermasculinity of much rock guitar performance. At last, perhaps, with this blues trio from Essex, some humour has framed the performance of 'hard' rock

'Hendrix after death is a growth industry'

Over the past 35 years, Hendrix has been reinterpreted, sometimes almost 'remade', across a wide array of merchandise and in histories, biographies and critical commentaries focused upon him. This is, as Tate (2003: 64) has suggested, a 'growth industry' in popular music. Nelson George (1988) sees this as an entirely 'white' concern. He locates Hendrix in the binaries of a racialized discourse, where 'Black' and 'White' constitute almost mutually exclusive domains. The result is an almost uncompromising dismissal of Hendrix, representing him as turning back (to blues) and isolating himself from the forward movement of black music. In George's account the black audience is characterized by a 'consumerism and restlessness [that] burns out and abandons musical styles'; meanwhile, 'white Americans . . . seem to hold styles dear long after they have ceased to evolve' (p. 109). In relation to this polarized construction of 'Black' and 'White' audiences, Hendrix's creativity was, in several senses, misplaced:

> Blacks create and then move on. Whites document and then recycle. In the history of popular music, these truths are self-evident . . . Hendrix drew from a style blacks had already disposed of . . . removed from the traditions of black America, Hendrix in London . . . emerg[ed] with a black based sound drenched in flower-power rhetoric that had little in common with the soul consciousness of James Brown or Aretha . . . Unfortunately, Hendrix fatally damaged his connection with black audiences because of his innovative brilliance on the electric guitar, an instrument that, with the declining interest in the blues, fell into disfavor . . .
>
> (George 1988: 108–9)

George concludes his lament with 'you just couldn't dance to it' (p. 109). Mark Anthony Neal places Hendrix in much the same way, arguing that he was 'never claimed by the black community, in large part because of his own refusal to have his music reduced into any specific genre' (1999: 113).

Paul Gilroy (1993a: 93), implicitly accepting that Hendrix had little support from a black audience, construes Hendrix as 'made up' for white audiences in England:

Hendrix was reinvented as the essential image of what English audiences felt a black American performer should be: wild, sexual, hedonistic, and dangerous ... Sexuality and authenticity have been intertwined in the history of western culture for several hundred years. The overt sexuality of Hendrix's neo-minstrel buffoonery seems to have been received as a sign of his authentic blackness by the white rock audiences on which his burgeoning pop career was so solidly based.

In this perspective, Hendrix is, again as George suggests, 'misplaced' for a black audience. These are broadly convergent accounts, together suggesting that his music was anchored in a dying genre (blues) and an instrument falling into disfavour (electric guitar); that he did not produce music within a currently live and popular black genre; and that he was performing to a white audience in terms suggesting complicity with white fantasies about black sexuality.

But addressing the same issue – the apparent alienation of black audiences from Hendrix's music – David Henderson (2002: 313) attributes such tastes to the manipulative power of white-owned radio rather than to an 'authentic' expression of cultural preference or aesthetic sensibility. He believes that:

In many ways Jimi Hendrix's appearance in Harlem [September 1969] brought up the true paradox of his fame. Jimi was known world wide, but not in Harlem, his symbolic hometown. Both he and Eddie O'Jay knew that this reality was the result of corporate conferences. Eddie O'Jay nearly had to admit to the crowd that he did not control his own play-list (a horrible admission for any DJ). In fact, his play-list was controlled by the Sonderling Corporation of Dallas, Texas – a white corporation that owned a string of the biggest black radio stations in America and ran the stations as a component of specialised radio for black markets. Their seven-day, 24-hour air time was the heaviest advertisement-saturated format in radio. Their interests in the cultural development of their listeners did not rise above black R&B Top 10 and the most legally allowable ad density.
(Henderson 2002: 313)

For Henderson, Hendrix was unknown because he was unheard, not because he played blues, or the guitar, or too much for a white audience, or appeared to have embraced hippie rhetoric (see also Tate 2003: 30–1).

In common with all of the preceding authors, Greg Tate (2003: 8) doesn't question the argument that black audiences have shown little interest in Hendrix. But his project is to intervene. *Midnight Lightning* is:

> ... a Jimi Hendrix Primer for Blackfolk. A user-friendly introduction for all of My People who don't get that Hendrix was a Black man who came from several Black worlds to make extraterrestrial Black music for all God's children whether they got rhythm or not ... it is ... a Jimi Hendrix Reclamation Project. One that dares come demanding he be accepted in the fold of twentieth century Black icons by all who ever dared think he played 'white boy music'.

Tate, a performer as well as a writer, is implicitly aligned with a movement of musical recovery concerned to revisit the blues. Since Nelson George's apparently terminal judgement (1989), the blues has been the object of a 'rehabilitation by a new generation of black performers', actively challenging its 'dismissal by 1960s black power activists as accommodative and appropriated by whites' (Negus and Pickering 2004: 101).[4] Public Enemy's Chuck D, for example, figured prominently in a recent homage to Chess Records and Muddy Waters (Scorsese 2004). And by contrast with George, Charles Shaar Murray has also provided a detailed overview of the many disparate reworkings of Hendrix's music through the past 30 years (Murray 2001) suggesting, in effect, that Hendrix's music was far from 'backward looking'.

But Tate's project is more than a matter of *musical* recovery. Arguing that African-American culture tends to resist radical change, he construes Hendrix as living, prefiguratively, beyond 'race': 'Any book about Hendrix with race on the brain has no choice but to recognize him as a destroyer of our racialist worldviews. This holds for black and white folk alike' (Tate 2003: 11). As Tate further argues (p. 30):

> If Hendrix is a Black Icon, he is also a destabilizer of Black Masculine stereotypes from both within and without African American Culture. Hard where the culture says soft (the volume level of his guitar), relaxed where the culture says either 'ghost' or fly into a rage (when among mobs of white folk). For this reason I consider him a super-signifier of Post-Liberated Black Consciousness. Someone who tried to show by example what life as a Black Man without fear of a white planet might look like, feel like, taste like.

In some respects, Tate's Hendrix appears here as a precursor of other more aggressively masculine black men acting in defiance of a 'white planet': the 'blaxploitation' film *Shaft* (MGM/Shaft Productions, 1971) and more recently the many gangsta rappers openly asserting their right to sexual involvement with white women. Is the cover of the British edition of *Electric Ladyland* thus more appropriate than Hendrix himself acknowledged, in that it implies precisely this liberation from the fear of violent reprisal (castration, lynching) for the act of miscegenation? The difficulty here is that however 'relaxed' Tate suggests Hendrix may have been, the security of his position seems to have depended on precisely the racial mythology of black phallic 'superiority'. So, if this is liberation from the 'fear of a white planet' it seems largely dependent on an inflection of an image of black masculinity with a long history: just another black man/beast with a very big penis (Mercer and Julien 1988; Mercer 1994; Hall 1997: 262–3). Tate cites his 'Harlem-based girlfriend' Faye Pridgeon: 'There were times when he almost busted me in two, the way he did a guitar on stage' (Tate 2003: 56). David Henderson (2002: 326–7) similarly documents Hendrix's sexual reputation: 'for Hendrix the chicks were release, part of his creative fashion, a way for him to maintain his drive and keep his energy peaked. That Hendrix's sexual appetite was enormous made him more the pimp in Devon's eyes, the super-pimp, the master game pimp ... Hendrix's joint "was damn near big as his guitar"'.

Tate's 'recovery', like Henderson's, is thus not without problems. But any appropriation of, or tribute to, 'Hendrix' cannot evade this issue. Hendrix as the black stud can't be bracketed out from Hendrix as the blues 'innovator' or 'virtuoso' guitarist. This is an issue especially central to any consideration of white emulators of Hendrix, including, as I will discuss below, the Essex-based band the Hamsters. The selection of particular attributes to emulate in tribute performances and recordings necessarily entails a series of implicit judgements about Hendrix as a *black* musician/performer.

I want to turn now, albeit briefly, to outline the posthumous construction of Hendrix as hero in a variety of white authors' recollections and analyses of his influence. Some comment on him in the context of more broadly focused autobiographical reflections. For example, Sheila Rowbotham, born in the 1940s, uses a memory of Hendrix in performance to present a condensed image of an historical moment: 'at the Saville Theatre ... the wild energy of Hendrix on stage tearing up the American flag was accompanied by ear-bursting music exploding from the biggest speakers I had ever seen ... music was no longer just for dancing; it signalled psychic discovery' (2000: 131–2). Though a few years younger, Donna Gaines (born in the early 1950s) similarly associates Hendrix's playing of the 'Star Spangled Banner' with a liminal moment in 20th-century history:

> My lasting impression of burned-out 1960s idealism was the sound of Jimi Hendrix cranking the national anthem as the sun rose over Woodstock ... The culture of consumption had peaked. On a noise guitar note you understood the American Century was fading; the dream was over. In that moment Hendrix sounded the death knell for an economy predicated on consumption and waste.
>
> (1990: 106)

Gaines thus gives the memory of Hendrix a perhaps more negative inflection, implying both the apparent end to the long consumer boom of the 50s and 60s, and to the 'psychic discovery' located by Rowbotham just two years earlier. But elsewhere, Gaines (1990: 178) more straightforwardly contributes to the construction of Hendrix as hero, hailing him as: 'Zen master of the Stratocaster. Ruler of haircuts and dress codes, now as in the hour of our deaths. Undisputed King of our rock and roll universe'.

Germaine Greer, author of *The Female Eunuch*, speaking in the 1973 documentary by Joe Boyd and John Head, comments that:

> Well, he was a Black man in a white man's world, there's no doubt about that ... I put it down in a general sort of way to the impotence of the community he played for. We had no way of making him understand what he meant to us. He knew what the press thought, but he didn't know how much we needed him or what kind of energy he was giving us.
>
> (cited in Tate 2003: 55)

Like Rowbotham and Gaines, Greer construes Hendrix as a singular focus for a generation of white youth. An expressive 'energy' is located *in* Hendrix. Sheila Whiteley, in *The Space Between the Notes* (a title taken from an interview with Hendrix) argues that:

> The extreme use of noise, in conjunction with the hypnotic nature of the Hendrix sound with its overwhelming energy and drive, created a means through which he could tune into the 'collective unconscious' of his audience. This provoked the mass sexual ecstasy often associated with his concerts, which moved towards a corporeal sense of tribal unity.
>
> (1992: 25)

Here, as Greer foresaw, it is as if the intensity of meaning attributed to Hendrix's performance has to be reanimated, articulated years later, in what, especially from academic writers, is peculiarly 'excessive' language. These invocations of Hendrix's performance may appear so extravagant because they so persistently *intermingle* political and sexual imagery.

Others translate the 'intensity' of his playing more univocally into sexual hyperbole. Ruth Padel (2000: 81), for example, offers this graphic elaboration of the usual phallic metaphors:

> In Greek terms, a hero is a man with a bit of god in him, divinity that flares in heroic daring and the way women keel over before him. Hendrix was also a world-wide sex symbol, a guitar ejaculating over the world: far out innovation plus daring technique went with legendary sexuality. A guitar hero, brandishing the magic weapon that turned him into a god.

All of these writers happen to be women. But for George Lipsitz too, though embedded in some more dispassionate comments on 'technology' and 'technique', Hendrix is represented as extraordinary: his 'sensuality' is 'apocalyptic' (1990: 129).

Gilbert, a retrospective fan of the Velvet Underground, not Hendrix, and born in the early 1970s, is more sceptical of Hendrix's construction as a 'hero':

> Jimi Hendrix deployed the resources inherent in electronic amplifi-
> cation largely to extend the melodic range of his instrument and
> thereby to secure his place as the ultimate phallocentric guitar hero
> ... [the received image of Hendrix the lone guitar hero is in stark
> contrast to that of the four members of the Velvet Underground
> immersing themselves ... in the wall of noise].
>
> (1999: 42, 48 endnote)

Gilbert's acknowledged 'cheap shot at Hendrix' (Gilbert 1999: 48n.) is a productive interruption to the chorus so uniformly evident in writing from the earlier generation of critics. For example, while arguing, apparently le-gitimately enough, that white rock music in the 1970s 'progressed' by taking over, without acknowledging, the features of African-American musical per-formance he exemplified, both Iain Chambers and Robert Walser reiterate the attribution of heroic genius to Hendrix. Chambers portrays Hendrix as 'a black guitar hero in a very white world' (1985: 100–1). Walser reasserts Hendrix's place in relation to heavy metal as the 'first truly virtuosic hard rock guitarist', producing 'a virtuoso's vocabulary of extravagance and transgres-sion' (1993: 77).

There is an important paradox here. Both Chambers and Walser contest the 'denial' of Hendrix and yet at the same time draw upon and further Hendrix's reputation as a lone hero, a guitar virtuoso, a reputation not that they have to (re)establish, but which has already been constructed.[5] They identify the sound feeding progressive rock and heavy metal as Hendrix's alone, not of the Jimi Hendrix Experience, as the product of ensemble playing between three players. White and English, Mitch Mitchell and Noel Redding are erased here (though not entirely from either Henderson 2002 or Murray 2001). They thus further indulge an insistent fascination with Hendrix *alone*. All that is exceptional, intense and innovative is located only in the black member of the trio. It is Hendrix, not the 'Experience', that is most con-sistently hailed as the properly 'authentic' source for all that followed.

This is, in part, an effect of the individualizing, and essentializing, dis-courses of genius. Negus and Pickering (2004) trace the history of such dis-courses, linking later variants to 'race thinking' in the 19th and earlier 20th centuries. They refer, for example, to 'a romanticized ideal' involving 'an assumed raw, unspoiled vitality' and of 'primitivism' (in art) as speaking to 'a sense of lack in white subjectivity' (Negus and Pickering 2004: 142). Hendrix is constructed through a later inflection of this discourse. In effect, in the discourse through which he is constructed as a lone guitar hero, he is positioned as embodying a 'raw' power, oscillating in its expression between sexual and musical innovation, excess and transgression. His sidemen are just 'competent' (Gilroy 1993b). And when Bennett and Dawe refer to Hendrix as 'single-handedly pioneering a new style' (2001: 3), they further articulate the dominant discourse through which Hendrix is currently recalled.[6] Of course Hendrix produced some exceptional music but, as Negus and Pickering argue, it is possible to disentangle a recognition of exceptionality from an essentializing, and in Hendrix's case a 'racializing', mythology of creativity. They suggest that 'the sense of genius as an entire person' should be abandoned (2004: 159). Instead they emphasize that exceptionality 'depends upon a longer process of *becoming*, from which the exceptional creative act that is termed genius can emerge' (p. 158). Following this, and to break with the racializing tropes sedimented in the discourse of 'primitive' genius, Hendrix's musical innovations need to be located in both his own substantial prior experience in rhythm and blues and in the specific collaborations (with other musicians and with producers) in the period from late 1966 until his death.

The Hamsters

Following Manthia Diawara, Skeggs remarks that: 'the "Blues", as a form of music appropriated by white musicians, was the site where "cool" as an attribute was formed' (2004: 188). Of course blues in Britain in the 1960s had a substantial place alongside soul and Motown and, eventually, psychedelic rock. Blues, unlike other black music, was probably first encountered by many, both live and on record, as it was played by white performers. To play blues guitar was, as Skeggs suggests, a very cool thing to do. Transferred to the bodies of young white men, the dexterity and 'down' demeanour of blues playing bestowed a mystique and an understated (hetero)sexuality unlikely to be read off from the bodies of its (seemingly always already old) black performers. Take, for example, in the mid-1960s, Eric Clapton or Bert Jansch by contrast with B.B. King or John Lee Hooker. In some respects the 'cool' stance of white blues players implied a male sexuality both elusive and (dis)-passionate. It was serious, plain and accomplished.

In many respects, the Hamsters are inheritors of this version of 'cool' rather than, in any overt way, the dressed up, showy, sexualized performance style associated with Hendrix. And yet they are known as a band substantially devoted to performing and recording material produced by the Jimi Hendrix Experience. They play regular sets, sets dedicated entirely to Jimi Hendrix and sets combining Hendrix with ZZ Top, largely on a pub rock and beer, biker and blues festival circuit in England, and to some extent in Holland and Germany. But the Hamsters are not young men. They formed the band in

Figure 6.1 Barry Martin ('Snail's Pace Slim') at the Half Moon pub, Putney, London, 22 January 2005. Photograph courtesy of Chris Richards

1987 and are now in their fifties. They are thus men entering later middle age, largely playing music associated most strongly with the 1960s in Britain, when they were teenagers. Their most prominent spokesman is the lead guitarist and singer Barry Martin (known as Snail's Pace Slim). Andy Billups (Zsa Zsa Poltergeist) plays bass. Alan Parish plays drums and is also known primarily by a facetious pseudonym, the Reverend Otis Elevator.

Elements of self-mockery in their presentation, though not generally in their onstage musical performance, are persistent, strongly marking their distance from what they typically refer to as 'muso' culture. In interviews given to various music magazines,[7] they present themselves with a self-deprecatory humour and position themselves as addressing an audience construed neither as young nor with pretensions to musical expertise. Thus their drummer comments:

> I'm not a particularly technical player and there was a period in my playing life when I got very hung up about that ... and there were all these guys around the area where I was in, Southend, you'd go and see them and think, 'Fuck me, that was clever', but at the end of the day, does the guy in the street give a toss about that? Not really ... Put it this way, I'd rather send home 198 normal people happy and 2 musicians who don't think much of it.
>
> (Bateman n.d.)

In a lengthy interview for *Guitarist Magazine* (Marten 1991) Snail's Pace Slim similarly constructs their audience as *ordinary*: 'The last thing I ever want to do is play to a room full of musicians every night. We're a punter's band, we like people to come out and see us and go home saying, "Yeah, I had a really good time" '. Such an audience is ordinary according to a variety of implicit criteria, including being predominantly (though not exclusively) 'older' (perhaps 35 or 40 and above), mostly provincial, perhaps particularly male but also musically non-expert and primarily loyal to the genre of blues rock:

> I was working in a record shop when Dire Straits came along, and there were all these guys coming in who probably hadn't bought a record since Cream or early Fleetwood Mac, because they didn't like Gary Numan and Madness and The Clash. It wasn't the fact that it was a revival; it was simply that these people started hearing something they liked again...
>
> (Marten 1991)

The successful growth of the audience for the Hamsters in the early 1990s is substantially attributed to their inclusion of an increasing proportion of material from Hendrix. Slim suggests that their growing audience, and their expanded commitment to playing Hendrix, were complementary aspects of the dynamic defining their career in its first phase: 'We never had an audience ... it wasn't until we started playing a few Hendrix tunes that suddenly we uncovered this beast'.[8] Though represented as, in part, a recovery of an older audience, Slim also acknowledges an audience too young to remember his music: 'there are a lot of people out there who have never seen Hendrix ... the legend is so strong that there are now lots of young people who have heard about him'. But the music industry, like much of the media, is portrayed as both 'metropolitan' and as 'youth' obsessed, thus defining what constitutes popular music in narrow terms *obstructive* of a potentially stronger cross-generational appeal – suggested, emblematically, in a reference to 'fathers who were into Cream bringing their son with his Megadeth T-shirt on. And the Hendrix thing is the common thread' (Marten 1991).

> Let's face it, A&R people are all eighteen and nineteen years old and they're all trapped in this London thing, or now it's Manchester, and they think they've got to sell records to kids. Well there aren't any kids in comparison to what there were. People who buy records are older now and they've got more money to spend. And with a band like us it's the music that matters, not the hair-dos and clothes. The people who are interested in the kind of music the Hamsters play are the same people who bought Stevie Ray Vaughan records.
>
> (Marten 1991)

Recalling Nelson George (1989), the Hamsters appear to confirm his view of white audiences and the lamentable dead-end represented by Hendrix's success with them. The recovery and perpetuation of music from between 35 and 40 years ago seems unarguably backward looking, and the audience invoked in all three interviews appears to confirm such a view, being mostly composed of white men seeking to hear the music they listened to in adolescence (Frith 1987). Equally, there seems little evidence that the Hamsters have any interest in repositioning Hendrix as a distinctively black musician – as Greg Tate has advocated he should be. Indeed, Snail's Pace Slim, though acknowledging the crucial early influence of Little Richard on his musical tastes (Foster 2000), identifies even those blues guitarists of interest to him as mainly white – Stevie Ray Vaughan, Ronnie Earl, Anson Funderburgh, Duke Robillard, Robben Ford, Hollywood Fats (Marten 1991). In their repertoire, Hendrix is thus seemingly assimilated to a blues-rock tradition to which black players are by no means central.

However, it is crucial that the Hamsters do not emulate, in the sense of seeking to re-embody, Hendrix. Hendrix as an 'icon' (Tate 2003) is present as a visual motif: for example, his image is displayed on one of Slim's guitars, a T-shirt and a shirt imprinted with the cover art from *Axis: Bold as Love* (worn at the Half Moon, January 2005). But they do not dress or perform as if to replicate Hendrix himself nor, though they are a trio of bass, drums and guitar, to replicate the Jimi Hendrix Experience. The Hamsters' musical recovery implies a de-essentializing of Hendrix's music, asserting that 'it' can be played by others – not 'note-for-note' ('we're not necrophiliacs' – Marten 1991) – but as music stripped of the mystique of embodiment in Hendrix alone. The band has consistently constructed its own identity. They have developed their own stylized cartoon iconography – mainly featuring hamsters – and gestures to Hendrix are confined to the addition of bandannas, military jackets, left-handed guitars and playful parodies of album titles – *Electric Hamsterland, Band of Gerbils*. The band's name is traced back to punk and, according to Slim, was chosen partly to avoid 'macho posturing'.[9] While they tour widely within England, they are still also firmly located in Essex, in the South-East. The claim that 'we never set out to re-create Jimi Hendrix; we just set out to do us doing versions of Hendrix, that's all' (Marten 1991) positions them as reworking, without necessarily making innovative changes to, the music of the Jimi Hendrix Experience (Bennett 2000: 146). Slim adds: 'I don't actually think I play anything like Hendrix ... We just try and capture the spirit of what he did, and that slots nicely in amongst our rockier, bluesier things' (Marten 1991).

Indeed, at The Torrington (a pub in Finchley, north London), Slim wore a black shirt bearing the repeated imprint of Ozzy Osbourne's face, rather than Hendrix. At the Half Moon in Putney he wore a 'Sex Pistols' shirt for the first half of the set. They routinely end their performances walking among the audience, swapping guitars, while playing a ZZ Top track. Thus the Hamsters situate themselves in a larger web of musical references rather than seeking to 'reincarnate' Hendrix.

The Hamsters' 1995 *Jimi Hendrix Memorial Concert*, recorded live at the Robin Hood pub, Brierley Hill (West Midlands), includes interesting evidence of their relationship with audiences in the earlier phase of their career. On both 'Foxy Lady' and 'Purple Haze' the audience is drawn into a participatory relationship with the performance. Though this is no more than a matter of shouting out the chorus 'Foxy lady!' in the first case, with 'Purple Haze' there is a more particular invitation in that the singer (Slim) leaves lines incomplete – so that the audience can shout out the missing words: 'scuse me while I kiss the sky', 'put a spell on me', 'or the end of time'. The track fades with the audience chanting 'Hamsters, Hamsters, Hamsters!' Andy Bennett has drawn attention to how 'via processes of selective appropriation into types of vernacular discourse, popular music is continually being reaffirmed by audiences as their music and thus as a form of folk music' (Bennett 1997: 99). Certainly, it is possible that the songs in question (and perhaps others such as 'Hey Joe') have become a part of a popular repertoire, perhaps somewhat divorced from their original circulation. In this respect, their performance by the Hamsters could be seen as furthering such a 'divorce' rather than securing the audience's knowledge of the Hendrix performances. The Hamsters' first album *Electric Hamsterland* (1990) includes both 'Foxy Lady' and 'Purple Haze' and, for some, it may be that in the 1995 concert the Hamsters are heard as performing a version of their own recording rather than that of Hendrix. But hearing both simultaneously seems equally possible. The Hamsters' performance of their own previous studio recording need not displace the Hendrix recording, to which their own production is a response.

How current audiences for the Hamsters 'hear' their performances is obviously an elusive matter. Such audiences are not quite as exclusively male, or as middle-aged, as aspects of the Hamsters' earlier interviews may suggest. Though the first of their appearances I attended (the Cauliflower, Ilford) certainly seemed to be favoured by white men over 30 years of age, there were women present. At The Torrington there were also several much younger white women, in their late teens and early twenties, mostly located close to the stage.[10] Though still addressing the audience in characteristic informal 'pub band' banter (Bennett 1997: 99), and reaffirming a sense of belonging to a blues-rock 'tradition', Slim identified and placed songs, if only loosely, in the contexts of their initial circulation. It could be argued that their playing of a track from *First Rays of the New Rising Sun* (not released as such until 1997) and 'Manic Depression' (1967), and if also more predictably, 'The Wind Cries Mary' (also 1967), informed a younger audience of the wider Hendrix repertoire. Despite this, and their recognition of a cross-generational interest in Hendrix, the Hamsters' *primary* affinity is still with an older audience. Thus, in announcing a 50s rhythm and blues song, Slim pointed out, with mildly confrontational wit no doubt directed at the younger people present, that the rhythm and blues in question was not that of Beyonce Knowles (Destiny's Child), but of a much earlier genre.

The Hamsters do not play Hendrix as primarily a psychedelic or proto-jazz guitarist.[11] To the contrary, as I have argued, his songs are incorporated into a British blues-rock tradition through which, in both live performance and modest 'independent' recording, the Hamsters assert their musical authenticity. From some standpoints, such a relocation of Hendrix will imply a dis-authentification, a degradation and perhaps a whitening of his music. But the Hamsters revisit Hendrix's music as a 'source' rather than as the object of pastiche, parody or major elaboration. Slim insists: 'All we try and do is get the spirit of his music into what we do', and, perhaps refusing his 'heroic' status adds that 'Hendrix was a major innovator, but I've never looked upon him as a sacred cow', concluding firmly that 'we never set out to re-create Hendrix' (Marten 1991).

However, the Hamsters do venture into significant irony in reflections on their own relationship to rock's hard masculinity. When they play Hendrix's music, in a context framed by jokes about ageing and bodily failings, it can produce a distinctive, and subversive, 'disembodying' of Hendrix as hero. At the Half Moon in Putney, Slim ended the first half of their set with a reminder of the implications of 'prostate problems'. Their recent 'in performance' DVD is entitled *To Infirmity and Beyond* (2004). The ironic disparity between Hendrix's 'apocalyptic sensuality' (Lipsitz 1990) and the Hamsters' decidedly ungodlike self-presentation is well illustrated in the concert video, filmed in Milton Keynes in 2003. Slim's comic banter with the audience, addressed as ageing with them into their fifties, significantly inflects the meaning of the tribute:

> Thanks a lot folks ... It's usually about this time of night we stick a Jimi Hendrix thing in for ya ... For the uninitiated, we've always enjoyed Jimi's songs but we have encountered some criticism from the music press for playing Hendrix songs, they think it's uncool ... well I'm afraid they have confused us with someone who might give a shit. The real reason is we've got a combined age of 150 ... when you get that old you're far more worried about having to get up three times a night for a piss than what some spotty little virgin on the *NME* has to say about you ... and the other good thing about getting old is you don't have to do drugs anymore 'cause you get the same effect just standing up quickly ... anyway, as most of you know.
>
> (Slim, on *To Infirmity and Beyond* 2004)

The audience is addressed here with familiarity, acknowledging implicit loyalty to the band and distance from the music press, and inviting an awareness of ageing and its consequences. These are not performers putting their bodies on display. To the contrary, though they move rather more than some of the more austere 60s blues guitarists, their actions are more mundane, more routinely those of 'working musicians'. Even Slim's relatively extravagant gesturing with the guitar in his playing of 'Star Spangled Banner' is more a matter of technical necessity than of mimicry of Hendrix-as-bodily-performer. Though Slim's verbal style is jocularly abrasive,[12] there is, amidst the hard-rock playing and the evident 'mastery' of Hendrix's material, a paradoxically self-effacing refusal of the phallic posturing so often enacted by lead guitarists in that tradition.

Conclusion

The Hamsters are one among many of those who continue to recover, and variously pay tribute to, Jimi Hendrix and the Jimi Hendrix Experience. Their performances and recordings, though clearly adapting Hendrix to a British blues-rock tradition, also offer a convivial and determinedly unpretentious take on Hendrix's music. Moreover, as they work on into their fifties, they provide a wry commentary on a faltering masculinity, and thus an implicitly ironic counterpoint to the image of Hendrix as phallic guitar hero constructed in the late 1960s and after his death.

Coda

Of course I have often regretted not going to see Hendrix when he played in Hull, in 1967, just a few miles from where I grew up. I probably missed something extraordinary. But maybe it doesn't really matter that much as then, and since, I have never felt at ease in the face of rock machismo (see Reynolds and Press 1996; Gilbert 1999). And hearing the Hamsters perform their versions of Hendrix's music at least allows a recovery of the distinctive musical innovations made by the Jimi Hendrix Experience without indulging in the mystique of genius or an endorsement of the racialized othering of blackness.

Notes

1   Similarly, in an interview I recorded with David Cross (formerly of King Crimson), he remarked that 'It wasn't easy for me to identify with Hendrix, he didn't look like me'.
2   Simon Frith has argued that 'people do not idolize singers because they wish to be them but because these singers seem able, somehow, to make available their own feelings – it is as if we get to know ourselves via the music' (Frith 1987: 142).

3   I began buying Hendrix on CD following conversations, over the past three years, with the guitarist Tony Smith. Prior to that, all I had was a cassette, bought to play while driving in the early 1990s (*Cornerstones*, 1990 PolyGram International Music).

4   They cite Corey Harris, Guy Davis and Eric Bibb.

5   David Cross refers to him as 'deified' in the progressive rock scene of the 1970s (Summer interview 2004).

6   See, however, Dave Marsh's comments in *The Jimi Hendrix Experience* box set (MCA Records, 2000).

7   The interviews cited here can all be found on the Hamsters website: www.thehamsters.co.uk. The Hamsters can be contacted via email at: 3geezers@thehamsters.co.uk.

8   Slim has further complained that 'We're still saddled with the Hendrix tribute tag by some sections of the media, but they can't be blamed for that; we've used it to our advantage and it's been good to us' (Slim cited in Duncan 1997).

9   Slim further explains the reasoning behind the band name: 'The Hamsters was a name [the Sex Pistols] used on one gig. I just liked the irony of it – vicious group, cuddly name. I don't really go for these bands whose names are like trouser snake adverts. I find that whole macho posturing thing rather silly ... But the thing is, we don't take ourselves seriously, never have, but we're serious about what we do; we like to try and do what we do properly. And the reason we have our silly names is that we don't want people to think, "Oh ... more boring old musos"' (Marten 1991).

10 In all three of the London venues where I have seen the Hamsters perform, the audience was predominantly white: the Cauliflower, Ilford 20 August 2004; The Torrington, Finchley, 5 September 2004; and the Half Moon, Putney, 22 January 2005.

11 Slim actually speculates, in the Marten (1991) interview, that if Hendrix had lived 'he would have lost his audience and would probably now be playing jazz festivals with Miles Davis'.

12 At the end of the evening at the Half Moon, Putney, Slim closed the performance with 'If you didn't have a good time – bollocks!'.

References

Bateman, D. (n.d.) A different perspective of a working drummer, www.thehamsters.co.uk. (accessed 8 September 2004).

Bennett, A. (1997) 'Going down the pub!': The pub rock scene as a resource for the consumption of popular music, *Popular Music*, (16)1: 97–108.

Bennett, A. (2000) *Popular Music and Youth Culture: Music, Identity and Place*. Basingstoke: Palgrave.

Bennett, A. and Dawe, K. (2001) *Guitar Cultures*. Oxford: Berg.

Chambers, I. (1985) *Urban Rhythms: Pop Music and Popular Culture.* London: Macmillan.

Duncan, S. (1997) 'Rodent rockers', *Blueprint,* www.thehamsters.co.uk. (accessed 12 September 2004).

Dyer, R. (1985) Male sexuality in the media, in A. Metcalf and M. Humphries (eds) *The Sexuality of Men.* London: Pluto Press.

Dyer, R. (1997) *White.* London: Routledge.

Foster, M. (2000) *Play Like Elvis! How British Musicians Bought the American Dream.* London: Sanctuary.

Frith, S. (1987) Towards an aesthetic of popular music, in R. Leppert and S. McClary (eds) *Music and Society – The Politics of Composition, Performance and Reception.* Cambridge: Cambridge University Press.

Gaines, D. (1990) *Teenage Wasteland: Suburbia's Dead End Kids.* Chicago: University of Chicago Press.

George, N. (1988) *The Death of Rhythm and Blues.* London: Omnibus Press.

Gilbert, J. (1999) White light/white heat: *jouissance* beyond gender in the Velvet Underground, in A. Blake (ed.) *Living Through Pop.* London: Routledge.

Gilroy, P. (1993a) *The Black Atlantic: Modernity and Double Consciousness.* London: Verso.

Gilroy, P. (1993b) *Small Acts.* London: Serpent's Tail.

Hall, S. (1997) The spectacle of the other, in S. Hall (ed.) *Representation: Cultural Representations and Signifying Practices.* London: Sage.

Henderson, D. (2002) *Scuse Me While I Kiss The Sky: The Life of Jimi Hendrix.* London: Omnibus Press.

Lipsitz, G. (1990) *Time Passages – Collective Memory and American Popular Culture.* Minneapolis, MN: University of Minnesota.

Marten, N. (1991) The hard shell, *Guitarist Magazine,* www.thehamsters.co.uk. (accessed 11 September 2004).

Mercer, K. (1994) *Welcome to the Jungle: New Positions in Black Cultural Studies.* London: Routledge.

Mercer, K. and Julien, I. (1988) Race, sexual politics and black masculinity: a dossier, in R. Chapman and J. Rutherford (eds) *Male Order: Unwrapping Masculinity.* London: Lawrence & Wishart.

Murray, C.S. (2001) *Cross-Town Traffic: Jimi Hendrix and Post-War Pop.* London: Faber & Faber.

Neal, M.A. (1999) *What the Music Said: Black Popular Music and Black Public Culture.* London: Routledge.

Negus, K. and Pickering, M. (2004) *Creativity, Communication and Cultural Value.* London: Sage.

Padel, R. (2000) *I'm a Man: Sex, Gods and Rock'n'Roll.* London: Faber & Faber.

Perry, J. (2004) *Electric Ladyland.* London: Continuum.

Reynolds, S. and Press, J. (1996) *The Sex Revolts: Gender, Rebellion, and Rock 'n' Roll.* Cambridge, MA: Harvard University Press.

Richards, C. (1998) *Teen Spirits: Music and Identity in Media Education.* London: University College London Press.

Rowbotham, S. (2001) *Promise of a Dream: Remembering the Sixties*. Harmonds-worth: Penguin.

Skeggs, B. (2004) *Class, Self, Culture*. London: Routledge.

Tate, G. (2003) *Midnight Lightening: Jimi Hendrix and the Black Experience*. Chicago: Lawrence Hill.

Walser, R. (1993) *Running with the Devil: Power, Gender, and Madness in Heavy Metal Music*. Hanover, NH: Wesleyan/New England University Press.

Whiteley, S. (1992) *The Space Between the Notes: Rock and the Counter-Culture*. London: Routledge.

Discography

DVDs

Scorsese, M. (2004) *Martin Scorsese Presents the Blues: Godfathers and Sons*. Snapper Music (DVD).

To Infirmity and Beyond (2004) Filmed at the Woughton Centre, Milton Keynes, 28 February 2003.

The Hamsters CDs

Open All Hours (2004) Rockin' Rodent Recordings.

They Live by Night (2001) Rockin' Rodent Recordings.

Pet Sounds: 10 Years of Rodent Rock (1998) Rockin' Rodent Recordings.

Jimi Hendrix Memorial Concerts (1995/6) Rockin' Rodent Recordings.

Route 666 (1995) Rockin' Rodent Recordings.

The Hamsters (1993) Rockin' Rodent Recordings.

Hamster Jam (1991) Rockin' Rodent Recordings.

Electric Hamsterland (1990) On the Beach Recordings.

Condensed Hamsters (1989/90) Rockin' Rodent Recordings.

7 Fabricating the Fab Four: pastiche and parody

Ian Inglis

fabricate [fab'rik-at'] *v/t* to put together by art and labour; to manufacture, typically with deceitful intent; to produce; to fake or forge.

pastiche [pas-teesh] *n* a literary, artistic or musical work in a style that imitates that of another work, artist or period.

parody [par'a-di] *n* a literary or musical work that imitates the style of a particular author, composer or genre for comic or satirical effect.

For any artistic imitation to be successful, its audience must, first, be able to recognize the 'original' being imitated, and, secondly, possess sufficient knowledge of the original in order to appreciate and enjoy the imitation. Given these requirements, it should come as no surprise that the most frequently imitated popular musicians have been, and continue to be, the Beatles. In fact, there are more than 600 professional or semi-professional Beatles tribute bands[1] currently active across the globe. Around 200 of these are located in the USA (Rain, the Fab Four, the Blue Meanies); 60 in Japan (the Bad Boys, the Beetles, Strawberryfields), 75 in the UK (the Cavern Beatles, the Bootleg Beatles, the Backbeat Beatles) and 20 in Germany (the Bootles, the Silver Beatles, Beafore). In addition to these expected locations, they are also to be found in countries like Thailand (the Better), Hungary (the Beathoven Brothers), Paraguay (Madera Noruega), Croatia (the Bugs, the Beatles Revival Band), Kazakhstan (the Kazakhstan Beatles), Norway (Det Betales) and Costa Rica (Revolution).

One explanation for the remarkable profusion of these tribute bands lies, of course, in the Beatles' musical legacy and the extraordinary longevity of the songs that they produced between 1962 and 1970. However, to see the Beatles merely as a (hugely successful) pop group overlooks their significance at a number of other levels – the band as a historical event and cultural phenomenon, its members as musical innovators, surrogate intellectuals and political spokespersons. This wider significance cannot be divorced from the group's past (and present) musical achievements; rather, it helps to explain the continuing popularity of a group that effectively disbanded more than 30 years ago, whose last public performance took place in 1966, and of which two members have died. It also helps to explain the intense media interest in the detailed circumstances of the lives of John Lennon, Paul McCartney, George Harrison and Ringo Starr, and, increasingly, those of their friends and families. The Beatles have transcended the broadly defined world of entertainment in which they were primarily active, to become – almost uniquely – iconic figures of the 20th century. They have become so well known, to specialist and non-specialist audiences, that the reproduction of something as simple as a stance, a gesture, a phrase, a hairstyle, a chord or an item of clothing carries with it multiple references to place, time and person that are understood around the world.

In addition to the musical achievements and commercial and cultural impacts of the Beatles, there exists a particular, and very relevant, perception of the decade in which the group was professionally active. For many, the 1960s retain 'a collective image of modernity, a vision of bright lights and speed and vitality, in which every individual ingredient was simply part of the whole' (Booker 1969: 45). Thus, through the explicit use of music, Beatles tribute bands make an implicit reference to a sociohistorical period widely seen as buoyant, optimistic and exciting, and which is likely to be as attractive to those who wish to revisit it as it is to those who seek to visit it for the first time. In fact, the range of ages among their audiences is one of the most common observations of tribute band members, according to the Bootleg Beatles' Neil Harrison:

> We get young kids ... and I don't mean teenagers. I'm talking 10-, 8-, 3-year-olds, seriously, on their dads' shoulders. It's quite incredible. You really have got the lot – young kids, teenagers, students, 35-year-olds, and grandparents who remember them first time around.
> (Harrison interview 2003)

> Perhaps the majority of the audience we get are maybe people who can remember them, or contemporaries, but there are a lot of younger ones, who weren't even alive when Lennon was alive, let alone when the Beatles were still going.
> (Rick Alan, Cavern Beatles, interview 2004)

The combined weight of these musical, cultural, historical and social factors has helped to create a set of circumstances in which audiences' shared understandings, memories or expectations of 'the Beatles story' can be vigorously exploited.

Such exploitation, however, goes well beyond the activities of tribute bands. The representation and re-presentation of the Beatles' story has, since the mid-1960s, been evident across a number of genres (including art, literature and design, as well as music) and via two distinct, but related, forms:

'pastiche', which seeks to copy or imitate its target, and 'parody', which sets out to satirize the target (often through exaggeration and distortion). As contemporary cultural theorists have observed, these processes are not limited to musical subjects, but are central components of postmodernist practice; indeed, the concepts of parody and pastiche illustrate the processes through which modernist conventions have become postmodernist codes (Jameson 1991: 16–25). In a political and cultural (and musical) environment where the modernist ideologies of *style* have given way to a proliferation and fragmentation of *styles*, and where the only certainty is that there are no longer any certainties, engagement with the familiarities of the past has become ever more attractive, ever more inevitable. As Hutcheon has argued, 'parodic references ... textually reinstate a dialogue with the past and with [its] social and ideological context' (1988: 23). And similar historical connections are achieved through pastiche's 'ransacking and recycling of culture [and] the direct invocation to other texts and images' (McRobbie 1986: 57).

Pastiche and parody may be marked by a variety of forms (visual, literary, architectural, musical), strategies (burlesque, irony, metafiction, exaggeration, travesty) and motivations (homage, confrontation, promotion, criticism). Although broadly distinguished by the 'playful' intent of the former and the 'satirical' intent of the latter, it is, nonetheless, their common imitation of a unique work, artist or period that enables them to be bracketed together as 'part of a range of cultural practices which allude, with deliberate evaluative intonation, to precursor texts' (Dentith 2000: 6). In this case, those precursor texts are the songs, performances and careers of the Beatles.

Media: satires and imitations

Within the literary world, one of the first novels to draw upon the Beatles as its inspiration was *All Night Stand* by Thom Keyes, which told the story of the Rack – a four-piece group whose early career in Liverpool and Hamburg is followed by national and international fame, culminating in a wildly successful trip to the USA:

> There are four of us and we are called the Rack ... we have also been called the Big Noises and the Climbers but that was a long time ago, in very early days. There is Mick, who is the baby. Nobody could be more sweet ... he's got such a pretty face. And there's Gerry, who is the great chat expert, the joker, the thinker. As for Nick ... bloody moody bastard. He writes our songs, and he's good, and that makes up for a lot ... he's deep, you know. And there is me.
> (Keyes 1966: 7–8)

In order to effect the connection between the Beatles and the Rack, *All Night Stand* requires nothing more of its readers than a general familiarity with the main outline of the Beatles' story. Less obvious in its parallel narrative, but in similar vein was *A Picture to Hang on the Wall* by Sean Hignett. Set in the bohemian precincts of Liverpool in the early 1960s, including many of the places where real-life art students John Lennon and Stuart Sutcliffe lived and played, it seeks to strengthen those links by explicitly referencing them in its characters' conversations:

> 'As a matter of fact, that's what we were talking about. You know, pop music and the Beatles and that ... you think it's all respectable and cultural and it's not. It's bloody good pop music and I like it and that's what it is. And the only difference is it comes from here and not the United bloody States and we're proud of it and we'll only spoil it if we make it respectable ... some of us have been with it for years only now everybody's trying to get in on the act and pretend it's cultural and bask in reflected glory. And it isn't. It's POP and it comes from Liverpool, that's what.'
>
> (Hignett 1966: 75–6)

In contrast, the 'alternative history' of the Beatles contained in Mark Shipper's *Paperback Writer* assumes a much greater, detailed, 'insider' knowledge of personalities, events, and their repercussions:

> Epstein, holding his injured foot, hopped around the room until the pain stopped, then turned to Harrison.
>
> 'What's this all about, George?'
>
> 'I'm not going to remain in a group whose rhythm guitar player claims he's bigger than Jesus. I want out.'
>
> 'Hold on a second now.' Epstein's toe was throbbing. 'John isn't even sure he *said* that in the interview.'
>
> 'It doesn't matter. I asked him about it last night, and right to my face he said, "We *are* bigger. What Jesus album ever sold a million copies??" He really thinks we're bigger than the Lord.'
>
> 'What do you care what he thinks? Let him think whatever he wants, and you can think whatever you want.'
>
> 'No, I'm sorry. We're a partnership. Musical and financial. My duty to the Lord is clear. I have to resign. I can no longer be associated with the Beatles.'
>
> 'Bloody Christians,' Epstein muttered to himself. Now they were in a fix.
>
> (Shipper 1978: 76–7)

That depth of knowledge is also assumed in Doctor Lev's 'fictionalized history' of the Beatles, *Billy Shears*:

Brian paused as everybody was on their toes listening. 'I'm proposing that we secretly replace Paul ... and not tell the world at all ... let me call in Billy Campbell. We'll all have a chance to look at him and interview him. Then we'll decide. In the meantime, maybe we could get away with some out-of-focus photos with Billy just to alleviate any suspicions or leaks of the accident.'

George Martin continued on Brian's train of thought. 'Let me also remind you boys again that we still have a couple of songs that Paul was working on that we could finish and release in a short amount of time.'

John became slightly intrigued by the prospect. 'Okay, okay, but what about Paul's family and Billy Campbell's family and friends? What about any witnesses to the crash?'

George Harrison added, 'And what about the papers? Do you know for certain that they haven't already printed something up?'

Brian was quick to remind the others about the strong and re-liable links EMI Records had with the British MI6 Secret Service.

(Lev 2001: 47–8)

These passages also clarify the distinction between pastiche and parody. The first two aim to reproduce the popular music environment (or an 'authenti-cized' version of it) in the Liverpool of the early 1960s; this reproduction, or imitation, is the central plank of pastiche. The second two excerpts employ exaggeration and distortion. The first case conflates John Lennon's comments about Christianity in 1966, George Harrison's introduction to the Hare Krishna movement in 1967, and his decision to temporarily quit the group during the recording of *Let It Be* in 1969. The other excerpt (through its references to the rumours that began to circulate in 1969, alleging that Paul McCartney had been killed in a car crash three years earlier, that an actor named William Campbell had been hired to replace him, and that the Beatles had planted numerous clues to the conspiracy in their music and lyrics) lampoons the group's activities through the creation of a comic – but es-sentially false – environment.

The two traditions can also be seen in art and design – specifically, in album cover design, 'a field full of homages, in-jokes, sly parodies and all manner of elliptical quotations' (de Ville 2003: 8). Some of the many imita-tions of Beatles covers are straightforward examples of pastiche. London band Roogalator scrupulously copied not only the shadowed black-and-white photograph of *With the Beatles* on its *With the Roogalator* EP (1977), but also the lettering and layout on the back of the sleeve. New York City's *Soulful Road* (1973) duplicated the cover of *Abbey Road*, and Booker T and the MGs' *McLemore Avenue* (1991) repeated its cover *and* its music. By contrast, satire and ridicule distinguished the cover of *We're Only in it for the Money* (1967) by the Mothers of Invention, which extravagantly mocked the design of *Sergeant*

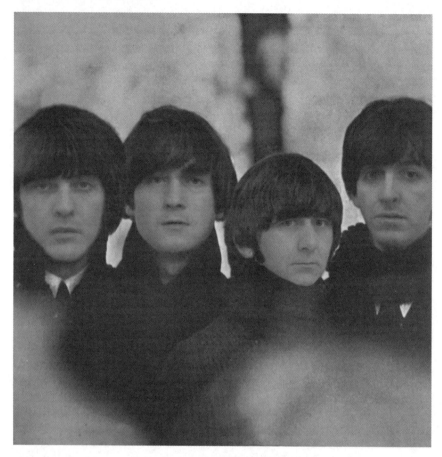

Figure 7.1 The Cavern Beatles invoke Robert Freeman's photographs used for the *Beatles For Sale* album cover of 1964. Photograph courtesy of the Cavern Beatles

Pepper; the group poses in drag, the shrubbery which adorns the original cover is replaced by garbage and rotting vegetables, and the figures in the tableau surrounding the group include Rasputin, Nosferatu, Captain Beefheart and Lee Harvey Oswald. The same satirical intent defined the Red Hot Chilli Peppers' *Abbey Road* EP (1988) on which the band march naked across the famous zebra crossing. Imitation may or may not be the sincerest form of flattery (see Figure 7.1), but there is little doubt that 'Beatles sleeves have produced more look-alikes, homages and pastiches than those of any other rock group' (de Ville 2003: 88).

Musically, the most famous example of pastiche came with the creation of the Monkees. After auditioning, rehearsing and launching an American group whose roles coincided exactly, and unashamedly, with the public perceptions of the four Beatles (wisecracking leader Micky Dolenz/John

Lennon; romantic lead Davy Jones/Paul McCartney; boy-next-door Mike Nesmith/George Harrison; clown Peter Tork/Ringo Starr), television producers Bob Rafelson and Bert Schneider, and music publisher Don Kirshner, were rewarded with a TV series freely recalling the antics and adventures of *A Hard Day's Night* (Richard Lester, 1964) that won two Emmy awards, and an internationally successful pop group that sold tens of millions of records between 1966 and 1970. Following the Monkees, though not as directly imitative in their recruitment and assembly, was in fact much of the music created by groups in the 1970s like Electric Light Orchestra and Wizzard, and, in the 1990s, by Britpop bands like Oasis. Of the former, it has been claimed that they 'based [their] entire careers' (MacDonald 1994: 175) on the cello parts of 'Strawberry Fields' and 'I Am The Walrus'; and the conspicuous presentation of the latter has prompted similar comments:

> Indeed, to scrutinize the visual style of popular Beatles admirers like Oasis is to witness a near perfect synthesis of fashions culled from different periods of the Beatles' career and reassembled into a bricolage of styles which evokes a disturbingly schizophrenic sense of undifferentiated time ... the Britpop revolution of the mid-1990s (of which Oasis are clearly key players) has at its core a nostalgic pastiche of the Beatles' abstract lyrical allusions and harmonic structures.
>
> (Neaverson 2000: 159)

The same parity of casting that distinguished the selection of the Monkees was also evident in former *Monty Python* member Eric Idle's creation of the Rutles in 1978, but here the intent was spectacularly satirical. Neil Innes (Ron Nasty/John Lennon), Eric Idle (Dirk McQuickly/Paul McCartney), Rikki Fataar (Stig O'Hara/George Harrison) and John Halsey (Barry Wom/Ringo Starr) were billed as the Prefab Four. On television and record, the group's career parodied, in painstaking detail, that of the Beatles, blending fictitious albums (*A Hard Day's Rut, Sgt Rutter's Darts Club Band, Tragical History Tour*) and genuine releases (*Archaeology*), fashioning new songs that paralleled original Beatles' tracks ('With a Girl Like You'/'If I Fell', 'Ouch!'/'Help!', 'Piggy in the Middle'/'I Am The Walrus') and placing coverage of derived personalities (Leggy Mountbatten/Brian Epstein, Gertrude Strange/Yoko Ono) alongside genuine contributions from the Beatles' peers (Paul Simon, Mick Jagger). The group (without Eric Idle) toured the UK as recently as 2004:

> Well, *Rutland Weekend Television* was Eric Idle's TV series and he asked me if I'd be interested in doing it with him. One of the things I came up with was ... a Beatles spoof called 'I Must Be In Love'. And I got into it a bit, and that's how the Rutles were born ... I started to write songs based on different eras they went through ... George had only friendly things to say ... I heard John was fascinated and kept

watching it ... Ringo liked the happy bit and not the sad bit ... Paul was forever saying 'No comment' about the Rutles.

(Neil Innes cited in Somach and Sharp 1995: 241–3)

Music: tributes and celebrations

Only by positioning the current discussion within historical traditions of pastiche and parody that were in place long before the emergence of tribute bands themselves in the 1980s and 1990s can we hope to fully understand the significance of the contemporary roles and functions they perform. At a simplistic level, of course, there is no mystery about the attraction that such bands have. Unlike other groups from the 1960s, such as the Who, the Rolling Stones and the Moody Blues, who continue to tour today (albeit with fewer and fewer of their original members) the Beatles *per se* do not exist. While their studio recordings and their film and television output are readily available, there is no opportunity for audiences to see the group in live performance. Tribute bands fill this gap by supplying a facsimile or fabrication of a live Beatles concert. And this fabrication is achieved through meticulous preparation and exhaustive rehearsal:

> Our job is to convince people, over the course of two hours, that we're the Beatles. Obviously, they don't *really*, deep down, think we're the Beatles, but they can be teased into it in some sort of way ... and by the time we get to 'Hey Jude' people have just accepted that they've seen the Beatles.
>
> (Harrison interview 2003)

> We'll all decide, 'OK, we're going to do *that* one as a new one, and *that* one as a new one'. So we'll all go away and learn them at home, so when we get together and have a live rehearsal with all the gear, we've all done our homework and we all know what we're going to do before we get there. So there's a lot of listening gone on, and we get to the room and do the rehearsal, the four of us, and then we'll go back to the reference point, which is the CD or album. So it's do your homework, get together in the room, and then fine-tune it. And of course, then you can start doing what you've got to do when you *perform* it, because we're not just four bodies on a stage. We'll look at the *Anthology* material and ask, 'Well, how did they do it?' And they would have a live arrangement, specifically to do it on stage, which was not like the recording. So we'll often look at that as well.
>
> (Roy Hitchen, Cavern Beatles, interview 2004)

In this respect, Beatles tribute band concerts are marked by a sympathetic collusion between performers and audiences, in which both are willing to temporarily, and knowingly, step outside a contemporary reality in order to participate in a mutual celebration. The fact that so many visual records of the group abound assists the fabrication; there is a considerable stock of common assumptions from which both can draw:

> The Beatles, and that era, were such a rich and fecund time ... we've got this wonderful period from 1962/3 to 1969, and they changed so much that we can do five or six different looks and they're all recognisable – John Lennon with glasses, the white suit, Pepper. And you'd be surprised – we make jokes maybe about Jane Asher or Yoko or whatever, and people do know. They're not experts ... but people do know the Beatles story.
>
> (Andre Barreau, Bootleg Beatles, interview 2003)

However, the Beatles' performing career, as is well known, ended long before their recording career. Following their show at San Francisco's Candlestick Park on 29 August 1966, the group never again gave a live performance (save for a 20-minute rooftop concert at their Apple offices in London's Savile Row in January 1969). In fact, more than half of the songs they recorded over their career (the six albums from *Revolver* to *Let It Be* and the ten singles from 'Eleanor Rigby' to 'Let It Be') were never performed on stage; this clearly presents considerable obstacles for tribute bands whose task is to reproduce those (non-existent) performances without any obvious reference points to guide them:

> There are some things ... 'Get Back' or 'Hey Jude' on David Frost's show. And we mix images – John Lennon in his white suit, George Harrison in his denims from the *Abbey Road* cover – so that people find it very natural to see us playing.
>
> (Barreau interview 2003)

> Where we don't have any record of them playing live, we try to imagine what they would do. But there aren't that many songs that we play that they didn't play live, really ... once the Beatles stopped touring and went into the studio, doing so many overdubs, they could no longer play – just the four of them – what was on the records. So we're kind of the same. We just play what you can play without having other people.
>
> (Alan interview 2004)

The stock of available information documenting the Beatles-as-performers has been supplemented by the publication of accounts exhaustively chronicling the songs they played in their live shows (Lewisohn 1986) and the instruments they used on stage and in the studio (Everett 1999,

2001; Babiuk 2001), which help to increase the verisimilitude of the tribute bands' performances:

> The thing with the instruments, and the look of it, and the whole thing ... very few of the audience seem to know that they are the right guitars. But I think if you get it right, the more you make the picture *look* right, then subliminally, the audience will appreciate it. And I think that's the same with the music.
>
> (Alan interview 2004)

> We try and make it as historically accurate as possible ... on this tour, we've added an Indian instrument we bought when we were out there last month that we've added to 'Strawberry Fields', the descending bit. And we worked out how the Beatles would have tuned it, in a completely non-Eastern way ... and it sounds just like the record when we play it.
>
> (Barreau interview 2003)

The attention to detail is not only necessary because of the audience's familiarity with the music, appearance and history of the Beatles, but also because the unprecedented exposure of the group during the 1960s (and since) has created a public who believes that it knows the Beatles themselves. Often based on the kind of choreographed and stereotyped characterizations that informed the creation of the Monkees, there nonetheless continue to exist succinct understandings of the nature of each individual Beatle, in a way which is not seen in equivalent perceptions of the group's contemporary rivals, some of whom enjoyed comparable success in the 1960s; it is hard to imagine an intimate public awareness of the personnel and personalities of the Dave Clark Five, the Hollies, the Rolling Stones, the Searchers, Herman's Hermits or the Kinks.

Consequently, tribute bands seeking to fully replicate the experience of the Beatles are required to be effective actors, as much as they are to be competent musicians; in particular, they are obliged to reproduce the conditions within which the very real warmth and affection that audiences directed towards the group are made believable. A principal strategy is to create a genuine interaction with the audience:

> We spoke to the audience ... that was the real difference, that we actually took on the Beatles' personas, you know, how they would introduce the songs. I remember that being the most difficult thing ... it's all very well singing the songs like them, but to actually impersonate them demanded more of an acting ability.
>
> (Harrison interview 2003)

There's a fair bit of banter between the songs. It's generally good-natured and people do tend to quite like it. We don't go out of our way to make them laugh, but there might be a tiny little mistake, a look on stage, someone might have said something from the front row, and there's normally a bit of chat.

(Hitchen interview 2004)

The success of the tribute band show is therefore predicated upon a sympathetic collusion (or suspension of disbelief) that allows audience and performers to contribute to the fiction of a Beatles concert in the 21st century. However, the process is complex, and disentangling the negotiations that produce meaning is difficult. For example, there are four overlapping meanings that can be attached to the applause that punctuates and closes a typical concert: audience members are applauding the tribute band's own musical expertise; audience members are applauding the tribute band's ability to mimic the Beatles; audience members are applauding the Beatles; audience members are applauding themselves. This last response, which permits an audience to actively congratulate itself for the role it has just played/for the performance it has just given, may lead to confusion when the show is over, the collaboration ends, and 'normal' relations are reinstated: 'They really don't know what to do. They want to meet you, but we don't exactly look like the Beatles when we don't have all our gear on ... we walk in and they don't quite know what to do. It freaks them out a little bit' (Hitchen interview 2004). As the Bootleg Beatles' Neil Harrison has observed, 'I think [the fans are] rather let down ... they'd quite like the fantasy to continue' (interview 2003).

As noted earlier, cultural theory's insights into the nature of the postmodernist condition provide another explanation for the popularity of Beatles tribute bands. At a time when nostalgia and fantasy have become central components of the culture industry (Ritzer 1999; Bryman 2004), the ability to re-enter the past and engage some of its leading figures and events demands the existence of some relatively accessible guides to what is often difficult terrain. Tribute bands provide such a guide, and enable us to, temporarily at least, 'try to freeze some knife-edge moment' (Mills 1959: 168) in order to know it better.

In this sense, the primary goal of the tribute band is not dissimilar from the primary goal of the historian – to offer an account of the past. Frith has provided a useful distinction between the ways in which the specific history of popular music may be written: as *progress*, where new acts replace old ones, performers develop and improve their skills with each record, and audiences become more knowledgeable; as *cycle*, where styles are repeated, patterns and parallels are observed and recognized, and the music of today freely recycles the music of the past; as *hidden*, where unexpected connections are revealed, and new explanations offered (1996: 4–6). Within these terms, Beatles tribute bands are practitioners of a form of history-as-cycle, employing the (musical) resources of the past as devices for entertainment today, and utilizing the (commercial) resources of the present in order to offer a rare glimpse of the sights and sounds of a previous era:

> When we first started, people would ask us, 'Why are you doing this? Music is always developing ... there'll be another Beatles. What do you want an old Beatles for?' But of course, history's proved that isn't the case. We create a sound that people don't expect to hear again on a stage.
>
> (Barreau interview 2003)

> In the first half of the show – last year and this year – we concentrate on one year. Last year was the fortieth anniversary of Beatlemania, so we just did everything from 1963. This year, we're doing all 1964 stuff. We put one year under the microscope, so we can play songs that people wouldn't get to hear live that often – 'Devil In Her Heart' or 'Anna' or 'Misery' or things like that.
>
> (Alan interview 2004)

Yet the primary rationale for the success of Beatles tribute bands remains the absence of the Beatles themselves and the desire of an enthusiastic public to see and hear a plausible substitute. It is, therefore, entirely appropriate to consider whether the group's continued presence after 1970 would have discouraged the growth of tribute bands. As anyone who has attended their recent live performances will testify, Bob Dylan, Brian Wilson, the Rolling Stones *et al.* include in their repertoires far more music from the 1960s and 1970s than from the 1990s and 2000s. Whether this reflects performers' own evaluations of their output or audiences' preferences for the music of their youth, the implications are clear: those Beatles contemporaries who continue to tour today are, through the obligatory performance of hits from the past, acting as their own tribute bands (see Introduction). This applies with equal accuracy to Paul McCartney, whose current live repertoire contains many more songs from his eight years as a Beatle than from his 35 years as an ex-Beatle.

The proper investigation of Beatles tribute bands therefore has to be situated within a number of interrelated contexts – musical, commercial, cultural, historical and personal. Either through pastiche or parody, the fabrication of a (more or less) credible reproduction requires inputs from performers and audiences alike. Far from being a passive spectator *at* an event, the audience member is an active participant in the creation and celebration *of* the event; and the familiarity of the Beatles story to so many adds to the clarity with which that celebration is articulated: 'We obviously can't go around as Beatles when we're in our forties', declared George Harrison in 1963

(Epstein 1964: 109). He was right; they cannot, and, furthermore, they need not, when there are so many Beatles tribute bands who are happy to do it for them.

Notes

1   Throughout this chapter, I draw extensively on interviews I conducted with members of the Bootleg Beatles (19 December 2003) and the Cavern Beatles (28 August 2004) during my research. Many of my ideas were prompted or refined by their insights, and I am deeply indebted to them for their generous participation.

References

Babiuk, A. (2001) *Beatles Gear*. San Francisco: Backbeat.

Booker, C. (1969) *The Neophiliacs*. London: Collins.

Bryman, A. (2004) *The Disneyization Of Society*. London: Sage.

de Ville, N. (2003) *Album: Style and Image in Sleeve Design*. London: Mitchell Beazley.

Dentith, S. (2000) *Parody*. London: Routledge.

Epstein, B. (1964) *A Cellarful Of Noise*. London: Souvenir Press.

Everett, W. (1999) *The Beatles As Musicians: Revolver Through The Anthology*. New York: Oxford.

Everett, W. (2001) *The Beatles As Musicians: The Quarry Men Through Rubber Soul*. New York: Oxford.

Frith, S. (1996) Backward and forward, in C. Gillett and S. Frith (eds) *The Beat Goes On*. London: Pluto.

Hignett, S. (1966) *A Picture to Hang on the Wall*. London: Michael Joseph.

Hutcheon, L. (1988) *A Poetics Of Postmodernism: History, Theory, Fiction*. New York: Routledge.

Jameson, F. (1991) *Postmodernism, or, The Cultural Logic of Late Capitalism*. Durham, NC: Duke University Press.

Keyes, T. (1966) *All Night Stand*. London: W.H. Allen.

Lev, D. (2001) *Billy Shears: The Secret History Of The Beatles*. Pittsburgh, PA: Dorrance.

Lewisohn, M. (1986) *The Beatles Live*. London: Pavilion.

MacDonald, I. (1994) *Revolution in the Head*. London: Fourth Estate.

McRobbie, A. (1986) Postmodernism and popular culture, in L. Appignanesi (ed.) *Postmodernism: ICA Documents 5*. London: ICA.

Mills, C.W. (1959) *The Sociological Imagination*. New York: Oxford.

Neaverson, B. (2000) Tell me what you see: the influence and impact of the Beatles' movies, in I. Inglis (ed.) *The Beatles, Popular Music And Society: A Thousand Voices*. London: Macmillan.

Ritzer, G. (1999) *Enchanting A Disenchanted World*. Thousand Oaks, CA: Pine Forge Press.
Shipper, M. (1978) *Paperback Writer*. New York: Grosset & Dunlap.
Somach, D. and K. Sharp (1995) *Meet The Beatles ... Again*. Havertown, PA: Musicom.

Discography

Booker T and the MGs (1991) *McLemore Avenue*, Stax Records.
Mothers of Invention (1967) *We're Only In It For The Money*, Verve.
New York City (1974) *Soulful Road*, Chelsea.
Red Hot Chilli Peppers (1988) *Abbey Road*, EMI.
Roogalator (1977) *With The Roogalator*, Stiff.
The Rutles (1996) *Archaeology*, Virgin.

8 'Smoke gets in your ears': the Marlboro Flashback tour as agent of change in the Netherlands

Lutgard Mutsaers

This chapter explores the tribute phenomenon within the Netherlands, a country that is strongly tuned into US and UK popular culture, and where overseas artists are often privileged at the expense of home-grown musical talents. Its capital, Amsterdam, is the main gateway for live acts, with the rock venue Paradiso, opened in 1968, gaining a reputation for hosting innovative performers and styles. Here I consider how the growing popularity of a particular commercial enterprise – the Marlboro Flashback tour – changed local understandings of the music cover and tribute. The Marlboro Flashback tour operated between 1996 and 2002, sponsored by tobacco company Philip Morris. Managed by the Dutch-based theatre and concert booking agency Companions, the tour consisted of approximately 400 gigs by 47 different acts, in eight smaller venues, in eight different cities across four different regions.

The tour was a phenomenon that enjoyed a national reputation for combining established performers with 'hot' new acts. Given the increasing popularity of tributes within contemporary live music scenes, this is not surprising. However, in hindsight, its success depended upon overcoming entrenched local ideas (evident in both audience and musicians' circles) about 'authentic' performance and the appropriation of rock and pop 'standards'. This included disdain for 'commercial' cover bands in a national industry which had produced few international successes. This chapter traces the emergence of tribute performers in the Netherlands, which arguably provided fertile local conditions for the later Marlboro tours. I also consider the tour's unique relationship between sponsor and touring agency, where a tobacco company was able to find a means of reconnecting with its youth market. The tour acts' choices of imitation and adaptation reflected not only personal or shared band preferences; they engendered a 'feedback' loop between original and tribute act that in one case provoked a reformation of the original band.

My main sources for this chapter consist of the national rock magazine *Oor*, a serious critical medium founded in 1971 and published twice a week; and the promotional Marlboro Flashback tour magazine *BackStage*, issued 13 times as a two-monthly full colour 36-page magazine, between February/March 1999 and May/June 2001.[1] Before 1999, *Oor* paid attention to the Marlboro Flashback tour in the live review section. After the demise of *BackStage*, *Oor* also reported Marlboro Flashback 'newsflashes' and announcements until the tour itself was abolished. These magazines played a significant role in the creation and maintenance of tribute audiences, and changing discourses about imitation. The Marlboro Flashback venture remains unprecedented in the Netherlands in its ability to provoke a national 'discussion' about the (commercial and aesthetic) worth of the tribute and cover musician.

Warming up: 1989–92

For arguably longer and more fanatically than any other western country, the Netherlands' critical rock audiences have held on to particular ideological beliefs about what is regarded as 'authentic' rock music. Ideally, 'authentic rock' came from the US or UK, preferably revealed some deeper meaning, and focused upon lyrical reflection, rather than its potential as dance music. Band members were expected to take an anti-commercial stance in interviews with the rock press, know their musical roots and acknowledge the canonized movers and shakers of pop and rock history. A sidestep like Sonic Youth's ironic project Ciccone Youth, covering some of Madonna's hits, among other material, on *The Whitey Album* (Blast First, 1988), was met with dismay for its perceived frivolity and banality. With no original repertoire of their own, local cover bands were placed at the absolute bottom of Dutch rock's hierarchy of authenticity. Broadly oriented for the sake of variety in moods and grooves, their working space was the party circuit, where they made excellent money.

This spell was broken in 1989 by a pioneering tribute band operating from Utrecht, consisting of experienced professional musicians in the theatre circuit. Playing covers from many 1960s and 70s sources in mainly music cafés for audiences not knowing what to expect, the band renamed itself Surfin' Safari, and embarked on a mission to pay tribute to the Beach Boys' early repertoire of sun, sea and surf material. Surfin' Safari brought the Beach Boys' look to the stage, with a painted blue sky sheet as backdrop, cardboard sand dunes, inflatable palm trees, Hawaiian shirts and white jeans (see Chapter 12). Their publicity campaign stressed these features, while the band sought to meticulously replicate the Beach Boys sound. Their performances at summer beach parties and in the nostalgia (so-called 'Back to the Sixties') circuit were nothing short of stunning. However, disillusioned by the lack of critical success, the group disbanded in 1991, before the later popularity of wider tribute circuits.[2] In 2001 Dutch band the Travoltas performed a tribute to the Beach Boys in the Marlboro Flashback tour. By this time, Surfin' Safari had regrouped, but did not fit within the Marlboro Flashback's formula that exclusively showcased acts with original repertoires of their own, national exposure and a solid fan base. Moreover, Companions, the promoter of the Flashback tours, retained tight control over the selection of their acts. In a few cases, this included suggestions about song selection for bands on the tour.

Tributes started to rise in the public eye when they were presented as retrospectives of bands that no longer existed, or coupled with a respectable or charitable theme or cause, or both. The Red Hot Aids Benefit Series which began in 1990 with the CD *Red Hot and Blue, A Tribute to Cole Porter*, opened doors for other tribute CD projects. The 1990s saw an increasing number of retrospectives, tributes and reunion tours. The success of the Bootleg Beatles' 1990 British tour also played an important role. The British pop music press, always highly influential in the Netherlands, picked it up, and this turned out to be decisive for the acceptance of tribute bands. Coinciding with the mainstreaming of 'alternative' acts in US rock and 'Britpop' in the UK, new audiences, bred on rap and dance, discovered the sound of 1960s rock/pop. The road to the cultural repositioning of 'total' tributes (incorporating efforts to not only sound but also look like the original) was short.

Hans Dulfer, idiosyncratic tenor saxophonist and father of alto saxophonist Candy Dulfer (who has played with Prince and Dave Stewart), had unorthodox views. On 21 December 1989 he concocted a Rolling Stones tribute night in Paradiso, and was joined on stage by his daughter. This was followed one week later by a Dutch 'Prince & the Revolution' tribute event. On 20 December 1990, a tribute to country icon Hank Williams was performed by various well-known Dutch pop artists. A tribute to Dutch language popular song on 12 June 1991 was groundbreaking for its attention to local scenes and influences. A Jimi Hendrix Memorial Night took place on 20 September that year. On 13 November 1992 the Hendrix tribute was continued as the Jimi Hendrix Music Festival, with international artists such as Snowy White and Arthur Lee. These events remained different from the new wave of tribute bands that started touring the usual rock circuit venues, among them the Australian Abba tribute band Björn Again (Mutsaers 1993).

The great tribute hoax

On 26 November 1992, Björn Again played the Amsterdam Paradiso. The enthusiastic reception they enjoyed deeply annoyed the ideologically rooted staff at the venue. The event triggered a response from one of the venue's booking agents, together with a leading radio DJ of a left-wing Dutch broadcasting corporation and rock magazine *Oor*. Paradiso fake-booked the

Bohemians for a performance on 30 December 1992, and announced the act as a Queen tribute band from New Zealand. *Oor* cryptically announced that 'Anyone who wants to know who the real Champions are, must see this show!' (Mutsaers 1993: 153).

Some 400 people turned up on the night. The familiar Queen power chords sounded over the PA and a smoke machine clouded four mannequins on stage, but there was no live show. After a brief moment of suspense the DJ took the stage to tell the flabbergasted audience never to make the mistake again to go and see a tribute band: 'We do not settle for copies! The music of Queen lives on, that's all we have left!' The 'public lesson' caused a small riot; people demanded their money back, and threatened to sue the venue. The Paradiso defended the decision to stage the event for the sake of 'the integrity of pop', against the 'attack' of the tribute bands.

Oor followed up in early 1993 with an in-depth article on the rise of tribute acts, still referred to as 'cover bands'. 'Second hand emotions is not what we're waiting for' was the general sentiment (Adrichem 1993). The mastermind of the Bohemians hoax posed the rhetorical question: 'What is the difference between a cover band and puppets?' (Adrichem 1993). According to *Oor*, the tribute craze started when Erwin Navest, a Dutch fan of the Doors, in January 1991 accidentally walked into the middle of a performance in Los Angeles of 'Unknown Soldier' by the Doors tribute band Wild Child: 'I experienced the whole concert as a real Doors concert ... I can imagine that someone of 45, who has witnessed the Doors, thinks you must leave the past alone. But the generation of today also has a right to that piece of music history' (Adrichem 1993). Navest decided to book Wild Child on the occasion of the 20th anniversary of Jim Morrison's demise in Paris, in addition to ten gigs in the Netherlands: 'I was in the wrong place at the wrong time', he said about the financial fiasco of his private enterprise (Adrichem 1993). The Netherlands obviously was not ready for tribute bands on the regular rock circuit.

One successful booker of tribute bands, Rudolf H. (who at the time of his interview in 1993 wished to remain anonymous for tax reasons), stated that record companies, songwriters, musicians, publishers and fan clubs were happy with tribute acts. Referring to the Bohemians hoax, H. stated that 'The only people making negative noises are one club programmer playing God and the left-wing journalism front' (Adrichem 1993). H. had introduced Crazy Diamond (a Pink Floyd tribute), Dirty Ol' Men (a 70s tribute), Happy Tunes (a 60s 'flower power' band), and Block Busters (a Glam rock tribute) to the Netherlands. All the people quoted in *Oor* agreed that in terms of their own creativity, tribute bands all enter a 'deadend street'; yet they all saw a great commercial future for these types of bands (Adrichem 1993).

The quality venues in the Netherlands, however, collectively decided not to jump on the tribute train, at the risk of losing audiences who obviously were interested in tribute bands, especially if the original groups chosen for imitation no longer existed or toured. However, the train could not be stopped: around the time Tori Amos and Sheryl Crow, among others, contributed to the CD *Encomium: Tribute to Led Zeppelin* (Atlantic 1995), the final barrier for tributes as a new live art form in the Netherlands disappeared.

The Marlboro Flashback tour

A small column in *Oor* of 27 January 1996 announced the start of the Marlboro Flashback tour in February, in eight so-called grand cafés, in Eindhoven, Delft, Amsterdam, Rotterdam, Maastricht, Nijmegen, Utrecht and Groningen. It was advertised as a step 'back in time', and offered a variety of tribute acts for 15 guilders. With the exception of the summer months, these venues hosted tributes for one year, creating considerable local interest. Remarkably, the gigs were never held on Fridays or Saturdays, and therefore did not interfere with regular rock venue bookings. In the same issue *Oor* also reported that Iggy Pop and the Stooges were regrouping 'to make new music with the same people' according to Iggy himself. This would have a later impact, when the disbanded Dutch group Doe Maar, covered by Bløf as part of Marlboro Flashbacks, decided to follow Iggy's philosophy to 'make new music with the same people'.

From the *Oor* issue of 23 March 1996, Marlboro began inserting its immediately recognizable full-page ads of photo collages of the live gigs, in the Marlboro brand colours of black, white and red (see Figure 8.1). The first ad asked rock fans: 'Where the hell were YOU?', spread over the page. It introduced the Flashbacks slogan 'Small Places, Big Music', with pictures of the first Ten Sharp tour with their 'Woodstock heroes', a variety of cover songs with the 1969 Woodstock festival as the binding theme.[3] The first critical *Oor* review was on the occasion of Hans Vandenburg of Gruppo Sportivo performing Frank Zappa and the Mothers of Invention songs in March 1996 with other musicians than those of his regular band.[4] Vandenburg had characteristically announced his tribute enterprise as 'The Rubbers of Prevention': It was 'an entertaining evening full of Zappa-sentiment, by pointing out exactly where the early Gruppo Sportivo took its cues from. Mission accomplished. Herman Brood is the next one to give it a go; he will tackle Frank Sinatra with a reggae beat. Let's wait and see' (Ammerlaan 1996).

Almost from the very start, critics created the tour's momentum. The musicians themselves were therefore motivated to be better, and more surprising in their song choices and performances than their predecessors in the tour. National rock and roll animal Herman Brood had caused a small sensation in 1996 by his unusual choice of Sinatra for imitation, but it turned out he had lied a bit to heat the fire of expectation.[5] He only did two songs associated with Sinatra, and filled the rest of his show with covers of Iggy Pop, George Michael, Chet Baker and mostly reggae classics. He did not perform

Supersub flashback to Paul Weller

Bijna 20 jaar Britpop op z'n best. Supersub speelde Paul Weller, The Changingman. Het energieke en rauwe van The Jam, afgewisseld met het ingetogene en melancholieke uit zijn solotijd. Ze deden het helemaal in stijl, van de gitaren tot en met de kapsels. They really did something to us.

You want more? Dat komt goed uit, want er volgen nog meer optredens van bekende bands die voor één keer teruggaan in de tijd. Dat doen ze in kleine zalen. Er is maar een beperkt aantal kaarten. Die kosten slechts ƒ 15,-. Als je wilt weten wie waar en wanneer optreedt, bel dan 0909-2026069 (45 cpm).

The heat of the moment

Marlboro FLASHBACKS

Figure 8.1 Marlboro Flashbacks advertisement, *Oor* magazine 14 November 1998, p. 11, depicting the band Supersub performing a combination of Paul Weller/the Jam/Style Council sounds and images, complete with guitars and amplifiers of the times

with his regular band, but had hired professional reggae musicians. The reggae reviewer of *Oor* believed that Brood's choices were 'daring', with their delivery on stage 'a real accomplishment' (Franssen 1996).

In his own inimitable, anarchistic way, Brood had ruined the strict formula before it had really taken off. The production company Companions saw to it that it was reinstalled, however, within a more elastic framework. Marlboro Flashbacks in all revealed 39 tributes dedicated solely to the music of one act; two tributes that centred around performers leading two major bands consecutively (Split Enz/Crowded House and the Jam/Style Council); and one 60s tribute uniting both the Beatles and the Rolling Stones in one programme (in later presentations, the Beatles and the Stones were treated as separate acts). The tours also produced a Dutch nostalgia programme with greatest hits by Dutch acts; one highly original tribute of a 'Year in Pop' (1978); a rough-and-tumble Dutch language version of the Who musical *Tommy*; a 'Story of Hip Hop' tribute by Rotterdam based Cape Verdian gangster rapper E-Life; a 1970s funk tribute by Candy Dulfer and her band Hot Stuff; and a 'Dance Classics' tribute to the 1970s and 1980s by international DJ Ronald Molendijk and his new live band Soulvation. For Molendjik and Soulvation, the Flashbacks performances provided an important base for future success. From Bob Marley to Radiohead, from Skunk Anansie to Madonna, from Rod Stewart to Public Enemy, Nirvana to Björk, the Supremes to the Velvet Underground, the Flashbacks performances knew no stylistic uniformity, nor the artistic snobbery so symptomatic of pre-1990s scenes.

Tour participants were not even afraid to follow the real touring artists in their fresh footsteps. In the summer of 1996 Neil Young gave concerts in the Netherlands, followed in the autumn by Hello Venray doing their Neil Young Flashback tribute. For Hello Venray it was the beginning of a Neil Young tribute love affair. In 2000 the band released their CD *Roll Another Number* (Inbetween Records), a series of live recordings of Neil Young songs. The first Marlboro Flashback tour act to record (part of) its actual tour tribute was Bettie Serveert, with its female lead singer Carol van Dijck, in 1997. The CD *Bettie Serveert Plays Venus in Furs and other Velvet Underground Songs* was recorded live in the Paradiso; the venue had by this time abandoned its opposition to tributes and worked with the Flashbacks tour after its first year of high visibility and artistic acclaim. Ilse DeLange followed in 1999 with *Dear John* (songs by John Hiatt) and Trijntje Oosterhuis released her tribute to Stevie Wonder, *For Once in My Life*. In 2000 Kane released a CD and DVD of their tribute to U2; in 2002, Racoon produced a CD single performing songs of Faith No More. These are only the official releases. Bootlegs are circulating, for instance, of Herman Brood's reggae project in 1996, and E-Life's The Story of Hip Hop in 2001.

Tour highlights 1999–2001

In 1999, *BackStage* was launched and had a circulation of 10,000 per issue and an even larger potential readership. The magazine was not for sale in the regular pop magazine outlets, but was exclusively distributed to its subscribers. All you had to do was give your name and address during a Flashback night, and the magazine was mailed for free. It was definitely a must-read for those within the national rock scene.

International tobacco giant Philip Morris never sent direct mail brochures or advertisements for their products to the subscribers to *BackStage* or in any other way took advantage of its mailing list. Contributing artists were increasingly enthusiastic about the formula and even started to comment on the phenomenon when interviewed about their original material in the regular media. Remarkably, no references were made to Philip Morris as a cigarette brand or in any other way (presumably, none were necessary, given the distinctive red and white branding of the Marlboro product).

'Flashback to the Sound of Motown' was offered by alternative rock trio Caesar in the spring of 1999. Interviewed for *Oor* in August 1998, songwriter Roald van Oosten, then 29, surprised the journalist and readers by revealing his recent 'discovery' of Motown act the Four Tops. Van Oosten had randomly taken out a Four Tops CD from the local music library and was stunned: 'I heard it for the first time. Great music!' (Van den Berg 1998). From all the reasons to pick a particular act, there was a distinct advantage to cover songs that are far removed from any connection with the original band's history or personal favourites, even if it takes guest musicians (in this case) to recreate the Four Tops' sound. In September 1999 Trijntje Oosterhuis followed the Motown trail of Caesar with her 'Flashback to Stevie Wonder', with special guest Keith John, backing vocalist with the Stevie Wonder band. Unlike Van Oosten, she claimed a longstanding, deep knowledge of Wonder's repertoire. John's presence added a touch of 'the real thing'.

The 'Marlboro Flashback to John Hiatt' was the enterprise of Ilse De-Lange, in May 1999. Hiatt was not her true favourite (her preferred performers at the time were James Taylor, Dale Watson and Bonnie Raitt), but her band had made the choice to cover Hiatt. He is hugely popular in the Netherlands, more so than in other parts of the world, and therefore it would mean something special to do him for the tour. Immediately preceding her Flashback, *Oor* featured DeLange, who had just released her debut CD *World of Hurt*. She was the first Dutch pop/country singer to land an American record deal, and it did not seem very logical to immediately embark upon tribute work. The *Oor* interview focused on her original work, because not much could be said about John Hiatt, whom she only knew 'vaguely': 'If I like a song, then it is because it touches me directly. Because I feel the song. Not because the songwriter has witnessed a murder with an axe twenty years earlier' (Van der Horst 1999a). The interviewer for the magazine was 'totally taken by her crushing honesty'. Just like Emmylou Harris, Rosanne Cash and Kelly Willis, DeLange was musically at home covering Hiatt songs, especially the ballads. Her live reputation was thus established through her skilful covers of Hiatt's material at the time of her own CD debut.

Tribute acts had clearly gained ground and respectability thanks to the tours, and this also became evident in projects that operated parallel to Marlboro Flashbacks. In March/April 1999 'Dreams to Remember, A Tribute to Otis Redding' created a small sensation in the different format of musicians from various bands (ten in all, including a horn section), put together for the occasion:

> There is no direct reason to do this tribute ... That's no problem, the love for Redding's work is all the more real. [With] Lead singer Ross Curry ... no other white Dutch singer could have brought the sound of Otis Redding more to life; even the crack in Redding's dark brown voice is imitated without being irritating ... Soul fanatics better watch the agenda these coming weeks.
>
> (*Oor* 1999b: 21)

Another tribute event was *Cover Contests*, organized by the local branch of Columbia Records, Kink FM Rock Radio and the Paradiso venue. 'Clash of 99' had the Clash as the subject to be covered. The winner and four runners-up played live at the Paradiso; the winning cover version was released as a CD single. In the meantime the Paradiso staff member behind the Bohemians hoax in 1992 had completely altered his (public) opinion towards covers and tributes. What's more, on behalf of the Paradiso he claimed in *BackStage* that the venue had initiated the tribute scene for the Netherlands:

> We used to have session nights with local musicians covering their favorites. They dealt with icons like Chuck Berry, Gram Parsons, Ray Charles, Buddy Holly and their likes. Marlboro Flashbacks have moved tributing to more recent times, with topical artists. The Flashbacks have created an institution ... Since the 1960s it is not done for a band to play covers, but if you now see a band like Claw Boys Claw play Iggy and the Stooges with total dedication, then that's wonderful of course.
>
> (*Backstage* 2000: 30)

Just as remarkable, his rock journalist co-conspirator had joined the Marlboro Flashbacks enterprise in 1999 as MC.

Doe Maar

The nation's fevered anticipation of the millennium celebrations became more frenzied upon word that the most popular Dutch group of all time, Doe Maar (the leading band between 1980 and 1983), would regroup. On Monday afternoon, 1 November 1999, dozens of journalists flocked inside the Dutch Rock and Pop Institute in Amsterdam to witness the comeback announcement made by the four Doe Maar group members. It turned out that the Marlboro Flashback tribute to Doe Maar by Bløf had been the reason to contemplate the reunion.[6] Two Doe Maar members had been in the audience, enthusiastically singing along to their own hits. This had caused them to decide then and there that they could still do their own songs at least as well as Bløf. Doe Maar announced the release of a new CD and two gigs at a large venue, with a promise to disband again, for good, in May 2000 (Mutsaers 2001: 871–8).

After the news had sunk in, *Oor* went to the source of the story and asked Bløf how it had all come about. Early in 1999 the group was approached by Companions to join Marlboro Flashbacks, and was asked to pay tribute to their most important source of inspiration. This could be read in various ways. According to keyboard player Bas Kennis:

> We were told to play songs by a legendary band, preferably not existing any more. Usually everybody falls back on English-language music. In our case we contemplated John Hiatt and Counting Crows as options. But then you think: what was legendary in the Netherlands? A band that does not exist any more? That's Doe Maar! They sang in Dutch, just like we do. Somehow it clicked perfectly.
>
> (cited in Van den Heuvel 2000)

Lyricist and bass player of the group Peter Slager took some time to warm to the idea: 'When I was fourteen and Doe Maar peaked, I did not think it was cool to dig them. I ridiculed their songs, they sounded so simplistic. But when we started playing them, they turned out to be very sophisticated, sometimes even brilliant. I did not expect that' (cited in Van den Heuvel 2000). After the hugely successful Doe Maar Flashback performances, *Oor* called Doe Maar 'the Dutch equivalent of the Beatles' in terms of their popularity, and the sense of mania generated. They revised their initial critical bias towards Doe Maar: 'The music press – *Oor* included – was not impressed. But the fans knew better' (*Oor* 1999b: 13).

A new millennium

In the first half of 2000 the Doe Maar reunion overshadowed all other music news. The reunion grew into monstrous proportions, with the planned two concerts expanded to 16 sold-out gigs (in addition to four try-out performances and two gigs in Belgium), and huge sales figures for the new CD *Klaar* (*Finished*). Doe Maar kept its promise and disbanded, more unforgettable than ever.

The Postmen, named after 'African Postman' by Burning Spear, from Rotterdam were the first to hit the Marlboro Flashback tour in 2000. Their debut album *Documents* (Top Notch/V2 Records) had been released in October 1998. It was very well received. Critics praised its depth, originality and dance aesthetic. The Postmen's admiration for Bob Marley resounded heavily in the music and in interviews (Van der Horst 1999b). In January 2000 *Oor* produced a feature article about the legacy of Bob Marley, on the occasion of the release of the CD *Chant Down Babylon* (Island 1999) with remakes and remixes of Marley songs by various artists, which helped to prepare audiences for the Postmen's Marley tribute in the Flashbacks tour. The Postmen had also contributed to the CD *Trillend op mijn Benen: Doe Maar door Anderen* (*My Legs Are Shaking: Doe Maar by Others*), tribute performances of Doe Maar songs by Dutch artists, released in early 2000, to benefit from their reunion as 'the event' of the new millennium. The Postmen's version of 'De Bom' (The Bomb) from the CD was a hit.

The group was awarded the most prestigious annual pop prize of 1999 in January 2000, the BV Pop Prize (the Dutch equivalent of the British Mercury Awards). They had already been included in the Special Edition of Marlboro Flashbacks performance at the Paradiso Millennium Party before embarking on the tour with their tribute to Bob Marley. However successful, the Postmen were reported to have regretted the energy put into the Marlboro Flashback tour; at the height of their fame, they felt they should have toured and exclusively showcased their own compositions. The Postmen's chart success soon declined in spite of the huge expectations surrounding their debut.

End of an era

When the Marlboro Flashback tour started in 1996, it was already illegal to sell tobacco products to people under the age of 16 years. From 17 June 2002, at the start of the festival season, it was also prohibited to hand out free cigarettes to the public, ending an era of introducing young party- and festival-goers to this particular rite of passage (Horeca 2004). At this point Philip Morris shut down its Marlboro Flashback tour in anticipation of the final reinforcement of the new Tobacco Law on 2 November that year: the brand name could no longer be used as a label for the tour; and any reference to the Marlboro product in word and image would incur heavy fines. Tobacco brands until then were the most important sponsors of rock festivals, together with the big beer brands like Heineken. Many cultural events suffered from the new laws on smoking-related advertisements; some disappeared altogether – such as the Drum Rhythm Festival sponsored by another tobacco conglomerate, Drum – due to a lack of alternative big sponsors. As the promoter, Companions in this case worked for Philip Morris and was not in a legal position to continue the tour with another sponsor. It was really the end of an era in terms of audience awareness of the considerable role commercial sponsorship played in staging live popular music. The end of the Marlboro Flashback tour was deeply regretted by both audiences and critics. A unique live event with high visibility and excellent continuity over six and a half years, it was cut short well before the formula had worn thin.

Similar initiatives – multiple, relatively cheap tribute concerts on regular rock stages – soon emerged. For the local tribute musicians, it was a relief that their performances were now fully accepted and even required in the live scene. Tributes were integrated into the nation's live music scene.

The 'mega tribute' event

It did not take long before the Netherlands, with its history of global trading and profit making, and its role as a 'crossroads' for touring bands from the US, UK and continental Europe, became a site of a 'mega tribute event'. On 3 July 2004 in the Rotterdam arena Ahoy', a Tribute Band Night was held for the first time. The event lasted three hours, with tributes to the Beatles, Robbie Williams, the Police, Madness, U2, Guns 'N' Roses, Queen and Abba. The event was sold to Dutch audiences as the best lookalike tribute bands of the world with the following rhetoric:

> The Tribute Band Night is a rather new phenomenon for the Netherlands. We Dutch are proud of our originality and for having our own free spirit and independent opinions. If we can't invent the wheel ourselves, we try to make a difference by our own idiosyncratic choices. Other countries took a different stance. Outside of the Netherlands there already exists a tradition of bands who choose to pay homage to their idols. They are not 'normal' cover bands that bring together the greatest hits of a variety of big artists of the past in one show, but bands that focus on one particular artist or band and copy their songs and entire concerts in their live shows. In the same stage costumes, with the same hairdos, the same movements, vocal sound, dance steps and often also the same jokes.
>
> (Tribute Band Night 2004)

Table 8.1   Marlboro Flashback tour

Year	Act	Tribute to
1996	Ten Sharp	Woodstock Heroes
1996	Hans Vandenburg	Mothers of Invention
1996	Herman Brood	a.o. Sinatra
1996	Pilgrims	Beatles, Rolling Stones
1996	Ernst Jansz	Otis Redding
1996	Henk Westbroek	Kinks
1996	Jazzpolitie	Joe Jackson
1996	Hello Venray	Neil Young
1997	Tröckener Kecks	Dutch Nostalgia
1997	Loïs Lane	Abba
1997	Raymond van het Groenewoud	Lou Reed
1997	Ten Sharp	Crowded House/Split Enz
1997	The Scene	1978
1997	Gorefest	Deep Purple, Black Sabbath, AC/DC
1997	Treble Spankers	The Shadows
1997	Bettie Serveert	Velvet Underground
1998	Daryll-Ann	The Byrds
1998	Van Dik Hout	David Bowie
1998	Marcel de Groot Groep	The Beatles
1998	Claw Boys Claw	Iggy Pop
1998	Raggende Manne	Tommy (the Who)
1998	Supersub	The Jam, Style Council
1998	Skik	Rolling Stones
1999	Volumia!	Joe Cocker
1999	Bløf	Doe Maar
1999	Caesar	The Sound of Motown
1999	Ilse DeLange	John Hiatt
1999	Trijntje Oosterhuis	Stevie Wonder
1999	Is Ook Schitterend	Dire Straits
1999	Special Edition in Paradiso (Sylvester Party)	
	Ten Sharp	REM
	Nits	Leonard Cohen
	Bløf	Counting Crows
	Loïs Lane	Supremes
	Postmen	Bob Marley
2000	Postmen	Bob Marley
2000	Billy The Kid	Rod Stewart
2000	Nilsson	Queen (with female lead)
2000	Heideroosjes	The Ramones
2000	Kane	U2
2000	Grof Geschut	The Police (with female lead)
2000	Candy Dulfer	70s Funk
2001	E-Life	The Story of Hip Hop
2001	Dilana Smith	Skunk Anansie
2001	Handsome3Some	Björk
2001	Travoltas	The Beach Boys
2001	Green Lizard	Nirvana
2001	Birgit	Lenny Kravitz (with female lead)
2001	Ronald Molendijk	Disco & Vinyl (dance classics of the 70s & 80s)
2002	Racoon	Faith No More
2002	Rudeboy + L.O.E.G.	Public Enemy
2002	16Down	Radiohead
2002	Judith Jobse	Madonna

The Tribute Band Night's second event occurred on 18 June 2005. As in 2004, the format was 20 minutes for each act, with only greatest hits allowed in the three hours: a true singalong paradise. The Ahoy' venue in Rotterdam has a capacity of 10,000 people. Ticket prices range from 31 to 35 euros, less than the regular ticket price for just one world-class original touring band (and only five times the price of a Marlboro Flashback tour gig with just one Dutch band on stage). Fake-U2's singer Paul Collyer stated in a television interview that the real U2 had never seen or contacted them. In the meantime Collyer was happy with his female fans and the other accoutrements of fame, while complaining that he did not enjoy as big a salary as Bono (RTL Boulevard 2005). The Tribute Band Night offers special arrangements, including parking, a three-course dinner, drinks, VIP seats, hostesses and a post-concert party, for those willing to spend on upgraded tickets. The event sponsors a local Rotterdam charity project, perhaps as a means to silence critical noises about tributes, as a leftover discourse from the 'Bohemians hoax' days.

Conclusion

Imitation is increasingly evident in other forms. Radio orchestra outfits with added drums and electric (bass) guitars now offer programmes with tributes to historical heroes of popular music in symphonic big band arrangements. On the musical stage, the song repertoires of Abba (*Mamma Mia!*) and George Gershwin (*Crazy for You*) create new fans for old music. The Hollywood movies *De-Lovely* (MGM 2004) and *Ray* (Universal 2004) about Cole Porter and Ray Charles respectively, similarly introduced film audiences to older popular repertoires. Even as a reference only, the phenomenon of tributes is popular: the national 'tearjerker king' Jan Smit, for instance, performs his own repertoire live with the Tribute to the Cats Band – the Cats being a legendary, defunct, best-selling Dutch rock group of the 1960s and 70s. Smit and the Cats all come from the village of Volendam, a location steeped in national folklore regarding fishermen, sea shanties and pop successes.

Contrary to strong scepticism about the concept of cover/tribute acts, the Marlboro Flashback events successfully mobilized rock and pop artists and audiences. They transformed the musical practices of tribute performers, and how they were received. Critical audiences and the serious music press embraced something they thought they'd never even consider. By the early years of the 21st century, the dominant bias against tributes had vanished and tribute acts were booked at the *walhallas* of pop snobbery, such as the Paradiso in Amsterdam. The Marlboro Flashback tour was unique for the Netherlands. Through its formula of an original band doing a well-publicized tribute to a famous act and/or repertoire of their choice, the art of the tribute achieved musical respectability. Due in no small part to the creative mixture of local and international 'flashbacks', tributes are now everywhere within the

Netherlands' live music scene. They are the proverbial smoke of real fires. Audiences of today who did not stand by the fire when it was hot, now thankfully inhale 'the next best thing' without any health risks.

Acknowledgement

The author would like to thank Wally Cartigny for his inside information on the Marlboro Flashback tour, Companions and *BackStage*.

Notes

1 I have drawn upon the range of *BackStage* material that discusses the Flash-back tour, and tribute/cover acts more generally, between 1999 and 2001; and *Oor* coverage of the tour since its inception in 1996. Some details in regard to titles and authors are incomplete within the period of magazines canvassed.
2 First-hand witness account.
3 Dutch rock/pop duo Ten Sharp, founded in 1984, had a worldwide hit record with 'You' in 1991.
4 Dutch pop group Gruppo Sportivo was founded in 1976; it disbanded and regrouped several times. Songwriter/lead singer Hans Vandenburg is a national icon of musical idiosyncrasy and humour.
5 Herman Brood (1946–2001) made his name in the 1960s as a blues and rock piano player and later singer with his band Wild Romance (1976–2001) and made no secret of his rock and roll cliché (drugs, sex, booze) lifestyle.
6 Soundalike of the Dutch word 'bluf' which means bluff. Bløf was founded in 1992; from 1998 onwards the group is the nation's Dutch-language top rock band.

References

Adrichem, P. Van (1993) De opmars van de coverbands, *Oor* (4).

Ammerlaan, E. (1996) Herrie, *Oor* (7), 6 April.

BackStage (2000) (9): 30.

Berg, E. Van den (1998) Caesar, *Oor* (16): 22–6.

Franssen, P. (1996) Herman Brood goes reggae, *Oor* (8), 20 April.

Heuvel, H. Van den (2000) Bløf interview, *Oor* (1), 18 January: 50–5.

Horeca (2004) Horeca (Netherlands hospitality industry site), www.horeca.org (accessed 22 December).

Horst, H. Van der (1999a) Ilse DeLange interview, *Oor* (9), 1 May: 28–32.

Horst, H. Van der (1999b) Postmen, *Oor*, 17 April: 60–3.

Mutsaers, L. (1993) *25 Jaar Paradiso, geschiedenis van een podium, podium van een geschiedenis 1968–1993*. Amsterdam: SPN, Mets.

Mutsaers, L. (2001) De Nederlandse taal in de popmuziek, in L. Grijp (ed.) *Een Muziekgeschiedenis der Nederlanden*. Amsterdam: Amsterdam University Press.

Oor (1999a) 8, 17 April: 21.

Oor (1999b) 18, 4 September: 13.

RTL Boulevard (2005) Paul Collyer interview, RTL 4, broadcast 23 March.

Tribute Band Night (2004) Tribute Band Night website, www.tributebandnight.nl (accessed 6 December 2004).

9 Yearning for *eleki*: on Ventures tribute bands in Japan

Keiji Maruyama and Shuhei Hosokawa

Introduction

Musicians can express their respect for great artists in a variety of ways. Composing variations of the original, sampling a one second-long soundbite, inventing alternate chord progressions, quoting signature passages, writing lyrics about and naming song titles after the artist are some common means. The tribute band is another form of homage that is widespread in local rock scenes. This type of performance practice is hard to find outside rock culture, though learning skills through copying appears to be a fundamental proce- dure for individual musicians almost everywhere. Jazz or blues players, for example, may drill a particular solo of Sonny Rollins or Muddy Waters, but not reproduce the entire group performance. Can a classical pianist pay 'tri- bute' to Benedetti Michelangeli by 'copying' him? Who dares to replay Public Enemy's 'Fight the Power' by using the same turntables, sampled discs and microphones?

The affinity between rock and the tribute band form can be explained by several factors:

1   the relative accessibility of basic performance techniques;
2   a wide range of listening publics who can recognize tributes as such;
3   relaxed performance settings that allow laughter among the audience;
4   a visibility of bodily actions in contrast to the obscure processes of computerized sound-making;
5   the function of a 'band' as a form of group expression and collective identity;
6   the ideological authenticity of 'live' performance.

The tribute band is a special form of canonizing, as well as fetishizing of a band that is usually long defunct or who tour infrequently. The aesthetics of tribute bands depend heavily upon the artists to whom tribute is paid, rather than upon the idiosyncrasies of particular band members. In other words, who is playing is less decisive for the shape of the resultant sounds than who receives tribute. The public usually enjoys, rather than condemns, performative differences between the original and the replica. Some tribute bands exaggerate these differences for humorous effect, while others try to minimize them.

The object of our research is the Ventures tribute band community in Japan. Compared to Led Zeppelin, the Beatles, Queen and other tribute communities in Japan, Ventures tributes are distinctive in terms of their core age group, their engagement with a particular vintage guitar market, and the marginality of the Ventures in rock history textbooks. This raises a number of questions about the types of act chosen for imitation, and the imitators. After 20 or 30 years' dormancy, why do male, middle-aged non-professional musicians purchase vintage guitars to play the music of a seemingly obsolete band? How is their social space and identity as 'Sunday musicians' shaped? How does this music-making make sense at this particular point in their life cycle? We will first provide a history of the reception of the Ventures in Japan. The second section of the chapter deals with the overall organization of the tribute band community, with an emphasis on the processes of socialization and learning. The subsequent section discusses controversies concerning copying and creativity among the players. We conclude the chapter with an argument about how guitar collection is complicit with the Ventures' revival. Overall, we seek to understand more of the motivations, value systems, interaction, socialization and joys of amateur music-making. It is our intention to go against the tendency in popular music studies to prioritize *youth*, originality and professional practice.[1]

An adventurous story: how to make it big in Japan

As an instrumental group that formed in 1959, the Ventures are ranked among the most successful of the surfing genre bands. They pioneered the use of the distorted fuzz box (Hicks 1999: 18f, 67f), although standard rock and electric guitar histories have given little credit to the genre in general (see e.g. Waksman 1999). This is not the case in Japan, where the Ventures still tour nationwide every summer and over the years have played more than 2000 concerts.

Their unusual story starts in 1965 when their Japanese tours in January and July–August caused a huge sensation. In this summer tour, the group successfully performed 57 concerts. This nationwide tour firmly established the fame and annual tour practice of the band. It was considerably different from the modest media attention to their first Japanese tour in 1962. By 1965, the Ventures were able to capitalize on a surfing music boom triggered a year before by the great success of the Astronauts' instrumental number 'Movin'' and its Japanese cover version, with added arbitrary lyrics. Some local surfing bands were formed around the same time.[2]

This was the first time that the electric guitar became both an object of admiration and an abomination. When in the late 1950s Elvis-like singers brought about a moral panic, vehement criticism was directed at the odd fashions, foolish stage actions, 'untuned' vocals and noisy drumming of the performances. However, the electric guitar at that time was exempt from adults' blame. The instrument was not considered as a 'decadent' youth accessory, nor was it thought to be an influence upon the 'delinquent' behaviour and minds of teenagers.

The Ventures changed this view. Most of the criticism was not of their fashions and behaviour, but of the 'unbearable' sound of the band. This is understandable because electric guitars featured prominently, rather than the band's particular outlook and stage actions. The musicians' jargon for the instrument *eleki* (the abbreviation of 'electric') became a household word. This term denotes both the instrument itself and the surfing music genre. The Ventures craze was highly intense, yet transitory. The Beatles' June 1966 concerts steered local popular music fashions from instrumentals to vocal bands. The new bands were keenly conscious of hairstyle, stage uniform, gesture and other forms of visual appeal, so that instrumental groups were marginalized.

Many of the loyal fans were young males who played (or at least, aspired to play) with imitation bands. The Ventures became, so to speak, amateur musicians' musicians. They could have been forgotten if not for 'Futari no Ginza' ('Ginza Lights'), a Ventures piece sung by the duo of youthful film stars (Masako Izumi and Ken Yamauchi) over a pre-recorded instrumental track made in the US in 1966. Reduced to commercial and musical oblivion at home, the band reinforced their Japanese connections. From 1965 they have extensively toured the country every single summer (except in 1969), usually for five to eight weeks. They have played almost all of the country's major public halls. 'I was touched by hearing the Ventures in a public hall of my [depopulated] home town', says a town hall officer who passionately listened to the band on radio when he was 12 (in 1965), put together a tribute band in 1987, and was responsible for his home town concert (Ugaya 1995: 42). He is among many who have loyally supported the Ventures, even during their 'cold' seasons.

Throughout the 1970s and 80s, journalists systematically viewed the Ventures as an obsolete band. The band members, they asserted, did not play the music any longer at home but toured Japan only as 'seasonal workers' lured by 'easy money' who repeatedly played the old stuff (*Shûkan Shinchô* 1978; *Sandê Mainichi* 1980; Kako 1981). The articles scorned not only the obvious 'Big in Japan' phenomenon, but also the low taste of fans. The Ventures, in some journalists' views, exploited ignorant Japanese fans. For all these harsh words, the band continued to conduct annual tours, playing to their loyal public in the provinces (which remained invisible to Tokyo journalists).

This sombre key was transposed towards the end of the 1980s. The reevaluation derived not only from nostalgia, but also from a contemporary revision of the surfing sound as proto-rock, and from an overall awareness of the ageing ('maturation') of rock music. Journalists now praised their longevity, comparing them with the Rolling Stones (*Focus* 1990). What had been formerly belittled as mediocre was now applauded as showing persistent belief in the music they created. The annual summer tour was no longer considered a 'seasonal job', but a steadfast act which could not be accomplished without a deep empathy with Japanese culture and its people. Playing midsized and small towns for over 30 years – an unusual trail for a foreign band (as indeed for any Japanese artist) – was especially praised. Being 'big in Japan' turned into a positive sign of their closeness to the hearts of Japanese people, with the band embedded in national and local rock cultures. As the *Aera* report concludes: 'One can deride them as "seasonal workers" or "a past band". But they live for performing and meeting their fans, and Japanese have kept on loving them for thirty years. This mutual happy love is good and sufficient' (Ugaya 1995: 45).

Play it again, old boys

The *eleki* boom stimulated the birth of electric guitar manufacturing in Japan. The number of manufacturers skyrocketed from 6 in 1962 to 40 in 1965, and the total product multiplied over 13 times in the same three years.[3] The vast majority of buyers were schoolboys and college students inspired by the Ventures and their Japanese imitators. Some companies supplied both guitars and amplifiers. The principal manufacturers co-sponsored band contests which were broadcast on primetime television. It is no exaggeration to say that every junior and senior high school had its Ventures copy bands between 1965–8. Some cities and schools banned the electric guitar, and the label of 'rebel' or 'anti-adult' leisure item only attracted more juvenile players. Twenty years after its defeat in war, Japan's economic potential was about to explode and the *eleki* craze was indicative of the establishment of a youth music market. With the demise of instrumentals, however, a majority of amateur players gave up pursuing their initial inspiration. 'There was a period when I felt shame to say I was playing the Ventures. Then others were doing Led Zeppelin, for example', remembers Ken Otani, a professional guitarist from the 'oldies' (50s and 60s US/UK pop) band Red Zone (Otani interview 2003). Throughout the 1970s and 80s, the Ventures were totally ostracized by the popular music press and only a small number of aficionados maintained tribute bands, with no connecting organization.

In keeping with the revitalization of the Ventures in the 1990s, amateur *eleki* bands surfaced again. The weekly *Aera* (Ugaya 1995: 46), for example, highlighted three extreme cases: a 52-year-old father who trained his four sons to form a Ventures cover band that played as a support act for the

Ventures themselves; a 39-year-old man who once had 'chased' the Ventures, retires from the office to open an 'oldies' bar, where he sometimes plays Ventures tunes by himself with karaoke backing tracks; and a bar owner who invested 1 million yen ($US 80,000 at that time) in presenting a Ventures concert with lead guitarist Nokie Edwards in his city, with shows of his own solo performance (with rhythm machine and bass pedal accompaniment) to his Ventures guitarist god. The article portrayed them as eccentric yet pure enthusiasts, who realized the dream of their adolescence. Sensitive to this trend, in 1997 NHK (the Japan Broadcasting Association's Fukuoka division) launched a band contest, *Nekketsu! Oyaji Batoru* (Hot Blood! Battle of the Middle Aged Men). Its special rule was that the average age of band members should exceed 40 years. A year later, *Eleki Guitâ Bukku* (the *Electric Guitar Book*) series, the first periodical targeted at *eleki* guitarists, was launched. It almost exclusively covers national and international *eleki* artists, together with vintage instruments and Japanese amateur band circles; a guitar lesson is included in each issue.

The core age group of these new *eleki* bands is over 40 years, the generation that was in its low or middle teens between 1965–8 (the Japanese counterpart to the American baby boomer generation). Many of our interviewees state that stable life conditions have allowed them to again start playing the instrument they had left in the closet or sold so many years ago. They are often motivated both by the mediated presence of their imagined peers (on television and in magazines), immediate experiences of listening (at amateur band gigs and meetings with old band members, or a Ventures concert) and finding the guitar they had aspired to buy in their teens in an instrument shop. In addition to financial and domestic stability, the increase in hobby guitarists may have much to do with the leisure-conscious lifestyle (that critically reviews previous workaholic lives) that has prevailed since the 1990s among the Japanese middle aged. According to this new life plan, leisure activity is deemed to be as valuable as work. Having a good hobby (fishing, social dancing, sports, cooking, DIY, painting and music-making) is recommended, especially for middle-aged men (*oyaji* as they are both scornfully and affectionately called) who are starting to think seriously about their life after retirement. One of the Ventures tribute circles, accurately named the Oyaji Band Club, proclaims that playing this music prevents them from succumbing to senile dementia (*Teketeke Oyaji no Ereki Juku* 2004: 122). Since the 1990s, *yutori* (having economic and temporal 'space' in one's life) has become a national slogan and the 'worker bee' lifestyle has been gradually rejected by the middle aged (although on the flipside of affordable middle age, one sees an increase in *karôshi*, or sudden death from overwork, among male office workers since the 1990s). Playing *eleki* music is a good option because the community is in practice confined to the same age group (so it is undisturbed by younger people); training results in public concerts where the players are spotlighted; members are decisively compassionate and the music sounds joyful. The presence of supportive audiences and their fellow players boosts self-confidence. The 'harmful noise' of 1965 has been completely converted into healthy music-making.

All of our interviewees played the music in their youth, and the vast majority of them gave up band activity after several years because of disagreements among members; high-school and university entrance exams; shifting concentration to sports and other activities; and loss of interest in music. Important life course events such as moving, sickness, employment, change of business, marriage and the birth of children have tended to distance them from music playing (and listening). Only the most fortunate and obstinate could keep on playing music into their 20s and 30s.

The 'old beginners' are concerned less with how to play guitar, than with how to *recover* their skills. *Eleki* guitar books sometimes warn against the gap that lies between what readers believe they can do and what they can really play, underlining the lost dexterity that results from decades-long dormancy. Some call their guitar practice 'rehabilitation', and one band is even named *Kenshôen*, or 'Inflammation of the tendons', a painful injury the non-habitual musicians suffered from when they overplayed the instrument. Until the mid-1990s the bulletin boards of instrument shops were almost the only available space for making contact with other amateur *eleki* musicians (*Guitar Player* and other guitarist magazines usually neglect the surfing sound), but today's newcomers can find their peers through local player organizations and websites.

The Ventures Club, established in 1997 in West Tokyo, is one of the better organized tribute circles and has approximately 300 members. They arrange rehearsal meetings called 'V Sound Seminars' a few times a year at public institutions. Usually 20 to 40 players and observers gather from the Greater Tokyo area. Amplifiers are provided by those members living nearby, and some bring their private vintage equipment (such as Fender Showmanship amps, the model that the Ventures used). The participants put their personal or stage names on shirts to create a friendly atmosphere. The rehearsal and concert that follows are useful for technical improvement, musical motivation and for consolidation of networks, particularly for beginners.

The gatherings are in part aimed at 'match-making' for the 'one-man Ventures' players who practice the guitar at home (mostly with headphones or unplugged), yet hesitate to perform in front of others because of a lack of self-confidence. Being able to play loudly is one of the most important advantages of participation in the group rehearsals. By plugging in, they re-live the memory of adolescence for, as many say to us, an overwhelming loudness was the first aural shock at Ventures concerts (though it was physically moderate compared to today's earsplitting gigs). Playing an instrument requires carefully coordinated bodily actions. Long interruptions in practice make it difficult to regain a sufficiently advanced technical level. Many regret that they did not play the instrument for decades but feel positive about restarting practice at a certain stage of life, where imagination supplements the actual lack of skills. The processes of self-imagining (fantasizing), in playing the role of their generational icon, is more important than the resultant sound.

The band members are chosen on grounds of their geographical proximity, level of technical skill, availability for rehearsals, and their preference for one or other of the Ventures' two lead guitarists (Nokie Edwards, 1960–8 and 1972–85; or Gerry McGee, 1968–72 and 1985–).[4] In addition, the inexplicable factor of congeniality is without doubt the most crucial one. The recruiting of the 'hidden' Ventures shows the grass roots nature of community: *more* players are wanted, rather than *better* ones. Such a friendly stance is common to all the organizations we encountered (contrary to the competitiveness of the 'cutting contests' in the African-American tradition). Since the style and repertoire are fully fixed, switching instruments and participation by extra players are not unusual. Bands have names such as the Hiroshima Ventures, the Knock Me Out (after a Ventures hit); the Uentures; the Hentures; and the Niwaka ('instant-made' or 'folk comedy') Ventures, while members have stage names such as Nokie Suzuki and Don Tanaka (after Don Wilson, the original rhythm guitar player since 1959). Some call their act 'the Ventures *gokko*' (the Ventures make-believe, or play acting as if the Ventures). The parodic art of self-naming, often mixing respect and locality with humour, is also reflected in parodic cover designs of their private CDs circulated within the *eleki* community. Deadly serious copying and playfulness (even childishness) exist side by side in the rehearsal and concert spaces.

The homework for participant players is aimed at committing chord patterns and other basic techniques to memory. Memorization through 'purposive listening' (Green 2002: 61) is fundamental for all the practitioners we interviewed. All of them can read music (notes, chord names and tablature) but copying by ear (*mimikopi*, literally 'ear-copy') is more practical. In the 'V Sound Seminar', one often sees the participants chatting about skills, while imitating the fingerings and playing posture. One also observes older players demonstrating how to improve the techniques of the less experienced. Bodily transmission appears to be more favoured than verbal and written communication. Criticism is kept to a minimum, and every teaching act aims at encouraging further development. Both 'peer-directed learning and group learning' (Green 2002: 76ff.) are seminal in the rehearsal.

Many interviewees underline the egalitarian character of the Ventures, and say that unlike bands that feature vocals or one virtuoso performer, the Ventures (and by extension their tribute bands) have no hierarchy among members. The lead guitar certainly 'leads' the band, yet the rhythm guitarist can show off with tremolo glissando in 'Pipeline'; while the drummer has solos in 'Caravan' and 'Wipe Out', two indispensable pieces for their concerts. The bass guitarist has fewer virtuoso opportunities, yet the technical accessibility of the bass lines encourages players with moderate skill to join in the ensemble. The band members feel that they are not backing someone else, but playing their own music. Such a shared belief ('everyone is a main player') is important for them to explain their special attachment to a band that remains marginal in both rock history and the music industry.

The series of Ventures communities, despite the egalitarianism proclaimed, are not only guitar-centred, but also male-centred. Female members are only found as keyboard players who in all cases were too young to experience the peak of the Ventures' success (the keyboard was only briefly used by the Ventures in the mid-70s). Many of the young women extol the persistent passion for music-making of senior band members. In contrast to the rehearsals, wives, daughters and women friends are usually present at the public performances (concerts, Christmas parties, local festivals) as if to show that they have authorized the men's expensive hobby. Egalitarianism, then, functions as an ideological marker of Ventures tribute bands that differentiates them from the vocal-centred (mainstream) tribute bands. Vocal bands may believe that instrumentals are boring and more difficult to play, while the *eleki* enthusiasts are not moved by the simpler role of the guitar in the vocal group: 'I don't like the Beatles, because they play badly' was a decisive comment made by one Nokie Edwards imitator. The difference in aesthetics sometimes brings about the split of the amateur circle. The Yokohama Planets, a circle of amateur 'oldies' bands (including Beatles' and Carpenters' copyists among others) was closed a few years ago in part due to the dissonance between the vocal and instrumental bands. The cleavage may be related to the age and gender structure of the Ventures fans that is much more restricted than those of the 'oldies', extending to teenagers and women. In terms of fandom, the Ventures remain special in the 'oldies' world.

Competing aesthetics: the complete copy vs. creative reinterpretation

Among Ventures tribute bands, two aesthetic tendencies compete with each other. One is to closely copy a recorded performance that incorporates the original musicians' mistakes, the instruments they used, their fingering positions, gestures and costumes. The other is to allow a certain amount of room for deviation from the original. The vast majority of players adhere to the former, and most refer to three 'Live in Japan' albums recorded and/or released in 1965: *The Ventures in Japan*; *All About the Ventures*; and *The Ventures on Stage*. The aesthetic judgment of a performance is based on the degree of its closeness to the original. Their appeal depends heavily on knowledge of the original shared by the audience. What underlies the practice of serious copying is, we guess, the philosophy of pattern (*kata*) learning in Japanese traditional arts. Although pattern learning is universal, within the Japanese arts it implies an absolute obedience of disciples to their master, a self-purposefulness of the learning process, rigour, belief in the establishment of a disciplined self through repetitive learning, and the spiritual worth of patterned forms (see Hosokawa 1999: 524). It may not be uniquely and exclusively Japanese, but it is imperative in school curricula, work training and other everyday practices. Copying the master, with an accompanying eye to incorporate a high level of detail is not an intermediary step – it is the ultimate goal for the tribute players. Copying the original note by note is sublimated to a discipline similar to the hand-copying of *sutras*. The inevitable gap between the copy and original is where their respect lies. The smaller the gap, they think, the more respect is shown. In other words, the more they train to copy, the more they perceive the incomparable superiority of the Ventures. The idol is always revered from below.

By contrast, a minority group coexists that is oriented to creative reinterpretation of the Ventures, particularly their material recorded after the 1970s. This faction includes professionals and advanced amateur players who have been playing consistently since their youth. For the owner of Paparock, a Mosrite guitar shop and a hub of the Ventures circles, copying a live recording's wrong notes shows 'disrespect for the artist' (Kawabata interview 2003). His own band is one of the few who try to copy the studio recordings of the Ventures, which are musically more complicated than the live albums. In his words, his band has 'graduated' from the primary level of tribute playing. A professional guitarist told us that he produces ad-libbing techniques after the copy has been worked out. Playing in a house band, he believes that repetition of the same performance material bores regular customers. What he seeks is a cover band as imaginative as the Ventures themselves. Only amateur bands can repeat the same old copy because they play more for their own pleasure than that of their audience. Hiroyuki Tokutake, a well-known *eleki* guitarist, while reflecting on his 'return' to the Ventures after his pilgrimage to rhythm and blues, country, blues and gospel, believes that the special groove of the Ventures cannot be made without going through the whole sphere of American music that the Ventures lived with. In his view, the exclusive copying of one band is not sufficient for making good music. A younger *eleki* guitarist affirms that Tokutake's sound is much more 'American' than those of amateur copyists, who for him sound too 'Japanese', despite their best efforts to reproduce the original (Tokutake and Naka 1999: 26).

These aesthetic discrepancies, however, are not insurmountable. After all, reverence and love for the Ventures unites all the members, and they are clearly conscious of the marginality of their niche in the music world. None of the amateur musicians we interviewed intend to turn professional. They prefer socializing with players who share their tastes, to the competitive world of professionals.

Figure 9.1   Ventures tribute rehearsals, Paparock guitar shop, Machida, West Tokyo. Photograph courtesy of Keiji Maruyama

The Mosrite guitar fetishism

Pursuing your idol's guitar – the ability to play the same instruments and amplifiers – is common among amateur players of all kinds; and a longing for the Ventures' sound is understandably synonymous with a longing for the guitars they used. Most Ventures tribute players believe that Mosrite, the guitar company the Ventures contracted as exclusive artists in the mid-1960s, is the most authentic brand made even more special because of its defunct and marginal status.

Mosrite went bankrupt in 1968, and there followed litigation by the Ventures, who still have a blatant aversion to Semy Mosrey, the founder of Mosrite (*Za Benchâzu Kessei Kara Genzai Made* 1995: 70f). Around the same time, a Mosrite guitar shop in Tokyo, Fillmore, became the general agency for Mosrite and was authorized to manufacture the Japanese models. On the other hand, the Kurokumo Manufacturing Company subcontracted the original Mosrite design, and had produced imitation models since around 1967 (under the name of 'Avenger' from the First Man Manufacturing Company). The subsequent business failure of Semy Mosrey made the licensing arrangements unclear. Both the Fillmore store's 'Mosrite of Classic' and Kurokumo's 'Mosrite of California' brands used a Ventures logo. In 1998 the latter sued the former for infringement of a registered trademark and lost. These events tell us of the power of the Mosrite signature line, and the complexity of the licensing business in the electric guitar industry. To make things more complicated, the Ventures themselves licensed and started using Aria's Ventures Models guitars (produced by Arai Trade Inc.) in 1990, but many followers still prefer to buy Mosrites. This twist may be exceptional to the rule of the 'signature' model that decrees that the fans choose the guitars authorized by their idol. The inclination toward Mosrite instruments shows how most Japanese Ventures fans fetishize the early Ventures, that is, the theme sound of their adolescence. Some bluntly remark that today's Ventures are nothing but a replica (probably the most authentic version) of the 60s Ventures.

Worship of Mosrite guitars can also be observed in the Mosrite Kids Club (MKC), an owners' club founded in 2002 by Fillmore. The 'Kids' in the name reveals the marketing aspirations of Mosrite that invite middle-aged musicians to relive their youth; Fillmore's objective is to showcase expensive guitars to inspire club members to purchase them. One amateur player-collector who owns all the models the Ventures played in the 1960s, assiduously copies Ventures recordings with the same model they used. He uses, for example, the candy red Mosrite for songs from *The Ventures on Stage* album, and the pearl white guitar for those from *All About the Ventures*. He is among many enthusiasts who meticulously research which instruments (and amplifiers) the band played on each track. The knowledgeable scrutinize microscopic differences in body colour, arm angle, logo, serial number, strings and so on. We gained the impression that in the MKC rehearsals, many fix their eyes more on which guitars are used, rather than listening to what kind of music is played. Using the 'authentic' guitar model is essential for the fantasy of self-metamorphosing into the Ventures. Performing and listening serves to articulate an alternative form of the self and create an imaginary identity.

In macroscopic terms, the age, economic standing and many other characteristics of the Ventures tribute guitarists are shared with the American baby-boom guitarists interviewed by John Ryan and Richard A. Peterson (2001): the first 'electric shock' in the 60s; withdrawal for decades; a return in their 30s and 40s; and a mixture of private playing, local band activity and guitar collection. Like Ryan and Peterson's informants (2001: 100), our interviewees collect the guitar not for speculation but for playing. One of them is proud that all his instruments can be played perfectly; he identifies himself more as a player than as a collector. Both groups have sustained a keen interest in their 'own' music that they first met in their teens. As one musician within Ryan and Peterson's study stated, the music remained 'a central element in how I define myself in terms of maintaining continuity between my youth and my current state of mind' (Ryan and Peterson 2001: 112).

Such a feeling of self-realization and achievement encourages these amateur players. Their music-making can be reflective of their own life course, passions, oblivion, memories, and a reaffirmation of the past and present.

Conclusion

Upon the release of a Ventures compilation CD in 1997, the London label Ace's bulletin described the worth of the Ventures as follows: 'They had a seemingly inexhaustible supply of good tunes and a gift for clever arrangements that would act as a *do-it-yourself template* for the booming number of aspiring guitarists and drummers' (Burke 1997: 1, emphasis added). Japan must be a model case of this endorsement. The quote is in harmony with Ryan and Peterson's idea about the popularity of the guitar among baby boomers, where 'the guitar fitted well with the "do-it-yourself" ethos of the youth of the day' (2001: 107). Schoolboys who took to the guitar to replicate the Ventures sound marked an important point of beginning for Japanese rock music.

Some 30 years on, a previous after-school teen leisure activity now gives them an after-work social life. In both life stages, playing with a band and listening to peer bands constitutes an alternative subjectivity that revives a particular closeness to other musicians. Making music is thus simply more than a pastime. It is far from the pragmatic routines in school, workplace and family, as a creative process that rekindles schooldays, identifies with past idols, relives old experiences with new friends here and now, and expresses personal inclinations and special skills to the band members and public. As Tia De Nora (2000: 66–7) notes, music serves as 'a container for the temporal structure of past circumstances', where 'musical structures may provide a grid or grammar for the temporal structures of emotional and embodied patterns as they were originally experienced'. This may well explain the fundamental pleasure of playing the music of one's adolescence in a social setting of relatively homogenous members. De Nora then develops her idea of 'musically composed identities', or the locating of 'me' (2000: 68) in the ongoing act of listening (and performing, in our argument). Both physically (through performance) and socially (through same age and gender groups with shared musical values), our tribute players relive the original experience of the 1960s. The involvement of bodily action in the process of remembrance makes their stance towards collective memory different from that of vinyl and memorabilia collectors. It provides a 'real' and intensive experience for them to participate in imagined forms of egalitarianism and adolescence, imagined forms of the communal and the emotional (see Frith 1996: 272ff.).

The Ventures' influence in Japan has been both short and long-lived. Their ephemeral nature has served as a generational marker for passionate fans, while their longevity helps the band to be a role model for the actively ageing. The consistency of the Ventures, and its semi-regular band lineup of more than 40 years' standing, teaches fans the worth of family-like bonding and banding. Ventures copyists not only pay tribute to the band, but also to their own life and generation.

Notes

1   This chapter is based on Keiji Maruyama's masters thesis, *Eleki eno Dôkei* (*Yearning for eleki*), submitted to the Tokyo Institute of Technology in 2004, supervised by Shuhei Hosokawa. The authors thank Nokie Kaneko, Yoshiaki Kawabata, Ken Otani and others who generously granted interviews. All the interviews were conducted from June to December 2003. We are thankful to Hugh de Ferranti for his editorial advice.

2   Takeshi Terauchi and the Blue Jeans, and Yuzo Kayama and the Launchers are the most famous. They are still covered by today's amateur groups. But we have not seen any tribute band that dedicates itself exclusively to one of these bands.

3   The Association of the String Instrument Industry (cited in Kitanaka 2002: 178) reports the annual total of electric guitars manufactured as follows:

Year	Total	Domestic sales
1962	51,823	11,064 (the Ventures' first Japan tour)
1963	99,511	55,910
1964	448,470	113,076 ('Movin'' and the surfing sound boom)
1965	684,101	305,701 (the Ventures craze)
1966	360,643	124,257 (the Beatles' tour)
1967	471,228	142,513 (the peak of 'Group Sounds')
1968	371,532	131,057
1969	232,247	22,773

These statistics show the exceptional year of 1965 and the great percentage of exported instruments (imported guitars are not counted here). The growth of the electric guitar industry coincided with that of the acoustic guitar because of the coeval folk song boom (inspired by Peter, Paul and Mary, the Kingston Trio among others). Both types of guitar contributed to the formation of Japanese rock music in the subsequent years.

4   The guitarist Nokie Edwards separated from the Ventures twice but has more followers than Gerry McGee, who replaced him. He continues making winter tours to Japan. In January 2005, he performed at the Osaka Blue Note, a jazz

venue. This shows that his performances are considered to be different from the 'festival'-oriented performances of the Ventures.

References

Burke, D. (1997) Adventures in Sound, *Right Track*, May, (27): 1.

De Nora, T. (2000) *Music in Everyday Life*. Cambridge: Cambridge University Press.

Focus (1990) Gôkei 208 Sai no Ereki Yarô (The Eleki guys of total 208 years old), 6 July: 48–9.

Frith, S. (1996) *Performing Rites: On the Value of Popular Music*. Cambridge, MA: Harvard University Press.

Green, L. (2002) *How Popular Musicians Learn: A Way Ahead for Music Education*. Aldershot: Ashgate.

Hicks, M. (1999) *Sixties Rock: Garage, Psychedelic and Other Satisfactions*. Urbana and Chicago, IL: University of Illinois Press.

Hosokawa, S. (1999) 'Salsa no tiene frontera': Orquesta de la Luz and the globalization of popular music, *Cultural Studies*, (13)3: 509–34.

Kako, A. (1981) *Renzoku 21 Nen no Rainichi Kaikinnshô Benchâzu (The 21-years' successive Japan tour of the Ventures)*, *Sandê Mainichi*: 146–7.

Kitanaka, M. (2002) *Gitâ wa Nihon no Uta wo Dô Kaetaka (How Has the Guitar Changed Japanese Song?)*. Tokyo: Heibonsha.

Ryan, J. and R.A. Peterson (2001) The guitar as artifact and icon: identity formation in the babyboom generation, in A. Bennett and K. Dawe (eds) *Guitar Cultures*. Oxford: Berg.

Sandê Mainichi (1980) Natsuno Teikibin Benchâzu (The summer scheduled service of the Ventures), 24 August: 147.

Shûkan Shinchô (1978) Nihon de Tsukamatta Benchâzu no Uchimaku (The back story of Ventures arrested in Japan), 24 August: 13.

Teketeke Oyaji no Ereki Juku (2004) (The Eleki School for Middle-Aged Men). Tokyo: Shinko Music.

Tokutake, H. and Naka, S. (1999) Grûvu Inochi no Saikyô Gitâ Insuto Bando Sorega Ventures (The Ventures are the Strongest and the most Groovy Guitar Instrument Band), *Rekôdo Korekutâzu (Record Collectors)*, September, (18)9: 22–7.

Ugaya, H. (1995) Natsuda! Natsurida! Benchâzuda! (It's Summer! Festival! The Ventures!), *Aera*, 7 August: 42–7.

Waksman, S. (1999) *Instruments of Desire: The Electric Guitar and the Shaping of Musical Experience*. Cambridge, MA: Harvard University Press.

Za Benchâzu Kessei Kara Genzai Made (1995) (*The Ventures Book: from the Beginning to the Present*). Tokyo: Kawade Shobo Shinsha.

Discography

Japanese releases of Ventures recordings:
The Ventures on Stage (1965, Liberty Records)
The Ventures in Japan (1965, Liberty Records)
The Ventures in Japan, Vol. 2 (1966, Liberty Records)
All About the Ventures (1966, Liberty Records)

10 All the King's Elvii: identifying with Elvis through musical tribute

Jason Lee Oakes

Do Elvis impersonators – collectively known as 'Elvi' or 'Elvii' in their proper pseudo-Latin plural form – really belong in a book about tribute bands? Many members of tribute bands would answer with an emphatic *no*, given that impersonators are routinely disparaged as campy, amateur mimics – the image in the collective imagination is of a veritable army of middle-aged white men sweating and gyrating in tight-fitting polyester jumpsuits. One member of a tribute band I interviewed went so far as to call Elvis impersonators 'garbage', which could very well be a not-very-euphemistic euphemism for 'white trash'. Another questioned their musical integrity by accusing impersonators of placing 'more emphasis on the image than on the music' and of 'hallucinating' that they are in fact the impersonated subject. This working method was then contrasted against tribute artists who are 'grounded in reality' and who 'interpret' rather than copy the original music and musicians.[1] The irony here is that popular music tribute bands grew directly out of the impersonator phenomenon from which they both borrowed, and set themselves apart. Thus, any discussion of tribute performers would not be complete without a study of their Elvii *doppelgängers*. With Elvii portrayed in such striking terms as the impure Other, the attitudes expressed towards them are quite likely to provide an indicator of tribute performers' anxieties concerning their own imitative behaviour.

The tribute–impersonator dialogue can also be quite revealing when it comes to practices of popular music fandom, with 'tribute' and 'impersonation' conceived as lenses through which fans *identify* with the voices, the bodies and the subjectivities of star performers. Even if one does not go so far as to impersonate one's musical idols, such identifications lie at the heart of what it means to be a 'fan' as the term is commonly understood. For instance, one tribute artist states that 'if you're a true fan … you identify with that artist so much that they actually feel like a part of you' (artist interview 2001). While this statement may seem a bit extreme, who can say they have never sung along with their favourite records and mimicked the singer's voice, or perhaps played air guitar in the mirror, or tried to copy the fashion sense of a popular musician? Just as singers commonly find their own voice by first imitating other singers, the fan also uses identification as a means for reaching self-actualization.

There are two schools of thought that differ radically on the significance of this identification. In one view – largely descended from the mid-century Marxist critics collectively known as the Frankfurt School – such identifications play a pivotal role in instilling the 'false consciousness' of capitalist ideology, and in reinforcing the hegemony of the culture industry. Lured in by the 'pseudo-individualization' of popular music stars, their individual 'trademarks of identification' (Adorno 1941: 24–8) are supposed to hide the fact that they make only slight and meaningless variations to a standardized formula. In the more positive reading – a reading that in academic circles has its roots in the Birmingham School and subcultural theory, and later in the discipline of cultural studies – identification is the very means by which consumers are able to transcend the commodity status of commercially recorded music. By identifying with and making the music 'their own', the fan is able to assert their own agency in a mass-mediated form, and to create bonds of sociability in the context of fan-driven music subcultures.[2]

Thus, identification is alternatively positioned as a form of mass exploitation or of individual empowerment, or quite often as both at the same time. This is probably why both the pleasures *and* the perils of fandom are so closely linked to identification: that is, being a fan is rewarding because of the close relationships that are formed with the music, with the star's image and with other fans; but there is also a pervasive fear that the fan–star identification can become pathological if taken too far (e.g. the cautionary tales of John Hinckley, Mark Chapman, Charles Manson and so on).[3] This schizoid discourse around fandom is further intensified in the realm of impersonators and tribute artists, given that they are even more explicitly concerned with identification and as such are positioned as 'uber-fans'. Finally, the pleasure/pathology dialectic scales even greatest heights when it comes to Elvis impersonators – perhaps because the phenomenon of Elvis fandom has been so routinely and thoroughly examined over the past 50 years, or perhaps because there are just so many Elvii out there. Either way, there are few recording artists, even today, who are so closely identified with their fans and their fans' behaviour.

So Elvii are both 'fun' and a little bit 'dangerous'. On the one hand, Elvii provide an easy means for injecting pleasure and enthusiasm into a given setting; they are near-guaranteed crowd-pleasers and almost always seem to bring a smile to the face of their spectators, even the non-Elvis fans. As one fan puts it, 'Elvis impersonators are great because when they're good, they're good, but when they're bad, they're still good' (interview 2004). Despite their lightheartedness, however, critics have made a habit of questioning the motives, the methods, and even the mental health of Elvii. In fact their image has been turned into a sort of cultural shorthand in much of the mass media –

portrayals of Elvii are often intended as symbols of kitsch, consumerism and/ or regressive nostalgia (perhaps this is somehow related to the 'Vegas Elvis' being a more common subject for tribute than the Memphis-era Elvis). To give one example, both sides of this coin are seen in the movie *Honeymoon in Vegas* (MGM, 1992) – the Elvii in the film are played both for comic relief and as a symbol of the superficiality from which the protagonist's girlfriend is rescued.

Since it is not only tribute performers but also much of the larger populace that emphatically place Elvii in the box marked 'Other' – that is, portrayed in distancing, exoticizing terms – we may find that these portrayals mask widespread anxieties related to the integrity of the self, projected onto the easy target of the impersonator. For in their world as well as in our world, the 'anxiety of influence' runs headlong into the 'culture of the copy' (Bloom 1973; Schwartz 1996). Judging by the amount of distress this collision causes, it must be recognized as a key contradiction of our times – at least for those living in heavily mediated cultures that provide more and more representations (sounds/images/personas) with which to identify and greater means for doing so, but which at the same time place an ever-growing premium upon autonomous subjectivity and unique 'authenticity'. Likewise, while the rise of identity politics and marketing demographics has driven individuals into ever more narrow and inflexible identity categories, these same marketers move additional products by promoting the belief that 'you can be whatever you want to be', or at least that you are infinitely transformable through the market.

Knowingly or not, Elvii and other tribute artists hold up a funhouse mirror both to the new freedoms and to the fraught issues faced by individuals in highly-commodified, media-saturated, 'postmodern' societies. For instance, the freedom of self-invention in modern societies is counterbalanced by a fear that such limitless freedom in constructing our 'selves' leads to a 'new kind of superficiality' or 'depthlessness' (Jameson 1991). Likewise, the increased ease with which we can copy and clone images, sounds and information has served to foster creative exploration, but some would say that copies have become *too* easy to make and that the sheer volume and flexibility of representation has subverted the very nature of representation itself. For instance, widely-read postmodernist theorist Jean Baudrillard (1981) argues that whereas representations once referred to some external referent out in the real world, now there is nothing but a plethora of signs and symbols referencing nothing but other signs and symbols. If he is correct that simulations have overtaken and replaced representations, then it could legitimately be argued that impersonators are far more 'real' than anything they could deign to impersonate.

Elvis and the birth of tribute culture

Presley is commonly known as the 'king of rock 'n' roll', a credit that has caused no end of controversy, but I would submit that an equally good case can be made for Presley as the 'king of musical tribute'. While this title is less likely to capture the public imagination, it is perhaps just as meaningful if not more so. The rise of musical tributes, as a mode of performance that works through a critical (although usually positive) *commentary* on previous music-making, is in keeping with other trends that have worked their way across the musical landscape. In more recent years popular music has become, in the words of Andrew Goodwin, 'more and more a producer's and programmer's medium' where 'music practice comes to resemble criticism' (1998: 130, 129). One finds this to be the case not only for music that utilizes sampling and remixing (e.g. hip-hop, electronica, mash-ups), but also in genres that still cling tenuously to an auteurist-Romantic aesthetic. As rock critic Simon Reynolds has observed:

> The curator-turned-creator is not an especially new phenomenon ... At some point in the mid-eighties, though, a shift began that led to the phenomenon I call 'record-collection rock', where a band's total sonic identity is reducible to its members' listening habits ... As the CD reissue and box-set boom escalated, and retro culture made the past available like never before, this mode of creativity became more common ... The aesthete weaving through this overcrowded bazaar of cultural jetsam becomes a figure for navigating through the chaos of urban postmodernity itself.
>
> (2004: 299)

Long before rock bands were routinely described through a Rolodex of influences (for example, Interpol = Joy Division + the Psychedelic Furs), and long before DJs trawled used-record stores looking for just the right oldies and obscurities to play back or sample, Presley turned his record collection into a career (and unlike someone like Pat Boone at the time, he did make a point of acknowledging and honouring his sources). Perhaps more than any previous recording artist of his stature, Presley approached his career as a *fan* of other artists with whom he identified, and he was said to be an omnivorous collector of everything from records to other memorabilia.

Besides the strong element of tribute in Elvis Presley's own music, Elvis fan cultures have played a major role in developing and popularizing the notion of 'tribute' well before it permeated the popular music mainstream. In fact, the parameters for the tribute versus impersonator differentiation were actually established within Elvii culture before it later became a means for other tribute bands to distinguish themselves from Elvis impersonators. One central pillar of Elvis fan culture is the annual Elvis International Tribute Week marking the anniversary of Presley's death. Since 1977, thousands of fans have converged on Memphis each year in the sweltering heat of late summer for a week-long series of commemorative events. From the sacramental overtones of the fans' pilgrimage to the culminating candlelight vigil at Graceland, Elvis Week is structured around the organizing trope of tribute, and one primary means of paying tribute at Elvis Week has been through impersonation. Beginning in the early 1980s, a marathon tribute was held over the course of Elvis Week at Bad Bob's Vapors, a bar and supper club in a rundown section of Memphis. The idea for the event came from Elvis' former veterinarian, Dr E.O. Franklin, popularly known as Doc, who was the proprietor of the club. Elvis tribute artist Robert Lopez describes his memory of these early shows:

> You could go from three in the afternoon to three at night and see impersonator after impersonator ... it was like psychotherapy on stage. It was people who had never been on stage before, who had this homemade belt made of paper clips, and these outfits – they've stuck little pieces of glitter and glue to make do what they could and don't have any sense of rhythm, can't sing but they were singing their hearts out just because it was a tribute to Elvis. And you'd see all these people really showing their hearts on stage, and it was great, because it was a really human drama of people paying tribute.
>
> (Fan interview 1995)

In 1987 the tribute was moved from the now-shuttered Bad Bob's Vapors to a ritzy hotel ballroom and re-christened the annual 'Images of Elvis' International Elvis Impersonator Contest. The change in venue coincided also with a shift in approach, with each Elvis now scored by a panel of judges. Performances have become increasingly ritualized with most of the competing Elvii relying on a central core of songs, gestures and costumes. Although witnessing the contest can still be an entrancing experience – one Elvis after another tinkers with the basic formula with the application of someone composing a fugue – it is a far cry from the freewheeling vibe described by Lopez (also see Rubinkowski 1997 for more on the Images of Elvis contest).

The particular inflection of 'tribute' employed by tribute bands took early shape among these performers, so that today most professional or semi-professional Elvii bill themselves not as impersonators but rather as 'a tribute to Elvis'. The emergence of the 'tribute' tag was no doubt in part a defensive move, an effort to break free of the freakshow depictions of impersonators common in the mass media. Also, if Elvii don't want to be sued by the Presley estate they make sure not to include 'Elvis' or any variation thereof in their stage name, settling instead for the 'tribute *to* Elvis' tag following their actual name. By implication, Elvii make a case for their own agency through their use of the word *tribute*, which implies a critical selectivity and commentary on their subject. Directly related to this, 'tribute' is a word that has high-culture associations. Tributes have long been held at Carnegie Hall and Lincoln Center, and classically trained musicians do not play 'cover versions' of Bach or Beethoven but rather they pay 'tribute' to the great composers.

Interestingly, it is the unabashedly amateur, anything-goes imitators of Elvis that have embraced the 'impersonator' tag. The populism and do-it-yourself approach of the impersonator is contrasted against the exclusivity and professionalism of the tribute artist, and thus many impersonators see themselves as having greater personal *agency* when it comes to their own interpretations. Also, their frequent campness and humour are contrasted against the musical tribute's occasional self-seriousness. This humour, often crossing over to self-parody, provides an alternative strategy for Elvii to defend against slander and ridicule, and it is also in keeping with the humour and occasional self-parody reportedly treasured by Presley himself and by early impersonators such as comedian Andy Kaufman. Finally, as opposed to Elvis tribute artists who have largely reconciled themselves to a singular standard of what constitutes a good Elvii performance – that is, to the point where they can be formally *judged* – impersonators tend to place a greater emphasis, whether by choice or by necessity, on variation and heterogeneity. So if the tribute artists at the Images of Elvis contest enact something akin to a fugue, then there are some impersonators at the other end of the Elvii spectrum that are more like free jazz improvisers on Presley's music and image.

Why Elvis?

Whether weighted more towards the former or the latter, Elvii culture is firmly rooted in a theme-and-variation structure. Throughout his career, both living and posthumous, Presley has been re-enacted in every conceivable form – from carbon copies to photo negatives to funhouse-mirror distortions – and his cultural impact seems to thrive on this sheer fecundity and overabundance. While one person dressed as Elvis and jumping out of a plane may not garner much attention, the Flying Elvii have achieved notoriety for staging events with dozens of skydiving Elvises. While impersonators often perform solo, the most prestigious and anticipated shows are those where scores of Elvii perform one after another. Fans who set up 'Elvis rooms' in their homes do not simply frame a tasteful picture or two of Presley on the wall; instead, the prevailing aesthetic is to fill a room with as many knick-knacks bearing the singer's image as it will hold – from Elvis stamps to Elvis lamps, from Elvis toenail clippers to Elvis bedroom slippers. Of course, such overabundance is not in keeping with arbiters of 'good taste' or 'refined' culture. As performance studies scholar Barbara Kirshenblatt-Gimblett notes, it is no coincidence that 'to refine' literally means to remove impurities from something through a process of pruning and polishing; on the other hand, 'bad' taste, and its association with 'low' culture, is unrefined in that it overspills boundaries and exhibits 'a tendency toward excess, amplitude, and abundance' that does not shun 'paradox, ambivalence, [and] mixture' (1998: 265). All of these qualities were noted from the very beginnings of Presley's career, and perhaps further underlined since he himself came from a lower-class background. When it comes to impersonation specifically, it is an activity that is often associated with mixtures and ambivalences related to race, gender, class and so on – think for instance of familiar modes of impersonation such as blackface and female impersonation (Lott 1993; Garber 1997), or how musicians (through accent, dress etc.) will often align themselves with a lower social class to appear more 'authentic' or a higher social class to appear more 'legitimate'.

Thus, in the world of Elvis fans just as in the world of Elvii, a theme-and-variation aesthetic holds sway, assembling collections of mass-produced Elvis ephemera that at the same time can be endlessly rearranged and customized. This formula holds true also for Presley's own music, for while he was an expert mimic he always introduced significant variations into the songs that he covered, and his stylistic eclecticism was unknown among any of his contemporaries. While it is typically assumed that Presley's mimicry is what made him a controversial figure early in his career – particularly his mimicry of rhythm and blues artists – it was just as much the variations that caused a stir in terms of Presley's re-framing of sounds and images. For instance, the first single released on Sun Records in 1954 included a version of blues-singer Big Boy Crudup's 'That's All Right, Mama' that transformed the swinging jump-blues original into a strummed, strutting 'hillbilly' tune. On the flip side was a version of bluegrass legend Bill Monroe's 'Blue Moon of Kentucky' that was even more radically reworked – its waltz-time bluegrass shuffle transformed into a sped-up 'rhythm' number in duple time with blues-style vocal glissandos. Considered by some to be a desecration, it was much more controversial at the time than the Crudup cover.

Even posthumously, Presley's musical career has continued to be grounded in repetition and variation. Up to the present day, RCA has maintained a regular release schedule of 'new' material that repeats, re-arranges and acts as a variation on previous releases (often including recorded out-takes and slight variations on familiar songs). In fact it could convincingly be argued that Presley is probably the most *compiled* artist in the history of recorded popular music. According to *All Music Guide* online, 395 LP or CD compilations of Elvis' music have been released officially (compare this with a relatively paltry 78 compilations for the Beatles), often according to some particular theme, genre or association. While other artists usually have greatest hits packages or a series of albums that are considered the core of their recorded repertoire, producers and listeners have shown an abiding interest in continuously rearranging the bits and pieces of Presley's recording legacy, not to mention actually remixing his songs, such as the 2002 JXL breakbeat-enhanced remix of Presley's 'A Little Less Conversation' that topped charts all over the world.

Given the constant *versioning* enacted by Elvis and among his fans, it is not surprising that the most contentious issues surrounding Presley tend to revolve around repetition and variation. In interpreting and re-inflecting black gospel, and rhythm and blues musical forms, was Presley ripping off the original music cultures, or did he help to break down racial barriers by providing wider exposure to other performers and genres? In re-enacting an Elvis Presley performance, do impersonators and tribute performers pay him tribute or exploit his memory? What rights do individuals and businesses have to profit from mass-produced reproductions of Elvis' name and image, and can a single trademark holder control these reproductions? While it is tempting to view this constant versioning of Presley's image and music as a cynical ploy (though undeniably true in some cases), I suggest that the process of repetition and revision points to something beyond mere marketing savvy or cheap manipulation, for the entire Presley persona has been built upon a series of comparisons, contrasts and even outright contradictions.

Again and again, fat Elvis is pitted against thin Elvis, Memphis Elvis v. Vegas Elvis, ladies' man v. mama's boy, racial integrator v. racist exploiter, working-class hero v. decadent superstar, musical iconoclast v. sentimental hack, and so on. Elvis stands as a prototypical instance of the American rags-to-riches mythos, yet he also helped establish the rise-and-decline narrative of rock stardom. He has been discussed alternately as a symbol of globalization (Jørgensen 1997; Kanchanawan 1997), American nationalism (Marcus 1975), Southern regionalism (Campbell 1997; Doll 1998) and youth culture individualism (Bertrand 1995). With his rural, working-class roots, Presley is for some a powerful icon of authenticity – he was at first marketed by RCA as a folk singer – but then again he's probably the most popular camp icon on the planet. Presley is often lauded by his fans for his modesty and generosity – from giving to charity to giving away Cadillacs – but with his famously voracious appetites for food, girls, guns and pills, he also acts as a potent worldwide symbol of American privilege and consumerist excess. Mojo Nixon half-jokingly and wholly insightfully observes that 'Elvis seemed to be able to do the coolest thing and the schlockiest thing in the same five minutes and not know the difference. That's what makes him great; that's what makes him the Great American Zen Riddle' (1992: xiv).

While one might think that the constant reiteration and versioning of Presley's image and music would eventually deaden their impact, the reverse appears to be true. Commentators from Greil Marcus (1991) to Gilbert Rodman (1996) have argued that the more Presley permeates popular culture, the more he seems to resonate as an iconic and impenetrable presence. According to one estimate there has been more written on Elvis Presley than on any other popular musician in history (Hinds 2001); by the turn of the millennium there were over a thousand published books and innumerable articles and editorials dealing with the man, his reception and his cultural impact. This has led to what Barbara Kirshenblatt-Gimblett calls 'semiotic saturation', where the wealth of meanings established around a particular cultural entity produces a saturation effect 'so overdetermined [that it] becomes underdetermined' (1998: 274). Like an image that's been Xeroxed too many times and starts to lose its clarity, the constant readings and re-enactments of Presley has caused some of his contours to *fade*, and thus they must be drawn back in by hand. In other words, the more that's known about Presley the less anyone seems to be sure of, and the more necessarily it becomes to construct *one's own meaning* out of the unbelievable overabundance of musical and discursive relics. Returning to my opening discussion, this is a task that may not be wholly unfamiliar to the modern subject who is at all times surrounded by a plethora of representations and identity-affiliations from which to choose. Impersonators and tribute artists may attempt to reconstruct the fractured whole, but even if all the King's Elvii can not put him together again, they do seem to have a lot of fun rearranging the pieces.

Alternative Elvii

Just as Elvis Presley cross-pollinated multiple musical influences, some of his impersonators also combine Presley's music with other outside influences. This is made literal when some Elvis tribute artists add a qualifier to set themselves apart from the other Elvii: such as the *lesbian*-Elvis (Elvis Herselvis), the *Yiddish*-Elvis (Elvis Schmelvis), the *environmental*-Elvis (Green E) and so on. Notably, a hyphen serves both to connect and to separate, and likewise these Elvii take on a unique challenge in navigating the tensions and continuities between multiple subject positions. These 'alternative Elvii' are defined through comparison and in counterpoint to what they perceive as the mainstream of Elvis culture. Alternative Elvii attempt to set themselves apart from the 'mass culture' of Elvis impersonators by expressing their own unique agency in the act of impersonation, and their own unique 'identity' in the act of identification. They take the established grammar of Elvis impersonation and play games with its syntax; they are fluent in the Elvis discourse but consciously re-inflect it and combine it with other discourses.

While many of the alternative Elvii have played in Memphis during Tribute Week and at other locales around the country, they have never been accepted in the official Images of Elvis contest held in the hotel ballroom near Graceland. Instead, they are kept somewhat in the margins, performing in clubs in downtown Memphis on Beale Street, and also in Carter-Young, a self-consciously bohemian neighbourhood in Memphis. In this betwixt-and-between state, the schisms and contradictions of the Elvis discourse are made more explicit, whereas in the mainstream these processes are more effectively obscured or taken for granted. The clashes and overlaps that alternative Elvii produce open up a highly productive space not only for the negotiation of the star-fan relationship, but also for articulating the complex relations between various cultural groups and social formations, relations that would otherwise remain largely concealed.

Probably the best known of the alternative Elvii is the 'Mexican Elvis', El Vez. El Vez is the creation of Robert Lopez (quoted above), a second-generation Mexican-American from Chula Vista, California. He began as a teen playing in seminal California punk bands such as the Zeros and Catholic Discipline, and later worked as an art curator travelling through Mexico to collect Day of the Dead iconography and other folk art. His involvement in curating a show of Elvis-themed art works led to submergence into Elvis culture which before long inspired the creation of El Vez, and which obviously inspired his curator-turned-creator approach to El Vez. At first, Lopez performed a straightforward impersonation of Presley with his songs translated into Spanish, such as 'That's All Right, Mama' transformed into 'Esta Bien, Mamacita' and accompanied by a ranchera-style accordion. Before long, though, Lopez utilized Elvis as a vehicle for what he labels a tribute in the truest sense – not only to Elvis but also to his other musical influences, and most of all to Chicano culture. While these might be seen as conflicted subjects for tribute, this was not true based on Lopez's own experience. He explains that, when growing up: 'I thought Elvis looked like my uncles [who] wore continental slacks and slight pompadours in that Elvis style. He looked Latin. The first movie I ever saw him in was *Fun in Acapulco*' (Lopez interview 1995). Also, just as Elvis Presley himself identified with voices that were racially diverse and diverse in other respects, Lopez likewise believes that 'Elvis is not just a job for a white man in his 40s any more; to be King is an equal opportunity kind of thing', and he also draws a parallel between the rise to fame of a poor, working-class Southerner in the 1950s – Presley was 'a poor man coming from nothing [who] became the richest entertainer' – and the plight of Mexican immigrants who come to the United States to pursue the American dream.

Not completely unlike Elvis Presley himself, Lopez interprets multiple musical genres and creates musical collages whose elements will at one moment flow seamlessly together and at the next moment create surprising juxtapositions. His songs act as musical palimpsests, like a malfunctioning mix tape preserving audible traces of everything ever recorded on it, its former contents bleeding into the newly-recorded songs. Elvis Presley is only one element in the mix, although he does serve as the connective tissue that holds the mess of other disparate influences and allusions together – with unexpected links and dissonances between Presley's songs and Glam rock, Mexican corridos, James Brown and so on. This musical layer cake is reflected also in a more literal sartorial layering. In his flamboyant and highly choreographed shows, El Vez mixes and matches iconography from Mexican,

Mexican-American and Elvis cultures. During 'Si, I am a Lowrider', a take-off on Elvis' concert version of 'C.C. Rider' (RCA, 1970), El Vez wears a white fringed Elvis jumpsuit complete with oversized 'phoenix' belt buckle, on top of which he wears a stereotypically working-class Chicano, or 'pachuco', headband and sunglasses. At the climactic point of different songs, he often strips off one layer of clothing to reveal another completely different outfit underneath, ranging from a Zapatista uniform to a gospel robe to Elvis' '68 Comeback Special black leather. In this way, El Vez performs a quite loyal tribute to Elvis Presley. Even if he takes far more liberties than more straightforward Elvii, on the conceptual level El Vez continues Presley's own practice of multiple identifications, stylistic hybridity, and theme-and-variation.

In another multi-layered musical interpretation, Lopez reworks Paul Simon's 'Graceland', taken from the 1986 album of the same name. The narrative of the original 'Graceland' describes the narrator's journey to Presley's famous Memphis home as a Mecca-like pilgrimage towards acceptance and reconciliation in the wake of heartbreak and a broken family. In place of Graceland, Lopez substitutes Aztlán, the mythical homeland of the Aztecs. In Chicano discourse, Aztlán is defined as the portion of Mexico that was annexed by the United States after the Mexican-American War of 1846, based upon the belief that the region was a point of departure for Aztec migrations to the south:

> And I say who has ever
> Ever seen this place, I am looking
> For a land that belonged to Mexico
> But now holds no time or space . . .
>
> For reasons I have explained
> I'm not a part of Spain
> I'm part Aztlán
> And I'm trying to get back
> To a place I've never been
> I'm trying to cross over
> Well I've reason to believe
> We all have been deceived
> There is an Aztlán.

Musically, Lopez certainly does 'cross over' – skilfully and seamlessly fusing the chord progression and melody of Simon's 'Graceland' to the chugging rhythm section from Elvis' version of Junior Parker's 'Mystery Train', another song that deals with a journey and with longing. Then, beginning about halfway through the song, additional quotations from 'Mystery Train' are included in parts of the guitar solo, and at the song's conclusion the entire instrumental groove and the final, jubilant shout are borrowed as the song fully morphs into its Elvis incarnation. Another layer of significance arises from the criticism that both Presley and Simon have received for musical appropriations. While today Presley is sometimes dismissed as a 'rip-off' artist who stole from rhythm and blues performers, Simon has more legitimately been accused of sometimes inadequately acknowledging or even taking credit for songs on 'Graceland' that were actually composed by South Africa's Ladysmith Black Mambazo and by the Los Angeles Latino band, Los Lobos (Meinjes 1990). Further building on the appropriations of Simon and Presley, El Vez transforms previously borrowed musical materials by adding new layers of musical influence and personal significance to the not-always-original originals. El Vez reappropriates music that was originally taken from others, and likewise the text of 'Aztlán' advocates Chicanos' reappropriation of land that was taken from Mexico. Thus, on numerous levels, this song is heavily infused with an 'anxiety of influence' both musically and culturally – in terms of musical borrowings that have been portrayed as exploitation, and in terms of an ancient place of origin whose culture has been wiped out and replaced by another.

In the song's text, El Vez struggles visibly with his own identity, 'trying to get back to a place [he's] never been'. This phrase could refer to something beyond his desire to reinvent the mythical homeland of Aztlán, for elsewhere El Vez contends that even though he was not born in Mexico and doesn't speak fluent Spanish, he can learn to be Chicano, much as Elvis impersonators, coming from many different backgrounds and with different histories, can learn to be Elvis. And finally, moving one additional layer out, we have the plight of the music fan/modern subject looking for their own mythical homeland, using identification with an absent Other as a pathway to self-fulfilment and actualization. This is not to suggest, however, that El Vez comes off as a depressive or as someone going through a desperate identity shift; most of his songs are very funny and his shows are absurdly fun. Furthermore, the identifications that make up the basis of his shows and his songs – identifying with Elvis, with Chicano culture, and with a plethora of other recording artists, pop cultural artefacts and political movements – do not seem merely compensatory, but instead are presented as revelatory.

This pastiche of multiple identifications is not employed to deconstruct stable identity as a postmodern commentator might assume, but for Lopez they serve to rebuild and stabilize identity. The excess, abundance and mixture of Lopez's cultural and social backgrounds are celebrated in his music. Take for instance the song 'Soy Un Pocho',[4] where El Vez reappropriates a pejorative term used by Mexicans to describe Latinos who don't speak Spanish and have, by implication, lost their roots. 'Pocho' literally means 'faded', referring to the feared cultural grey-out that could result from being overexposed to outside influences. El Vez instead uses 'pocho' as a positive identity marker, singing that 'to be a Chicano is more than a language/I'm not white bread but I am a sandwich'. Made up of multiple layers, El Vez is himself certainly not white bread, but he uses the 'white bread' of Elvis Presley to hold the rest of the sandwich together. Whereas the under-determined nature of Presley's posthumous 'identity' may lend itself to these multiple and flexible engagements – and the same may be said for many other musical styles and pop cultural references whose representational power is diminished through rampant overuse – once all of these influences and allusions are layered one on top of another, they have a tendency to become interwoven and to then provide a more stable basis for identity construction. Thus, the music fan and cultural consumer busy themselves with form identifications, to recognize relationships, and to put the pieces of the puzzle together in their own unique way – for the more connections that are made, the better they will be able to hold the whole mess together.

Elvis: dead alive

In his obituary for Elvis published in *Rolling Stone*, Greil Marcus persuasively argues for Presley as a key symbol of American mythology, a 'perfect all-inclusive metaphor' for the 'contradictions and paradoxes' that define the national character (1977). Here I would go further and suggest that Presley's impersonators also serve as a 'perfect, all-inclusive metaphor', but in this case a metaphor for the paradoxes and contradictions of fandom and, by extension, of global modernity. It may seem far-fetched, but consider how the pleasures and paradoxes of global capitalism are mirrored by Elvii in a number of interesting respects – the flamboyant society of the spectacle, the endless parade of signs and symbols it throws up, and the endless capacity for self-reinvention offered through these representations. In the 'Elvii economy', there is a shift away from the production of goods and towards the production of events (see Harvey 1989), with the job of being 'Elvis' outsourced and subcontracted to an army of temp workers. In the semantic debate between 'tribute' versus 'impersonation', one senses the nervousness with which many modern subjects approach their interactions with mediated representations that are viewed as 'unreal', and the anxious sense that they may be manipulated without their knowledge and lose control over their own thoughts and actions.

One can see then how Elvii and other tributes – as fun and silly as they are – enter headlong into these key debates in our time over identity, representation and simulation. The successful touring show simply called *'Elvis: The Concert'* can be considered as a final example. The show is a multimedia tribute that features a 'virtual' Presley backed by surviving members of his 1970s touring band. It's like karaoke in reverse, with live music accompanying Presley's vocal track which has been pieced together from various recorded live performances, and visuals projected onto a large video screen with footage taken from the same old concerts. Meanwhile, the band members also appear on the triptych of monitors – both as their younger 1970s selves and in their current manifestations as shot by roving cameramen on stage – so that they effectively play alongside themselves from 30 years previous. Meanwhile, behind the scenes a video editor and a sound engineer combine the pre-recorded and live audio-visuals into a seamlessly mesmerizing experience that looks and sounds better than most other large-scale concerts. So what is 'real' and what is a 'representation' in such a setting – what is 'live' and what is 'mediated' – or is it even possible to separate one out from the other?

At '*Elvis: The Concert*', 'impersonations' are performed by nearly everyone – the musicians who mimic a concert they performed decades ago, the audience who impersonate the behaviour of an 'Elvis Presley audience' (as seen on TV, most likely), and finally by 'Dead Elvis' himself who perhaps is the best Elvis impersonator in the world because *he is not even there.* Having witnessed '*Elvis: The Concert*' at Madison Square Garden in 2003, I can say that I have seldom felt so much energy and electricity at a 'real' live show, that is one featuring a living lead singer. The room was positively electric and it was impossible not to get swept up in the audience excitement – the frenzy of ovations and constant flash of camera bulbs – or the overwhelming aura projected by a singer who had been dead for over 25 years. None of this 'trickery' seemed to faze the crowd, however, and perhaps it is exactly this trickery that audiences identify with. '*Elvis: The Concert*' is not unlike the representational hall-of-mirrors that many of them may experience in day-to-day life, albeit distilled and intensified to even more spectacular effect. Thus, I would argue that it is not entirely productive to think of events such as '*Elvis: The Concert*' and live impersonator (tribute) shows as postmodern 'simulacrums'; rather, these events function as microcosms of everyday lived realities in a globalizing world, realities that modern subjects must learn to navigate and struggle to understand.

Notes

1   Quotes are taken from interviews of tribute band members conducted in 1994 in New York City.
2   Keith Negus gives a useful overview of this debate framed in terms of 'passive consumers' versus 'active consumers' (1996: 7–35).
3   See Joli Jensen's 'Fandom as pathology: the consequences of characterization' (1992) for an insightful reading of this anxiety and its larger cultural implications.
4   'Soy Un Pocho' is included on El Vez's 1996 album *G.I. Ay, Ay! Blues* (Big Pop).

References

Adorno, T. (1941) On popular music, *Studies in Philosophy and Social Sciences*, 9: 17–48.

Baudrillard, J. (1981) *Simulcres et Simulation*. Paris: Galilée.

Bertrand, M.T. (1995) Southern youth in dissent: rock 'n' roll, race, and Elvis Presley, 1945–60. Unpublished Ph.D. thesis, University of Memphis.

Bloom, H. (1973) *The Anxiety of Influence: A Theory of Poetry*. New York: Oxford University Press.

Campbell, W. (1997) Elvis Presley as redneck, in V. Chadwick (ed.) *Search of Elvis: Music, Race, Art, Religion*. Boulder, Co: Westview Press.

Doll, S. (1998) *Understanding Elvis: Southern Roots vs. Star Image*. New York: Garland.

Garber, M. (1997) *Vested Interests: Cross-Dressing and Cultural Anxiety*. New York: Routledge.

Goodwin, A. (1998) Drumming and memory: scholarship, technology, and music-making, in T. Swiss, J. Sloop and A. Herman (eds) *Mapping the Beat: Popular Music and Contemporary Theory*. Malden: Blackwell.

Harvey, D. (1989) *The Condition of Postmodernity: An Enquiry into the Origins of Cultural Change*. Cambridge, MA: Basil Blackwell.

Hinds, M.H. (2001) *Infinite Elvis: An Annotated Bibliography*. Chicago: A Cappella.

Jameson, F. (1991) *Postmodernism, or, The Cultural Logic of Late Capitalism*. Durham: Duke University Press.

Jensen, J. (1992) Fandom as pathology: the consequences of characterization, in L. Lewis (ed.) *The Adoring Audience: Fan Culture and Popular Media*. London: Routledge.

Jørgensen, E. (1997) From Denmark to RCA: on the road with Elvis, Scotty, and Bill, in V. Chadwick (ed.) *Search of Elvis: Music, Race, Art, Religion*. Boulder, Co: Westview Press.

Kanchanawan, N. (1997) Elvis, Thailand, and I, in J.L. Tharpe (ed.) *Elvis: Images and Fancies*. Jackson, MS: University Press of Mississippi.

Kirshenblatt-Gimblett, B. (1998) *Destination Culture: Tourism, Museums, and Heritage*. Berkeley, CA: University of California Press.

Lott, E. (1993) *Love and Theft: Blackface Minstrelsy and the American Working Class*. New York: Oxford University Press.

Marcus, G. (1975) *Mystery Train: Images of America in Rock 'n' Roll Music*. New York: E.P. Dutton.

Marcus, G. (1977) Elvis Presley (1935–1977): Blue Hawaii – tragic news from the mainland, *Rolling Stone*, 248 (22 September), www.rollingstone.com/news/story/_/id/5934883?rnd=1135132983223&has-player=true&version=6.0.8.1024 (accessed 14 June 2003).

Marcus, G. (1991) *Dead Elvis: A Chronicle of a Cultural Obsession*. New York: Doubleday.

Meinjes, L. (1990) Paul Simon's *Graceland*, South Africa, and the mediation of musical meaning, *Ethnomusicology*, 34(winter): 37–73.

Negus, K. (1996) *Popular Music in Theory: An Introduction*. Cambridge: Polity Press.

Nixon, M. (1992) Preface, in K. Quain (ed.) *The Elvis Reader: Texts and Sources on the King of Rock and Roll*. New York: St Martin's Press.

Reynolds, S. (2004) Lost in music: obsessive record collecting, in E. Weisbard (ed.) *This is Pop: In Search of the Elusive at Experience Music Project*. Cambridge, MA: Harvard University Press.

Rodman, G. (1996) *Elvis after Elvis: The Posthumous Career of a Living Legend*. London: Routledge.

Rubinkowski, L. (1997) *Impersonating Elvis*. Boston, MA: Faber & Faber.

Schwartz, H. (1996) *The Culture of the Copy: Striking Likenesses, Unreasonable Facsimiles*. New York: Zone Books.

11 Selling out or buying in? The dual career of the original and cover band musician

Guy Morrow

In the competitive live music circuit of New South Wales and in particular Sydney, musicians increasingly are creating cover/tribute bands to make a living as musicians and especially, and ironically, to fund original music projects. This strategy is common because the tribute/cover band circuit in Sydney is larger[1] and more lucrative[2] than the local originals circuit. Many within the industry believe that this practice is beneficial for the financial growth of bands as business entities, and for the development of performance technique, stage presence and musicianship, and ultimately for the production of original music. It is through this process that musicians can afford to pay for recording time and marketing campaigns. At the same time, however, artists are accused of 'selling out', with the view that they may never be able to cross over to have a successful career as an original recording artist (that will enable them to become a 'star'). Through this process their image and brand name will have been tainted by their start in tribute bands and, because the tribute/cover band circuit is the easier career option, the argument that these musicians are destined to remain on that circuit is fairly widespread. In order to avoid such a perception of 'contamination', musicians who employ this strategy are encouraged to keep their two operations entirely separate and to proceed with caution through this minefield of signification.[3]

This chapter concerns the operation of Sydney tribute band the Longboards, a band that primarily covers material by the Beach Boys. The commercial viability of this act, particularly within the New South Wales club circuit, will be compared with Sydney's original music circuit. Linking semiotics to branding theory, the rise of the tribute band phenomenon within the local live music scene in Sydney, and its interaction with other scenes, will be explored. Particular attention will be paid to self-managed musicians who work simultaneously in both tribute/cover[4] bands and original music acts, musicians who are caught within complex patterns of the signification of meaning. This chapter draws on my own experience working as a former drummer for the Longboards, and as a current drummer in other cover bands that subsidize an original band, Dion Jones and the Filth. I will compare the operation of the recycled brand image of the Longboards with that of the original band, addressing the common managerial strategy of using income derived from the lucrative tribute band circuit in order to fund original music projects.

Chris Harper is a pianist, vocalist, lead guitarist and founding member of Sydney Beach Boys tribute band the Longboards. He holds the view that local performance opportunities have evaporated[5] – 'In the early 80s I was working in a band that got work six nights a week and that's almost unheard of now'. Although many young rock musicians today are interested in performing their own original compositions and in using live performance as a marketing tool for self-financed CDs, the decline in original music venues is making it harder for the managers of these musicians and the musicians themselves (if they are self-managed) to make their small businesses financially viable.

The decline in local performance opportunities, particularly those involving original music, has reflected the concurrent growth in performance opportunities for tribute bands. Harper stated that:

> I was playing the live scene back in the 1980s and it was towards the late 80s and early 90s that tribute bands really seemed to come to the fore. There was a 'Fat Out of Hell' [Meatloaf] show, there was a Madonna show, the Doors show and a Blues Brothers show. These bands started to do really well and then other people started to get the idea.
>
> (Harper interview 2004)

For young talented Australian rock musicians, the local live circuit in Sydney operates in a way that almost forces them to work in tribute bands if they wish to make a living, or to earn something that resembles a wage, in the early stages of their career. The local original music circuit in Sydney currently operates in a way that makes it difficult for the musicians to make money. For example, relatively low-profile local bands are usually not paid by the actual original music venues they play. Usually these venues will be booked independently or by an agency that will negotiate a standard deal that will involve the musicians taking the door sales revenue (with production costs debited), while the venue keeps the revenue from beverage sales. Moreover, these bands can usually only charge between $5 and $8, and the venues that host shows at this micro-level of the music industry are by nature relatively small and can usually only fit between 100 and 120 people in them for a 'sell-out' show.[6] Therefore, if three bands on a bill charge the maximum entry fee that the market will bear for this type of show, and the event sells out, then the show will gross $960 ($8 × 120 payers) – if all of the audience members pay to enter.[7] As a maximum amount, this figure is above average for this type of show, and has to be split between the musicians in the three different bands. In contrast to this, if the original band learns enough material to be able to play a three- to four-hour tribute/cover show, compared to the 45-

minute to one-hour show they would normally play as an original band, and if the band owns their own PA system and thus can cover their own production costs, they can make anywhere between $450 and $2,000 a night with payment guaranteed.[8]

Although the originals circuit is financially weighted strongly in favour of the original music venues because they have not had to pay for the evening's entertainment and they have received income from bar sales and gambling revenue, live performance at these venues remains an essential marketing device for artists seeking recording opportunities. For artists in the initial stages of career development, these venues provide an opportunity for them to market their self-financed CDs directly to audiences. However, the cost of producing CDs that are of a competitive quality by far exceeds the income the musicians can expect to receive through touring their self-financed CDs around this circuit.

The following budget outline was formulated for an artist I co-manage, Dion Jones, a local Sydney musician who is the lead singer for tribute band the Longboards, the cover band Coverdrive, and an original band entitled Dion Jones and the Filth. This budget is an example of the costs local bands face if they wish to independently produce an EP or mini-album that is of a sufficient quality to gain the band a distribution deal and possibly airplay on national radio station Triple J.[9] In order to produce a nine-track mini-album, the band spent $8,286 on recording and mixing; $935 on mastering; $1,142 on manufacture; $1,500 on marketing and publicity and $1,500 on the design for the album's packaging. These expenses totalled $13,363 and were balanced against the income the band received from playing the tribute and cover band circuit.[10] Without the income from the tribute/cover circuit this small business entity would be financially unsustainable.

The Longboards

The tribute band the Longboards operates within this lucrative club, pub and function circuit in Sydney. When asked why he decided to form a Beach Boys tribute band in order to try and infiltrate this market, Chris Harper claimed that:

> I wanted to be in a viable working band so I needed to have some kind of product that was easy to get work with. I mean, it is never easy, though it helps if you have an angle. So I looked for features such as which concept was going to be saleable and beach music is pretty popular, as Sydney has a vibrant beach culture; it's good danceable material and it is quite fun to play. That's why I put it together.

(Harper interview 2004)

Harper stated that in the early stages of the band's existence it helped to have a specific angle to market the band. The concept of branding is fundamental to the role of music managers because, as the Sydney-based manager of Savage Garden, John Woodruff (2002: 1) has stated, 'a manager's job is to create the perception that the band is successful'. Indeed, with regard to musical consumption, the familiarity of the piece of music and the brand image it signifies is a surrogate for the quality ascribed to it – to like it is almost the same thing as to recognize it, and if the brand image has a point of difference then this aids the process of recognition. Harper believed therefore that there was a need to carve out a particular aesthetic position within the live market.

Through the process of branding, the unique quality of a musical act becomes instantly recognizable and condensed into a specific image that then becomes a trademark or brand name. This brand name then becomes ubiquitous across a variety of different forms of media, where it in turn connotes particular attitudes, values and beliefs. Although, for example, the circulation of the Coca-Cola brand is to a certain extent different from how music is identified, packaged and consumed, there are still similarities. While bands/genres come to be 'known for' particular aspects/attitudes/feelings, the music extends beyond its use/exchange value[11] (to be Marxist for a moment); it's more than a commodity.

However, Naomi Klein (2000: 4) has argued that branding has become the key to corporate success because the processes of production, that is, 'running one's own factories, being responsible for tens of thousands of full-time employees', have begun 'to look less like a route to success and more like a clunky liability'. Successful corporations are increasingly producing images of their brands (rather than products or 'things') and this has therefore shifted the emphasis from manufacturing to marketing. Klein claimed that the formula of *buying* products and 'branding' them, rather than *producing* products and 'advertising' them, has proved to be so profitable that companies are competing in a race towards weightlessness: whoever owns the least (through having their products made for them by contractors), has the fewest employees on the payroll and produces the most powerful images, as opposed to products, wins the race. This paradigm shift that she envisaged has started a trend that is leading to a new breed of marketers/business people proudly informing their consumers that Brand X is not a product but a way of life, an attitude, a set of values, a look, an idea (Klein 2000). Therefore non-music/culture-related organizations are also considering their products more broadly as being a means through which people create meaningful worlds in which to live.

As the manager of the Longboards, Harper did not have to generate a brand image from scratch because he effectively tapped into the vast resources that have been spent since the 1960s by the Beach Boys' management and label in order to enable their music and image to signify a certain lifestyle, concept and perceptions of success. Surf music articulates a series of

Figure 11.1 Promotional photograph of the Longboards, Sydney 2004

concepts, lifestyles and other qualitative phenomena that have in turn been used to sell associated surf products. Through engaging with semiotics, it may be stated that a brand name is a 'sign' that represents the metaphorical link between the material aspect of the sign and the sign's abstract potential. In this case, the Beach Boys' music is the signifier that provides the meaning surrounding the re-contextualization of the Beach Boys' music and image into the sign's abstract potential. The canonical status of the Beach Boys' music has been effectively used by Harper in order to find a niche for the Longboards within the local live music circuit in Sydney.

The surf music genre has traded on key lyrical signifiers about the 'good times' of summer that recalls beach parties and long days riding waves. For the Longboards, this is augmented by specific Beach Boys aesthetics: flower pattern shirts in the Hawaiian style and promotional shots of the band driving 1960s automobiles (such as the Deuce Coup of 'Little Deuce Coup' fame) and on the beach. On stage, the band employs an extensive range of harmonies in keeping with the Brian Wilson arrangements, with additional female vocalists and dancers.

Harper utilizes these signifiers in order to link the Longboards' performances to the Beach Boys' global brand image and also to translate and 'glocalize' (Robertson 1995: 28) this brand image within the specific surf/beach culture of Sydney. However, when interviewed, lead vocalist for the band, Dion Jones, noted that the Longboards' brand image was not just created in order to attain market differentiation. Rather, he stated that he has a genuine love for the surf music period; he is interested in experimenting with four-part vocal harmonies; and the vocal style of the band suits him, as he has a high vocal range.

In the case of the live music circuit in Sydney, the familiarity of an artistic brand image is a surrogate for the quality ascribed to it and therefore Harper is not alone in his attempt to use his band to signify the canonical work of another. When asked whether he believed that there had been an increase in the demand for tribute bands, Harper noted: 'Definitely in the last ten years or so – well – I don't know if there's been an increase in demand but there has definitely been an increase in supply which suggests that maybe there has always been a demand' (Harper interview 2004).

The rise of tribute bands in Sydney is partly due to the success of this business model and the way in which it enables audiences to readily identify with the core images and band narratives of canonical artists such as the Beach Boys. Original music also involves music managers coordinating the construction of the link between a musical act's signifier and its sign. Indeed, band managers are therefore also 'brokers of meaning' (Klein 2000: 25). However, in the case of tribute bands such as the Longboards, the musicians can use their band as a vehicle to generate revenue from live performance without having to spend the resources needed in order to generate an original brand image that will appeal to consumers.

The connection between musical signifiers and what is signified is discursively constructed and marketing simply sets up a point at which this identification or connection can be made in the first place. This process is becoming harder and harder to initiate because the amount of capital needed for an artist's marketing efforts to break through our increasingly saturated media landscape is perpetually rising. Klein (2000: 9) argued that the marketing world is always reaching a new zenith by 'breaking through last year's world record and planning to do it again next year with aggressive new formulae for reaching consumers'. She claimed that the advertising industry's rate of growth was so steady that by the year 1998 the total expenditure in the US was set to reach $196.5 billion (up from $50 billion in 1979), and that global advertisement spending was estimated to be $435 billion; according to the United Nations *Human Development Report*, the growth in global advertisement spending 'now outpaces the growth of the world economy by one-third' (Klein 2000). The most efficient way for local musicians to get consumers to create excitement and long-term interest in music lies in their ability to tap into and recycle such a longstanding and global brand name as the Beach Boys. Increasing competition between rival tribute bands on the Sydney circuit seems set to fuel the rise of this phenomenon into the future.

When asked whether he thought that the Longboards risked being overexposed within the surf music tribute market, Harper replied that:

I can't really see a time when it would be overexposed by the Longboards. I guess there's the potential for it to be overexposed by 'beach party bands' but I think that the market is big enough for more than one band. Endless Summer are probably the most well known beach party band. But there's enough work for them around and I think that there is still an untapped market for the Longboards because I don't think that we've achieved our potential yet.

(Harper interview 2004)

Rather than being built through the circulation of various discourses of authenticity, as with most tributes, the Longboards' brand name was built through the circulation of discourse that concerned how well they could re-create the identity of the Beach Boys. Rather than emphasizing a sense of originality or authenticity, or commercial success within the realm of mass culture, the band signified high-calibre musicianship and professionalism. This is exemplified in the Longboards' biography (see also Table 11.1).

The Longboards specialise in the Surf/Beach sound of the sixties. A beach party atmosphere comes alive with those familiar harmonies and well-loved guitar sounds. With the band churning out hit after hit, mainly from the Beach Boys, but also the Surfaris, Sunrays, The Ventures, Jan & Dean, and others, the audience will be partying on till closing time. To complement the focus on the Surf Sound era, the Longboards also provide an 8 song visit to the early Beatles rock'n'roll period with classics like Twist and Shout, I Saw Her Standing There, and Can't Buy Me Love. In tying off the night into a complete package, The Longboards include a selection of regularly requested party songs (old, retro & new) that never fail to keep the crowd on the dance floor. Examples are She's So Fine, Eagle Rock, What I Like About You, an Elvis Medley, Satisfaction, Born to Be Wild, Start Me Up, Echo Beach, Hot Stuff, Skater Boy, etc. The Longboards have a great track record of gigs – at pubs, clubs, corporate functions and outdoor festivals. Some venues & events include: Sweeneys, The Crest Hotel, Parramatta RSL, Club Merrylands, St Johns Park Bowling Club, Collaroy Services Beach Club, Pittwater RSL, Easts Leagues Club, Coogee Beach & Dee Why Beach (outdoor concerts), South Curl Curl Beach Sound Waves festival, corporate functions for Sunglasses Hut, AMP, Warringah Council, etc.

The way in which a music manager builds and then guides a musical brand name is best understood through the employment of the concepts of semiology advanced by Nattiez (1990). The different levels of Nattiez's framework, the 'immanent' (infra-textual), the 'poietic' (what the producers of the text understand it to mean) and the 'esthesic' (the set of meanings and

Table 11.1   Longboards' song lists, 2003

Beach songs	Beatles	Other party songs
1 Surfin' USA	1 Twist & Shout	*50s*
2 Surfin' Safari	2 I Saw Her Standing There	1 Johnny B Goode
3 I Can Hear Music	3 I Feel Fine	2 Elvis Medley
4 I Get Around	4 Day Tripper	
5 Surfer Girl	5 Eight Days a Week	*60s*
6 Do It Again	6 Can't Buy Me Love	3 I Only Wanna Be With You
7 Fun Fun Fun	7 I Wanna Hold Your Hand	4 Fortunate Son
8 I Live For the Sun	8 I Should Have Known Better	5 Higher & Higher
9 Little Deuce Coup	9 All My Loving	6 You Can't Hurry Love
10 Don't Worry Baby	10 A Hard Day's Night	7 She's So Fine
11 Dance Dance Dance		8 Rock Medley
12 Surf City	*Other ballads*	9 Bad Moon Rising
13 California Girls		10 All Along the Watchtower
14 In My Room	1 Have I Told You Lately	11 Brown Eyed Girl
15 Echo Beach	2 Love is All Around	12 River Deep, Mountain High
16 April Sun in Cuba	3 Unchained Melody	
17 Help Me Rhonda	4 Four Walls	*70s*
18 Darlin'	5 When the War is Over	13 What I Like About You
19 Surf's Up Tonight	6 Alison	14 Limbo Dance
20 Under the Boardwalk	7 (To Be A) Better Man	15 Proud Mary
21 Capricorn Dancer	8 Throw Your Arms Around Me	16 Eagle Rock
22 Hawaii		17 Rock 'n' Roll
23 Barbara Ann		18 Tush
24 You're an Ocean		19 Waterloo
25 Island in the Sun		20 Hotel California
26 Tide is High		21 Honky Tonk Woman
27 Walking on Sunshine		22 Old Time Rock 'n' Roll
		23 Bad Case Of Loving You
Beach instrumentals		
		80s
1 Pipeline		24 Start Me Up
2 Sleepwalk		25 All Fired Up
3 Wipeout		26 Candy
4 Wonderful Land		27 When Tomorrow Comes
5 Tequila		28 Alone With You
6 Hawaii 5–0		29 Papa Don't Preach
7 Apache		30 Hurt So Good
8 Walk Don't Run		31 Heart Of Glass
9 Shake 'n' Stomp		32 Beast of Burden
10 Bombora		33 Boys are Back in Town
		34 Mustang Sally
		35 What's My Scene
		90s
		36 (I've Got to) Fly Away
		37 The Way
		38 Sweet Child O' Mine
		39 The One I Love
		40 Mr Jones (and me)
		41 Wicked Game
		42 Better Man
		43 Torn
		44 Can't Get You Out Of My Head
		44 Murder on the Dance floor
		45 You Get What You Give
		46 My Happiness
		47 Complicated
		48 By The Way
		49 Drops of Jupiter
		50 I'm a Believer
		51 Beautiful Day
		52 Out of My Head
		53 Scar Tissue
		54 Skater Boy
		55 All Torn Down

perceptions of those who subsequently consume and/or criticize the text) are useful for an understanding of how music managers coordinate the 'departure point' for the constant construction and reconstruction of the metaphorical link between a musical act's sound structure and the identity, social structure or ideal that an act's brand name symbolically represents.

The poietic (production) discourse of professionalism evident in the Longboards' biography effectively formed the departure point for the construction of the band's brand essence, and had an impact on the way in which audience members at the esthesic level of musical reception interpreted the Longboards' music and identity. At an esthesic level, the Longboards are competent 'musical tradesmen' who are respected by other professional musicians who work the circuit. When considering the evolution of their brand name, it is clear that poietic discourses of professionalism and the band's tight performances have played a crucial role in the generation of such a response at the esthesic level. Rather than signifying an original and 'authentic' vision, the Longboards' brand image is attached to their reputation as musicians and entertainers.

The generation of a work of art is subject to a reliance upon a network of workers/players and 'art worlds' (Becker 1982). In a similar way, the generation of an artist's brand identity is dependent upon the interplay of music industry networks. While the discourses of professionalism concerning the Longboards' operation form a major facet of their brand identity, different perceptions remain about the 'original' and 'cover' musician. Although it is potentially advantageous for a musician to have a 'reputation' that is not solely attached to their 'original' product or to their 'cover' product, because this can enable them to add a seemingly infinite number of venues to their gigging circuit, at a time when many musicians are struggling for work, original musicians can provide some stability of employment through participation in the tribute/covers circuits. However, they run the risk of contaminating the original brand image they are trying to construct because the discourses of the inauthentic that surround their tribute/cover operation can undermine attempts to strike out on their own.

McIntyre (2001) has argued that the people who are involved in producing, engineering, promoting, marketing and selling cultural products become constituent components of the art world or field of contemporary western popular music, and as such can be seen to contribute to and affect the work. As such, the concept of the 'artist' is problematic, because an artwork or 'record' is the product of a community of practitioners. Musicians engaged in tribute and covers work need to be careful not to turn this broader community of original music practitioners away, because the discourses of in-authenticity that surround their work in tribute bands can generate the perception that these musicians have 'sold out' and that they are therefore failures.

A question of perspective

Hebdige (1979: 97) defines 'selling out' as being 'a process of incorporation into the hegemony ... [where] previously subversive sub-cultural signs (such as music or clothing) are "converted" or "translated" into mass produced commodities'. Tribute musicians employ the signifiers of previously 'successful' mass-produced commodities in order to generate their own potentially successful signs and therefore the process of forming a tribute band does not fit this strict definition of selling out. However, some practitioners within the originals scene have a problem with this process.

From his perspective as a musician who straddles both the originals circuit and the tribute/covers circuit in order to survive, Dion Jones, a musical collaborator of mine for the last nine years, believes that the strategy of working both circuits is beneficial for the financial growth of his original band, and for the development of his performance technique, stage presence and musicianship, and also for the production of his original music. The small amount of money and prestige involved often means that musicians like Jones are self-managed or they are managed by fellow musicians like myself. Jones and I have come to the understanding that this strategy is less risky and that it is beneficial because it generates 'organic'[12] growth and longevity. Rather than taking a large risk by investing the money required to 'inorganically' fertilize their careers in the hope that the gamble will pay off and they will eventually receive a financial return from their investment, myself, Dion Jones and the Filth use the tribute/cover circuit in order to organically develop our careers. Instead of taking the risk and going into debt through attempting to grow our business inorganically, we realize that if we do not 'make it' (which is highly likely) we will not be at a financial loss because our band will have been generating revenue the whole time. The idea of keeping our operation small and manageable is appealing to us because signed Australian bands rarely recoup recording costs (Johnson and Homan 2003); the larger a band becomes, the more expensive it is for it to tour, and thus larger entities can appear to be financially irrational.[13]

However, while the strategy of straddling both the original and tribute circuits is a way to 'buy in' to both the creative and commercial sides of the Australian music industry, many musicians see the strategy as blatantly 'selling out'. As a member of the Longboards, a cover band Coverdrive *and* an original band, Jones is a Sydney musician who has employed this strategy for a number of years. Rather than 'selling out', Jones and I employed this strategy as a way to 'extract revenge':

> Our plan at first was relatively simple. We wanted to extract our revenge on the music industry in Sydney, through infiltrating the lucrative covers circuit, through getting onto the books of various

> cover agencies that would book us shows at which we would play
> original music and a minimal number of covers. Therefore we'd be
> getting paid good money to play our own music.
>
> (Jones interview 2004)

For artists like Jones and me, the tribute/cover circuit presents one of the
few opportunities to 'buy in' to the music industry, given the decline in the
number of original music venues in Sydney. Like many artists who work the
originals circuit, Jones feels disdain toward the tribute/cover band circuit;
however, in line with the old saying, he believes that 'if you want to defeat
your enemy, sing his song' (Goodman 1998: 352). When asked whether he
has found gigs harder to come by in recent years, Jones replied:

> No. Once you've cracked the covers circuit and you start working this
> circuit as well as the originals circuit, the gig offers come flowing in.
> Keep in mind that if you're working a band around the covers circuit
> twice a week, and the same band is playing the originals circuit once
> every fortnight or so, the standard of your playing or your 'musi-
> cianship' steadily increases.
>
> (Jones interview 2004)

For Jones, the strategy of working both circuits simultaneously is a means to a
particular end: a sustainable career that provides the funding to attempt to
infiltrate the star system. At the same time, his career as a live performer
remains independent from the high-risk recording industry.

Dancing with the devil

A manager's role is to create a perception of success. While working both the
original and cover circuits is necessary, perceptions of commercial motivation
can lead to career death for rock artists who are interested in being known for
producing original music. This is why artists who employ this strategy are
encouraged to use a different name for their cover band. Chris Harper stated
that such bands need to keep their cover band operation 'a secret' so as not to
confuse their audience(s), and to ensure their original music is not tainted by
a discourse of 'selling out'. From his perspective as a working musician, Jones
stated that:

> Some people have a real aversion to cover bands. But the fact of the
> matter is that since the dawn of time musicians have gone from
> venue to venue or – if they were troubadours – they went from town
> to town, and they have played what people want to hear. They have
> been paid money for this service and then they have gone home. The

covers scene is the same. Sometimes you feel like a musical trades-man. I don't think that cover bands have led to the demise of ori-ginal music in Sydney, I think the fact that the general public in Sydney don't give a shit about original music has more to do with it.

(Jones interview 2004)

There are obvious commercial and creative dangers in playing across the covers, tribute and original circuits. On the one hand this strategy enables these artists and their managers to 'over-sell' their bands to the covers circuit because overexposure is not as much of an issue and their aim is simply to milk every last dollar out of these markets. Alternatively, they can 'under-sell' the originals market to make sure that their original shows have full capacity audiences, build excitement and generate a positive perception of their band. The idea is to attempt to make sure that demand for their original music remains unsatisfied, thus making it appear greater than it might be. While the idea is that this strategy can enhance and preserve their 'credible' careers on the original music scene through under-exposure, this can be problematic. Bands may generate the perception that they are more of a cover band than an original band, a perception that is reasonable because they do actually play more tribute/cover shows than original shows.[14]

John Brewster was a rhythm guitarist in the successful Australian original band the Angels (1976 – present) and he argued that the rise of the tribute band phenomenon has led to a problematic change in the Australian music industry's structure: '[Young bands] start off with all the right ideas about playing original music but then they leave school and realize that they need to earn a bit of money and they think "here's this cover band thing that we can do", and so they start to fall into this middle ground of mediocrity' (Brewster interview 2004).

Andrew Kelly is a Sydney musician who only plays his own music and therefore refuses to fall into the trap Brewster believes is present. Kelly is a multi-instrumentalist and performs under the stage name Andy Clockwise.[15] Through making an analogy between perceptions of cover bands and per-ceptions of sexual promiscuity, Kelly's attitude typifies that of many Sydney musicians who play only original music:

It's like being a slut, you know what I mean? Covers bands are like sluts. If somebody knows they're always able to have sex with you it's not very dignified is it? ... It's ridiculous to see that there's more money in covers than there is in original music. I mean what kind of backward country are we living in? It's a country in which people don't want to hear anything new and if they hear something new then it really annoys them. What is with that?

(Kelly interview 2004)

Kelly recalls that he 'went into a lot of debt promoting my record because I took out ads in the street press and paid for a designer and then I tried to just cut even on the door so I could pay back the debt ... once people have seen you a few times, you've got to stop doing gigs because you start to kill it through over-exposing yourself'.

Like Kelly, Brewster has concerns about the managerial strategy of using income derived from the comparatively lucrative tribute and cover band circuit in order to fund original music projects. He believes that original artists at a local level are better off going into debt:

> I know a girl who has a fantastic voice and she's writing great songs and then you find out that she's playing in restaurants doing covers. She has her MIDI tracks programmed and she's basically doing that glorified fucking karaoke thing – which I just can't stand because the backing tracks are always shit. [The problem is that] she loses the drive or the determination to get that original thing she's doing through somehow because this is such an easy way out.
>
> (Brewster interview 2004)

It is therefore risky for original artists to employ this strategy because if they want to succeed in the 'original' music industry they may struggle due to the prevalence of such attitudes.

Conclusion

The artists analysed in this chapter are located within an 'art world', though this art world has conflicting brand images within it. Artists such as Jones necessarily have to be located within this context/art world, although the 'art world' itself has the potential to kill their career because of the clashing process of signification that it generates. Johnson and Homan (2003) have argued that the local live scene in Sydney is widely regarded as an 'incubator' for artists seeking international success and that since the 1980s the local music industry has contributed significantly to the wider economy through the export of the live and recorded product that is produced by this industry. In 1991–2, the local music exports trade was estimated at $120.5 million (Price Waterhouse, cited in Johnson and Homan 2003: 2). The argument has been made that if musicians, managers and recording companies share a belief in the value of the New South Wales live circuit in preparing artists for regional/global success, and if there is a continuing decline in the number of original music venues and environments, then the crucial 'local music apprenticeships' will become more dependent on the local cover and tribute band circuits.

Economically viable music management practices at the local level of the music industry are crucial because it is here that recording and live performance careers begin, and where the overwhelming majority of working musicians operate. Within the star system, less than 10 per cent of musicians receive a return from income streams other than live performance. Rather than simply reacting to this change in industry conditions within the originals and tribute/cover circuits, the musicians who employ the managerial strategy outlined in this chapter are leading, rather than just managing.

It has been made evident throughout this chapter that an artistic identity or brand image is dependent upon its location within an 'art world'. Music management involves artist managers coordinating the development of, and then nurturing, a context or 'art world' in which an artist can thrive. However, the point has been made that in order for an original artist operating at the micro/local level of the music industry in Sydney to 'thrive', their management has to develop and nurture two separate and conflicting 'art worlds'. This means that the overarching context for such an artist's career becomes a minefield of signification, in that success remains a subjective concept. To progress within their art world, they have to rely upon music industry practitioners who have both positive and negative perceptions of their operation. Greater recognition is needed of the role that the tribute and covers sector plays in equipping musicians for the global stage, and of the pressures musicians are placed under through necessarily being located in an ambivalent position that involves them being bombarded by the discourse of 'selling out' and by the discourse of 'buying in'.

Notes

1   Of the hotels in New South Wales that host live popular music, 64 per cent employ cover and tribute bands as compared to 34 per cent that employ bands that play original music, while 57 per cent of clubs in the state that host live popular music employ cover and tribute bands while 43 per cent of such clubs employ bands that play original music (Johnson and Homan 2003).

2   It is my own experience as a working musician that (albeit with a few exceptions) cover and tribute bands play for a set fee that is guaranteed while local original bands play for the money they can make through a door charge in relatively small venues. Bookers of key originals venues in Sydney verified this claim. As the booker of the Hopetoun Hotel, with a capacity of 200 people, Loren McHenry noted that it is 'always a door deal at the Hoey'. The booker of the Annandale Hotel (450 capacity), Brent Lean, stated that 'it's a combination at the Annandale, though we try to avoid guarantees though it does depend on the calibre of the act', while Gaelic Club (900 capacity) booker Scott Leighton stated that 'the Gaelic club always runs with a door deal'.

3   All comments attributed to Dion Jones, John Brewster, Chris Harper, Andrew Kelly and Stephen White in this chapter are taken from personal correspondence with the author conducted in January, February and December 2004.

4   For the purpose of this study, the term 'tribute band' refers to a group of artists who attempt to replicate one original band's music and image, while the term 'cover band' refers to artists who replicate the original music created by an array of different original bands (but not necessarily their image).

5   Johnson and Homan (2003) reported that although within the last decade aspiring musicians have witnessed a dramatic growth in the variety and number of technical and further education, tertiary and private institution courses providing education and training, since the mid-1980s Australian musicians and audiences have experienced a decline in the number of music venues. Although popular discourse cites the liberalization of gaming legislation in New South Wales as the cause of this reduction, it is claimed that the causes also include changes in leisure culture, in popular music styles and formats, in financial and legislative frameworks, in the composition of audiences and in community demographics (Johnson and Homan 2003).

6   For example, the Sandringham Hotel in Newtown is a 100-person capacity venue and the Cat and Fiddle Hotel in Balmain is a 120-person capacity venue.

7   A significant number do not pay the door charge, including guests of the bands, media and music industry personnel.

8   Chris Harper stated that the Longboards average $1,200 a night while Dion Jones and my cover act Coverdrive average approximately $850 a night.

9   Triple J is the Australian national youth radio station that is operated by the Australian Broadcasting Corporation.

10   Some tribute bands also face these costs as some are producing CDs for sale at shows; however, these bands have bigger 'war chests'.

11   Use-value is the value that an object has for satisfying a want or need. For example, the value of a car is that it can transport people from place to place. Exchange-value is the value that a commodity has in a market. This is a socially created value. Exchange-value is the value that commodities are judged to have in relation to other commodities.

12   Within the vernacular of the Australian music industry the two terms 'organic' and 'inorganic' are often used. In the context of this chapter, the term 'organic' is being used to differentiate one particular strategy – which involves the musician's business investing in itself over time – from an 'inorganic' approach which would involve musicians investing their own savings or an outside entity (record company or otherwise) investing a large amount of capital up front in order to build the business.

13   Influential Australian music manager Stephen White (who currently manages the country artists Lee Kernaghan and Catherine Britt) believed that the cost of touring is relative to the status of the artist (in that there is a positive correlation between the two) (interview 2004).

14 For example, Dion Jones and I played about 12 originals shows in 2004, while I played 52 cover band shows and Jones played 110 tribute/cover shows in the same year.
15 I co-manage Dion Jones and Andy Kelly produced Jones' debut album.

References

Becker, H. (1982) *Art Worlds*. Los Angeles: University of California Press.

Goodman, F. (1998) *The Mansion on The Hill*. New York: Vintage Books/Random House.

Hebdige, D. (1979) *Subculture: The Meaning of Style*. London: Methuen.

Johnson, B. and Homan, S. (2003) *Vanishing Acts: An Inquiry into the State of Live Popular Music Opportunities in New South Wales*. Sydney: Australia Council/ NSW Ministry for the Arts.

Klein, N. (2000) *No Logo*. London: Flamingo/Harper Collins.

McIntyre, P. (2001) The contemporary western popular music industry as 'field', in D. Crowdy, S. Homan and T. Mitchell (eds) *The Proceedings of the 8th IASPM Australia – New Zealand Conference 2001*. Sydney: UTS Press.

Nattiez, J. (1990) *Music and Discourse*. Princeton, NJ: Princeton University Press.

Robertson, R. (1995) Globalization: time-space and homogeneity-heterogeneity, in M. Featherstone, S. Lash and R. Robertson (eds) *Global Modernities*. Newbury Park, CA: Sage.

Woodruff, J. (2002) Unpublished and untitled paper concerning music management presented at the Australian branch of the Music Manager's Forum's annual conference. Sydney, Novotel Hotel, 12 November.

12 *Toca Raul!* Praise singers on Brazil's central plateau

Jesse Samba Wheeler

I write this chapter from Brasília, the Bauhaus-esque leviathan that thrusts up out of Brazil's central plateau, a pop-up book of modernist blueprints of utopia. Planned, designed, organized and decorated largely by artists and aesthetically-minded technicians, the capital was abruptly torn from the coast, where it had been for more than 400 years, and erected anew, here, half a century ago.[1] It's mythic: in 1883 the Italian Saint Dom Bosco prophesied its existence, though it's doubtful he foresaw the swarm of 'apostates' of the most esoteric creeds, who believe Brasília to be Ground Zero come the Rapture. The whole area can be seen from space, its quartz glittering like a glean of herring at sunrise. And it's here where, on 23 October 2003, I stumbled upon a manifestation of a kind of passion I had never in my musical travels before encountered.

Invited by a musician friend to go to a show by his cover band, I trudged to the neighbouring 'Piauí Beverage Distributor' for a few beers, then, cheerier, shuffled down the sidewalk to Gate's Pub (in Asa Sul, the 'South Wing' of Brasília's Plano Piloto, or central 'Pilot Plan' area), meandering through throngs of youth on-the-make among cars parked with doors akimbo. The line to get in was long. Billed as 'Tributo a Santana', the band had drawn a good audience, and once inside I threaded my way towards the low stage. It was difficult to glimpse my friend, the drummer, Ticho Lavenère. I posted myself against a loudspeaker and thought, *Oh, well. Now I can tell him I came.*

Copies had always fascinated me – dioramas, holograms, reproductions of all kinds. When the fake stands in for the real, when what's real *is* the fake, it is possible to feel sated by the imitation and no longer desire the original. As a kid in Chicago, a perfect Saturday was a trip to the Museum of Science and Industry to marvel at the miniature of Cinderella's castle, then visit the vanished House of Horror to ogle gory displays of bloody waxen bodies and arcane instruments of torture. So why, then, my contempt for a cover band? Jazz, blues, samba and rap, with its use of sampling, have long been genres where paying tribute to other musicians and bands is considered *de rigueur*, if not proof of one's competence and credentials. Though one does not immediately think of them as being so, symphonic orchestras and operatic companies are institutionalized, pedigreed cover bands. The denigration that rock cover bands suffer includes the impugnation that the musicians are not 'real musicians'. If they were, the argument goes, they would be playing their own music.

That night at Gate's was meaningful for two reasons: Firstly, I became aware of, and began to let go of, my prejudice against rock cover bands, a species of copy I had unreflectively deprecated. Secondly, I started to think about them as something meriting critical study. Roberto Schwarz, in his 1996 essay 'Beware of alien ideologies', questions the naturalized notion that copies are inferior to their originals, that they are less creative and of less intrinsic value. Why is originality fetishized? Within popular music, grada-tions of originality are judged to evaluate a song or genre's 'new' features. A composition is judged to be original if it does not appear in too many ways too much like another known composition – a subjective criterion that values a certain set of differences over others.

Pierre Bourdieu (1984, 1990) would argue that the value placed on ori-ginality, and our interest in it, is arbitrary. As a category for the aggregation of symbolic capital – to be at some later time converted into economic capital – originality, I suggest, operates as a mode of 'distinction', whereby agents, in whatever their field, may express and reproduce social status (for Bourdieu: class inequalities). But such reproduction cannot remain naked; rather it must be disguised so as to appear intrinsically, objectively legitimate. Reading Schwarz against Bourdieu, I argue that the 'misrecognition' of the arbitrari-ness of originality (it appears to have natural and objective value) accounts for one part of the differential distribution of value throughout the art world.

In the musical field, bands playing original music tend to occupy the highest rungs on the ladder of taste. They are most often among those best remunerated.[2] Cover bands expose a 'system of valued difference' by con-tradicting it: they participate in a discrete and antagonic economy, where value is placed on strategic similarities. But just as valuing difference may veil instances of sameness, the converse holds true. A cover band's performance of an old favourite will invariably contain sameness and difference. Just as Thelonious Monk introduced a phrase from a familiar playground song into a whole-tone jazz piano solo, a creative act enjoyed and valued by his audience, the guitarist of a Led Zeppelin tribute band may weave difference into a studied Jimmy Page solo.

Cover bands also play with our understanding of authenticity and au-thorship, inviting us to re-evaluate these terms: the more authentic (faithful) my copy, the more I must give myself over to the original, the less I am the author. Fidelity and authorship appear to be inversely related. Yet, in order to perform it well, I must make the copy my own, thereby creating something unique: an original.

The argument I shall make in this chapter is that among musicians of cover bands, tribute band musicians (a distinction made below) represent a special class of musician and are involved in an activity that in important ways likens them to the *griots* of certain west African societies.[3] Through this reading one can more easily appreciate the complexity and social value of the tribute phenomenon. I shall also discuss issues of authenticity, fidelity and authorship, and suggest how the study of tribute bands can contribute to ethno/musicology and identity studies. Finally, I shall suggest how tribute bands expand the very definition of music itself.

Toca Raul! Rock, tribute and Brasília

In the United States, the cry of 'Freebird!' (a Lynyrd Skynyrd song) is so often heard at live rock shows that it has ceased to be a serious request for a cover. I chuckle whenever I hear it and wonder if it will continue even after Skynyrd is long forgotten. The word has a nice sound, and the playfulness with which it is lofted over heads towards the band makes me think it stands a good chance. In Brasília, and indeed, throughout Brazil, one hears the phrase '*Toca Raul!*' as often and with the same spirit. It means 'Play Raul', referring to Raul Seixas, the late rocker whose poetic and ludic lyrics and hippy-secessionist rhetoric earned him a place in nearly everyone's heart. But no one plays a cover of his on request; it's his memory that is honoured.[4]

Rock 'n' roll and Brasília are about the same age. Little Richard recorded 'Tutti Frutti' in 1955, the year in which the location for Brasília was chosen. The inauguration of the city in 1960 coincided with the inauguration of the US congressional investigation into 'payola' in the music industry (i.e. DJs accepting bribes to play records). Brasília prides itself on its rock 'n' roll history. In the 1980s and 1990s local rock bands like Plebe Rude, Capital Inicial, Legião Urbana, Paralamas do Sucesso, Os Raimundos, Little Quail and the Mad Birds, and PRAVdA injected the national music scene with a sincerity, a DIY aesthetic, and a punk edginess that earned Brasília the title 'the Capital of Rock', a phrase widely used by the media.

Rock's symbolic importance to the city was demonstrated in its *Carnaval* celebrations of 2005. The theme was the city itself, and two samba schools wrote *enredos* (songs) honouring Brasília's rock heroes. ARUC called their theme song 'A Cauldron of Cultures: From Dilermando Reis to Cássia Eller', the latter being the late, local, lesbian punk rocker. Aruremas paid tribute to Renato Russo, the late singer-songwriter who led Legião Urbana, one of the country's most famous rock bands. Their song was titled 'Brasília, A Star That Shines with Renato Russo': 'Smile Brasília . . . /Renato Russo is in this revelry/ Oh! How many songs we shall remember/From this boy who we so admire . . . In this sea of love/I will bathe/From your beautiful garden I want a flower/ Renato Russo you have not died/Your holy verses will be made eternal' (Pereira 2004).

Parallel to the traditional *Carnaval* parties, rock fans organized their own events featuring local bands, including 'Carnametal', 'Alternative Carnaval', 'Rock in Carnaval' and 'Carnaval of Rock'. This last event featured four days of rock covers. Cover and tribute bands are deeply ingrained in Brasília. 'Fuzzbox', a rock column/calendar in the main broadsheet, explained that: 'Because of a total lack of space, we prioritized the above events. But be aware that the usual cover bands continue to play the usual songs in the usual places' (Scartezini 2005: 5).

Celso Salim, a blues-rock guitarist I met when he participated in the 2003 'Tributo a Jimi Hendrix', compiled a list of over 70 cover and tribute bands in Brasília, both active and disbanded (I have since added at least 15 more). The musicians and bands honoured include Jethro Tull, Pantera, Lenny Kravitz, Santana, Queen, Whitesnake, Jamiroquai, Stevie Ray Vaughan, the Ramones, Rage Against the Machine, Bob Dylan, Lynyrd Skynyrd, Twisted Sister, Nirvana and Audioslave. Brazilian musicians covered include Cássia Eller, Raul Seixas, Gonzaguinha, Chico Science, Os Titãs, Elis Regina and Os Mutantes. Bands like Legião Urbana, the Wailers, Pink Floyd, Led Zeppelin, the Red Hot Chilli Peppers and Pearl Jam have inspired multiple tribute bands. Some have straightforward names, like Kiss Cover, and Clash Cover; others have punning names, like the Doors cover band Os Poortas (*portas* means 'doors'), the Alice in Chains cover band Alice in the Box, and the Let It Beatles.

On any given weekend the local papers may list shows for up to 20 cover bands. While original acts receive preference, some cover bands may have their promotional pictures displayed. Some hold down weekly gigs at one of the city's few bars with enough space for bands to play. The local cover scene has existed for approximately 25 years. The most fantastic instance of dedication to the *métier* of musician-cum-mime of which I have heard was the personal project of the owner of the now defunct bar Clube do Rei ('Club of the King'), named not for Elvis, but for Roberto Carlos, Brazil's highest selling recording musician. For many years, the bar's owner fronted a tribute band to 'the king' and underwent plastic surgery to look like him.

At the opposite end of the spectrum are Rosho, led by bassist and singer Duda Bello, who drew attention not for how they looked, but for how they sounded. Possibly the first tribute band to form in Brasília, they began in 1982 and gained renown for their faithful renditions of the Canadian rock band Rush. In 2001 a group of Rush fans organized 'RushCon 1', the first Rush convention, in Toronto, Canada. A worldwide call for 'demo' tapes of Rush cover bands was sent out, for which Rush themselves auditioned. Rosho was selected as one of only two bands to perform at the convention.

In Brasília, *banda de cover* literally means 'cover band'. It has both general and specific applications. Generally, it is used (as in English) to signify a band that plays the music of others. As such, it is differentiated from *banda de autoria*, an 'authorship band' (however, the term 'authorship' is problematic, as tribute musicians are, as we shall see, authors). This is the manner in which it is most often used by the general public. In its more specific usage, it

denotes a band that devotes itself full-time to making a living from the reproduction of the music of a single band or artist. The cover band may or may
not reproduce other aspects of a band's persona, such as looks, gestures or
performance style. When used in this way, the term excludes two other types
of band, the *banda de baile* and the *banda de tributo*. The former means literally
'dance band' and includes those bands that reproduce the music of multiple
bands in the course of a single show. Their repertoire may also include the
occasional original composition. The latter term translates as 'tribute band'
and refers to a band that comes together on a specific occasion to play primarily the music of a single band or musician. Tribute bands are comprised of
musicians who generally play in other bands.

The term *cover* usually connotes a reproduction in which musicians seek
to remain faithful to the original, though the degree of fidelity may vary
widely. *Versão*, or 'version', carries connotations of new approaches to a
previously recorded composition, usually by someone else. Thus, Brazilian
singer/songwriter Caetano Veloso's 2004 album of American pop hits, *A
Foreign Sound*, is a collection of versions, as each clearly bears his mark. The
related *interpretação*, or 'interpretation', may signify a version, though it may
also be the first recording or performance of a composition by another artist.
The late Cássia Eller, one of Brasília's most beloved musical daughters, did not
to my knowledge write her own music, but was known for versions and interpretations of others' songs, like Edith Piaf's 'Non, Je Ne Regrette Rien' and
Nirvana's 'Smells Like Teen Spirit'. What follows is an examination of one
tribute band, 7he Seven Rock Band.[5] Through 7he Seven we shall learn
something of the history of tribute bands in Brasília, including the contexts of
their formation, and their experiences of performing as a tribute.

The 'original' tribute collective: 7he Seven Rock Band[6]

In recounting the story of the birth of 7he Seven, the band's drummer Ticho
Lavenère told me the tale of Kiko Peres' climbing of Machu Picchu in 1995.
Kiko, a guitarist who for years performed with the nationally-known reggae
band Natiruts and one of Brasília's 'symbolic' musicians, according to Ticho,
recounted that with his funk rock band PRAVdA in tatters, and finding
himself with the need to do some soul-searching, he travelled seven days to
Machu Picchu, and climbed the highest peak:

> There [I was] on top, looking back on my life, meditating and
> mentalizing the goals I had. And one of the goals that I at that
> moment fixed in my head was to put together a tribute to Led Zep-
> pelin as soon as I returned ... It was a moment of mustering strength

and courage, really, to be at the head of this project, and a little audacity, too ... playing Led Zeppelin is a big responsibility.

(Lavenère interview 2005)

The show that resulted was foundational, invoking the first instance of the use of the word 'tribute' in Brasília. Only the word 'cover' was previously used, and it brought together diverse musicians for a single event to pay tribute to a single band.

The following year, in 1996, he realized another goal, a tribute to Jimi Hendrix, on the anniversary of the artist's death. Five years earlier, while he and his older brother Beto studied at the Los Angeles Guitar Institute of Technology, Kiko and the late Tonho Gebara went to the inauguration of Hendrix's star on Hollywood Boulevard. Neither knew much of Hendrix's music. There were few people, he remembers, but among them they recognized guitarists Vernon Reid, Steve Vai and Hendrix's father and brother. They felt a deep passion in the gathering: 'I came back a Hendrix maniac, a fanatic. I called Gebara in Rio a year later, and he had also turned into a Hendrix maniac. It was like we were baptized into a religion!'

7he Seven Band formed in the midst of this tribute excitement. Ticho told me the story of the band's beginning, and how it got its name:

> [In 1996] a big producer in Brasília called me, saying that he wanted to put on a show of only 70s music. And the name of the party was going to be 'Seventh' – 'How do you pronounce that?' [the 'th' sound does not exist in Portuguese]. 'Seventh', I replied. 'Seventh'. 'Mm-hmm'. And so he asked me, 'Do you have the band for that?' And I said, 'I do'. And I didn't. But I said I did ... because one week earlier I had talked with Beto Peres ... and we said, 'Let's put together a band to play songs we enjoy, that we like, and that the public enjoys and would like to hear'. And so when this producer called me, I said, 'It's time', and we set a date for the band's debut, and we rehearsed for two months, and our first show had 4,800 people ... So, what happened is that the band kind of got stuck with the name 'Seventh' – 'I don't know if I'm saying that right, but that's it'. 'You're saying it right', I assured him. At a certain point we decided to simplify it, pretty much because of the problem of pronunciation, and it became 'Seven', 'The Seven', '7he Seven Rock Band'.

(Lavenère interview 2003)

Beto stated that the name also echoed *The Magnificent Seven* film (MGM, 1960), conjuring up images of grandeur and warriors. He remembered the powerful feedback from the public and the feeling he got playing the music of the artists he had always admired: 'We kind of felt *incorporated* into the artists we were interpreting' (Peres interview 2005). Both he and Ticho felt there was

Figure 12.1 Some of 7he Seven Rock Band. From left to right: Jair Santiago, Henrique Ayres, Duda Bello, Ticho Lavenère, Alírio Netto, Bruno Wambier, Beto Peres. Photograph courtesy of Jesse Samba Wheeler

chemistry among the band's musicians, the public and the artists to whom they were paying tribute, and they decided to it again.

Ticho, Beto and a collective of rotating musicians including at least three guitarists, two bassists, five singers, two keyboardists and a saxophonist, gradually developed a repertoire of shows, each paying tribute to a different band, including Pink Floyd, Queen, Led Zeppelin, Rush and Deep Purple. They also developed a 'tribute to rock 'n' roll', with songs from the above shows and selections from Janis Joplin, Jimi Hendrix, the Allman Brothers, Lynyrd Skynyrd, Black Sabbath, Triumph, Dire Straits and Dio. With this repertory of tribute shows, 7he Seven played 52 engagements in the year 2000, just under half the number of shows played that year by Brazil's most active band, Charlie Brown, Jr. Their versatility, unique approach and consistent quality of reproduction and performance earned them unparalleled respect.

In a group conversation, the whole band traded stories. Beto recalled the time the producer of a New Year's Eve rock event arrived late and, standing at the door, from where she could hear the music but not see the stage, said to her co-producer, 'Two a.m. and [7he Seven] hasn't started?!' to which the other replied, 'That's the band playing'. She thought it was a CD playing.

Ticho remembered when a man in a wheelchair and two others approached the band before a tribute to Led Zeppelin concert they played in Rio de Janeiro: ' "Look, we saw the release of *Physical Graffiti* in '75 [stated to general, raucous laughter], and so we've come to see you guys". No friggin' way! We looked at each other like ... "Awesome!" And after the show they came back to congratulate us' (Band interview 2005).

The band members offered the following explanations about their desire to be in the group:

> I am paying tribute, giving what I owe to the people who influenced me, who invested in my musicality. And I want to give the public what we never had, what I always dreamt of, the chance to see Led Zeppelin.
>
> (Lavenère interview 2003)

> It's a consummation. Listening to 'Dazed & Confused' [from the Led Zeppelin I album] as a teenager, you wonder how they do it. Then you learn to play it, you understand what they were thinking, you become a member of the band. It's about pleasure, not money – a prostitute doesn't feel pleasure.
>
> (Keyboardist Bruno Wambier, band interview 2005)

> I learned to play rock 'n' roll with Jimi Hendrix and Jimmy Page. They were my teachers. They're why I learned to play guitar.
>
> (Guitarist Jair Santiago, band interview 2005)

> Jimi [Hendrix] is my idol, hero, master, guru, therapist. His music touches me deeply, it rescues my soul when I am depressed.
>
> (Kiko Peres interview 2005)

Celso is a musical colleague of several of the members of 7he Seven and summed up the meaning of 'tribute' this way: 'Tribute is a homage. I wouldn't play in a tribute to the Cure – I don't like them!' (Salim interview 2003).The musicians' approach of how to pay tribute is based largely on research, rehearsal and years of feeling the music. According to Bruno: '[*The*] *Dark Side of the Moon* took months to prepare, to get the sounds, parts and solos just right, to programme the keyboards. We don't have sheet music for this – it's [listening to] the CDs, LPs, and cassettes, over and over' (Wambier, band interview 2005). Alírio Netto, a vocalist for 7he Seven, similarly remarked that 'you dress yourself in the music, let it get into your blood, make it part of you'. The art of the tribute draws out different perspectives on attaining the 'right' copy:

> You have to listen so much that it becomes organic, that you 'think' drums like [Led Zeppelin's] John Bonham, so you play like him and not yourself. You get into the spirit of the music and express yourself through its language.
>
> (Lavenère interview 2003)

> It's dedication in getting both the details and the spirit of the music, the 'accent' of Jimi [Hendrix]'s musical language, in incorporating what they lived. Tribute is trying to get the soul of the music. It's much more important to get the spirit of the music, than to play it lick for lick. The best tribute to Led [Zeppelin] is to jam like they did. I love drinking whisky and playing Zeppelin stoned ... and [to] jam forever.
>
> (Salim interview 2003)

For the tribute to be successful, a combination of sincerity of intention, commitment to quality and fidelity to the music is required, which includes detailed attention to instrumentation, arrangements and sonority, especially timbres. All these ingredients are essential for the musicians to be satisfied with their homage:

> Sonority and tone color are fundamental. John Bonham used tremendous drums – his kick drum was 26 inches, his ride cymbal was 24 inches, his smallest [crash] cymbal was 18 inches, his hi-hat [cymbals] were 15 inches. I take the stuffing out of the kick drum when I play him. For Rush, heights of the drums are important, and I avoid rimshots. When I play Queen I open the hi-hat a little when I hit the snare – 'dun-dun-TCHA-tchi dun-dun-TCHA-tchi' – Roger Taylor does that constantly. If we're playing Rush, we can't play Led, we have to remove some drums first. But it's not just technique. It's performance, it's feeling.
>
> (Lavenère, band interview 2003)

> In their live shows Deep Purple used to do these guitar-keyboard duels. We improvise within their language, using their slang to maintain the same spirit and dynamic.
>
> (Wambier band interview 2005)

When questioned about the differences between tribute bands and the other kinds of cover bands mentioned above, the musicians took pains to distance their work – and by extension themselves – from that of non-tribute bands. The great effort to reproduce particular playing styles and feel is rewarded by a greater commitment to the band from audiences, who 'stand and listen, moved' (saxophonist Henrique Ayres, band interview 2005), as opposed to a cover band's show, where 'the crowd recognizes the song, but they don't feel it' (Beto Peres, band interview 2005). Duda summed it up this way: 'When we started to sing "There's no time for us" [in Queen's "Who Wants to Live Forever?"], your sister Molly started to cry. The role of music is to move people to project themselves back to a situation when they heard that song' (Duda Bello, band interview 2005).

Celso characterized the distinction with this popular conception of cover band musicians:

> Cover bands, you know the ones that play everything – 'Sultans of Swing', 'Rock 'n' Roll', 'Hey Joe', 'Stairway to Heaven', 'Smoke on the Water', 'Proud Mary' – the top ten from the 60s and 70s, just playing 'cause it's a job? [The guitarist] kind of plays every note, but it sucks, the Mark Knopfler solo note by note, but *sucks*. How is that possible?! 'Cause he doesn't have the *spirit*, 'cause he doesn't *listen* to Dire Straits! He knows only *that* song.
>
> (Salim interview 2003)

Netto also sang with Satisfaction, a pop-rock 'dance band', whose musicians, he felt, were not committed to the quality of their reproductions. This contrasted absolutely with 7he Seven's musicians: '7he Seven play with commitment to the music ... You look at the way Ticho plays – shit, dude! How could a guy like that not be committed? How're you gonna tell me he ain't feeling what he's playing?' (Netto interview 2005).

It became increasingly clear that 7he Seven saw their work as a vehicle by which both they and their audience could transcend the boundaries of time and space. This essentially emotional collective 'delivery' to the music's source, made possible by a combination of study and feeling, distinguished them from their colleagues in cover bands. This distinction is fundamentally made possible by a perceived emotional and musical proximity the musicians have with the artists to whom they offer tribute. This proximity both inspires the dedicated study crucial to faithful, heartfelt renditions and makes possible performances judged to be worthy tributes:

> For me it's an honour. I play [Lynyrd] Skynyrd and I leave the stage happy, and when the show goes well, I feel like I've paid homage. It's the collective energy, an offering to both the crowd and to Led [Zeppelin] when I play 'Going to California' – I love it so much. It really touches my heart.
>
> (Salim interview 2003)

> I feel such a strong connection to the artists, it's as if I had always known them, and I knew what they were feeling. Sometimes the song seems like it's just as much mine as Freddie Mercury's.
>
> (Netto, band interview 2003)

When pressed to elaborate on the experience of playing, to verbalize the sublime phenomenological aspects of tribute, the musicians resorted to spiritual, religious and supernatural tropes. They revealed that at the nexus of study, feeling and enactment lay the link to the artist:

> I remember once playing Jimi [Hendrix], I felt I did things that weren't me. I played a phrase that I had never played and I didn't know where it came from. Kiko said to me, 'Dude, what happened? You *incorporated* the guy!'
>
> (Beto Peres, band interview 2005)

> A ritual takes place, an energy moves back and forth between us, the public, and other places. For example, you're going to play Jimi [Hendrix], well, he's already on the top floor. You're going to play Led [Zeppelin], they got a representative up there, too. Janis [Joplin], Queen – it's ritualistic, the person's energy is everywhere. It's crazy.
>
> (Lavenère, band interview 2005)

Today 7he Seven play every few months. They also open shows for national touring artists such as Zé Ramalho, Alceu Valença and Marcelo D2. Most of the members continue to play in other bands, including 'authorship' bands. Alírio Netto sings with Khallice, an original prog-metal band. Ticho and Jair play together in Plástika, an original alterna-rock band. Beto plays in his brother Kiko's band. The main challenge they all express is finding a balance between the two sides of their careers. All of them find much more work with 7he Seven than with their 'authorship' bands. Their goals for the future are to stick to their 'original' plan of paying homage to the musicians to whom they feel indebted, but to expand their repertoire, hire roadies again, charge more for gigs, and to set the world record for playing the most number of hours live on stage.

Of *griots* and gurus – songs of praise

7he Seven Rock Band occupies a place of respect and reverence in local musical history, where they represent the elders of rock, recognized as individual talents and for their canonized repertoire. Why and how they have distinguished themselves are important questions that, if we keep in mind the symbolic capital attributed to the canonical rock bands, the following analysis of the musicians' narratives may partially answer. In order to elucidate what I see as values in the tribute phenomenon, and in 7he Seven's role as a specific instance of the same, that extends beyond mere appropriation of capital of famous musicians, I shall interpret tribute musicians as 'praise singers'.

Examining the musicians' narratives, we see several themes emerge. One is that the experience of playing tribute is one of paying *homage* to the artists they regard as heroes, idols, masters, gurus and therapists. Another is that to pay homage they must reproduce the music faithfully in order that they, and the audience, feel the *spirit* of both the music and the artist. Lastly, when they feel the spirit, they enter into a relationship with the artist that can be described as *incorporation*, a state in which the musicians experience the spirit of the artist enter their body. In the Afro-Brazilian religion *candomblé*, the imagery and terminology of which is commonly encountered in wider society, the phrase '*o santo baixou*' ('the saint descended') is used to describe the moment of the saint's possession of the body of the praiser.[7] The use of words and ideas usually associated with the sacred realm to describe this secular phenomenon recurs and underscores the musician's belief that there is something uncommon about their experience.

The praise singers of many West African societies, whom I refer to here as '*griots*', to imply all the societies in which they operate, are complex figures of historic importance. They are of low, if not the lowest, caste, although, like musicians everywhere, indispensable in their abilities and duties. They are musicians, historians and storytellers, and they play for socially and politically important personages, both living and dead. *Griots* have existed for centuries; Sundiata Keïta, founder and king of the Empire of Mali (1190?–1255) had his personal *griot*, Balla Fasséké. *Griots* today may sing songs praising the African warrior king Sundiata, such as 'The Bow Song', recounting the moment young Sundiata got to his feet for the first time (Niane 1982). They may also praise a wealthy businessman who wishes to appropriate, via the figure of the *griot*, something of the greatness of a king or respected contemporary figure. Musicians today, if descendants of *griots*, may be considered themselves *griots*, as is the case with Mory Kanté and Ami Koïta, though not Salif Keïta (whose name indicates that he is of a noble caste and, therefore, should not be a musician).

Tribute bands in Brasília, as exemplified by 7he Seven Rock Band, play a role in Brazilian society that is similar in important ways. They sing the praises of musicians whom society has invested with exceptional importance, musicians like Jimi Hendrix whose music is regarded as canonical, as 'classic rock'. Like the *griots*, who put to song a personage's praiseworthy acts, 7he Seven invoke the presence of these musicians by reproducing their acts, playing the music they created and focusing collective admiration for their skills. In doing so, they, too, are revered and honoured. Both *griots* and tribute musicians succeed through their veneration of canonical musicians to maintain the ascendancy of those musicians and their own livelihood.

As historians they tell the stories that people want to hear by playing the rock canon, the old favourites that everyone knows and wants to hear again. As *griots* remind people of the greatness of past warriors and kings, 7he Seven keep alive the spirit of those that made rock what it is. They serve to remind people of past events through, for example, their playing of a 'Tribute to Rock 'n' Roll' show to celebrate the genre's fiftieth anniversary. There is even similarity in the ambience of their performances: *griots* are often hired to animate parties, where they sing and play loudly yet eloquently. Tribute bands in Brazil typically play in highly celebratory environments, such as that of Gate's Pub, and do so with the greatest of skill and talent.

Finally, both are in paid service and respond to socioeconomic pressures. *Griots* are increasingly finding that new economic structures are forcing them to change what, where and why they play (McLaughlin 1997; Hearn 2004). The musicians in 7he Seven find that they earn more playing tribute shows than when playing in a *banda de autoria*. Market forces and industry trends in Brazil are two economic factors that have created a greater demand for cover bands than for 'authorship' bands.

Why is a reconsideration of the role of tribute bands important? Firstly, seeing them as *griots* focuses our attention on the stories they tell about popular music's heroes. Heroes, like archetypes and monuments, are loci of archived cultural meaning (Connerton 1989; Nora 1989). Tribute performances may act as ritual (in the sense that they are repeated and interactive) occasions for the reinforcement or critique of systems of value. 7he Seven become producers of culture. Secondly, the fantasizing that tribute bands stimulate in audiences is an element in the enactment of ideas about self and other. Tribute musicians channel fans' fantasies and desires that intensify their own feelings of incumbency, honour and worship. Thirdly, an analysis of tribute performances can reveal both practised and unintended stylistic differences, where tribute acts may construct new identities in the interstices between original and cover.

Performance analysis would also promote useful reconsiderations of authorship and authenticity, as it invites us to look beyond Romantic ideas of both concepts. Passion, as alluded to by 7he Seven's musicians in their testaments of deep emotional involvement in the music, can be a great creative force; however, as an emotion (thus implicitly irrational, inferior to reason), it does not receive the attention it merits in the study of the composition, performance or appreciation of music, either by postmodernists or those who would conserve the prejudices of the Enlightenment (cf. Nehring 1997).

The idea of tribute musician as *griot* opens a new angle for critical analysis of the market forces and industry decisions and directions that affect live music, as well as the performers' responses and proactive moves that generate change in the aforementioned fields. Members of 7he Seven and other tribute bands find that people are not coming out in sufficient numbers to support their authorship bands, while their tribute work is in obvious demand. By working within the domain of tribute work and re-signifying it as something valuable and not vulgar, they are transforming traditional ideological and aesthetic positions. The economic effects of such change and the effect it has on musicians' creative output require further analysis.

Finally, as 7he Seven's bassist Duda stated, through faithful, passionate performances of known songs tribute musicians are capable of transporting audiences back to a time and a place where they heard them before. It is as if a 'play' button were pushed inside their heads, and they hear both what they want to hear and what the band is playing. The widespread popularity of cover bands and karaoke indicates how desired this experience is. This combined internal and external musical experience is simultaneously individual and collective, intimate and public, unique and common. Music is, then, everything Anthony Seeger (1991) said it was, and more. It is also this chronotopic oscillation, the perception of being here and there, of having access to all eras.

Interviews were conducted with the following musicians: Ticho Lavenère (11 December 2003); Alirio Netto (16 February 2005); Kiko Peres (28 February 2005); Celso Salim (10 December 2003); and a group interview with 7he Seven Rock Band (22 February 2005).

Notes

1   According to MacLachlan, 'Uninterrupted by traffic lights, streets flowed throughout the city, passing by seemingly magical glass buildings, reflecting pools, and decidedly modern statuary' (2003: 125). Among the artists involved were architect Oscar Niemeyer, sculptor Alfredo Ceschiatti, landscape gardener Burle Marx, ceramicist Althos Bulcão and composer Claudio Santoro.

2   I believe it is possible to discern through the work of cover bands how the fetishism of originality quietly reproduces the status quo of capital inequalities in society by observing firstly how they are regarded (often with denigration) *vis-à-vis* other categories of value, such as technical mastery; and secondly, the distribution of symbolic capital conferred through repertoire.

3   They go by a variety of ethnolinguistic names. For example, they are called (in the plural) *gewel* in Wolof, *jeliw* in societies speaking Mande languages, and *awlube* among Fulani speakers. *Griot* is a French-derived term that does not specify society of origin.

4   Many of his lyrics were written by pop author Paulo Coelho. A song of his appeared on the *City of God* (Miramax, 2003) soundtrack.

5   The spelling '7he Seven' is consistent with the band's practice.

6   If interviewees' words are followed by 'group interview', they derive from an interview with 7he Seven Rock Band in 2005, and may have been paraphrased or reordered: see interview details above.

7   Called the saint's 'son' or 'daughter' in *candomblé* terminology.

References

Bourdieu, P. (1984) *Distinction: A Social Critique of the Judgment of Taste*. Cambridge, MA: Harvard University Press.

Bourdieu, P. (1990) *The Logic of Practice*, trans. R. Nice. Stanford, CA: Stanford University Press.

Connerton, P. (1989) *How Societies Remember*. Cambridge: Cambridge University Press.

Hearn, A.H. (2004) Guardians of culture: the controversial heritage of Senegalese griots (1), *The Australian Journal of Anthropology*, 15(2): 129–43.

MacLachlan, C.M. (2003) *A History of Modern Brazil: The Past Against the Future*. Wilmington, DE: Scholarly Resources.

McLaughlin, F. (1997) Islam and popular music in Senegal: the emergence of a 'new tradition', *Africa*, 67(4): 560–82.

Nehring, N. (1997) *Popular Music, Gender, and Postmodernism: Anger is an Energy*. Thousand Oaks, CA: Sage.

Niane, D.T. (1982) *Sundiata: An Epic of Old Mali*, trans. G.D. Pickett. Harlow: Longman.

Nora, P. (1989) Between memory and history, *Les Lieux de Mémoire, Representations*, 26: 7–25.

Pereira, C. (2004) Brasília, uma estrela que brilha com Renato Russo. Unpublished *tema enredo* for Aruremas, Recanto das Emas, DF, Brazil.

Scartezini, B. (2005) Fuzzbox, *Correio Braziliense*, 4 February.

Schwarz, R. (1996) Beware of alien ideologies, in R. Schwarz and J. Gledson (eds) *Misplaced Ideas: Essays on Brazilian Culture*. London: Verso.

Seeger, A. (1991) Styles of musical Ethnography, in B. Nettl and P. Bohlman (eds) *Comparative Musicology and Anthropology of Music: Essays on the History of Ethnomusicology*. Chicago: University of Chicago Press.

PART 3
COVERS AND ADAPTATIONS

13 *Tian ci* – Faye Wong and English songs in the Cantopop and Mandapop repertoire

Tony Mitchell

Introduction: covers without stigma

This chapter examines the reconstruction of a number of western pop and rock songs in the Cantopop and Mandapop repertoire, with particular emphasis on the musical output of the Beijing-born, Hong Kong-based 'empress' of Cantopop and Mandapop, Faye Wong, who has generated more interest in the western world than most of her peers, outside the relatively closed diasporic world of Mandarin and Cantonese-language pop music. She is known in the West mainly as an actress in Wong-kar Wai's 1994 film *Chungking Express*, which included a music video featuring her Cantonese version of the Irish group the Cranberries' song 'Dreams', and to a lesser extent for her role in director Wong-kar Wai's star-studded 2004 film *2046*. Faye Wong has gradually amassed a significant body of western fans, known generically as 'Fayenatics',[1] despite only rarely performing or recording songs in English.

Wong has recorded and performed versions of songs in Cantonese and Mandarin by US, UK, Scottish and Irish artists such as the Cranberries, Tori Amos, the Sundays, Everything But the Girl and the Cocteau Twins, in the process negotiating an 'in-between' position linking mainstream Cantopop and alternative rock music. Her incorporation of both mainstream and non-mainstream songs and musical elements into her repertoire led her to be referred to in the Chinese music industry press in 1994 as *Faye Chu Lau Tze Yam*, a term meaning 'the voice of Faye's mainstream', but also 'the voices of the non-mainstream' in spoken Cantonese, which could also be translated as 'Fayestream'.[2] This indicates that she could almost be said to occupy her own category in the Chinese pop music spectrum, and she has continued to combine mainstream pop songs with more 'alternative', even avant-garde oriented tracks throughout her career.

There are many examples of reinterpretations of western pop songs in Cantopop and Mandapop, drawing on what Witzleben (1998: 472) has called a 'venerable and well-respected tradition in Chinese opera' called *tian ci*, in which pre-existing melodies are set to new lyrics. Importantly, as Witzleben has observed, the adherence to the *tian ci* tradition of appropriating the tunes of western and foreign songs in Cantopop is a long-standing one, 'and has never had the stigma which is attached to the term "cover version"'. This is partly a byproduct of the craft of song lyric writing in Cantopop, which is practised independently by a large number of artists and generally considered as a quite separate art from musical song composition. Lin Xi, who has worked extensively with Faye Wong since her debut album *Shirley* in 1989, is considered to be one of the most distinctive Hong Kong-based lyric writers, and as Fung and Curtin have noted, his highly impressionistic and poetic lyrics 'are charged with metaphors and allegories' (2002: 281) which are often very difficult to translate. In a biography of Wong which appeared in the People's Republic of China (PRC) in 1998, *Brave to Be Myself*, Lin Xi's lyrics were described as '"imagistic" like prose poems. Their language is not fixed, in places its meaning is vague. It takes you into an hallucinatory world of sensitive intelligence' (Wong and Lan 1998: 102). The comparison to prose poems is noteworthy, given that two of the English song lyrics Wong has adapted, by Tori Amos and Ben Watt, were also written as prose poems.

Distinctive examples of *tian ci* in Cantopop include the late Cantopop actress and singing star Anita Mui Yim-Fong's controversial song about seduction and the frustrations of sexual repression, 'Bad Girl' ('Huai N'Thai'), first recorded in 1985, a Cantonese version of Scottish singer Sheena Easton's song 'Strut'. This song, which contained Chinese lyrics written by Lin Zhenqiang which are completely unrelated to Easton's original song, became an Anita Mui signature tune throughout the Chinese diaspora, although its English language source was completely unknown. 'Bad Girl' did contain a chorus in English, 'why, why, tell me why', which rhymed with the Cantonese title, and segued into the Cantonese for 'Why can't I let myself go?', as well as incorporating other English words, 'Help me' and 'Midnight'. 'Bad Girl' was banned in mainland China in the 1990s for its perceived salacious content (see Witzleben 1999), but remained in Mui's concert repertoire as part of a medley, sometimes introduced in English as 'Bad Girl', until her death in 2003 (and was included in her final Sydney concert in that year). It even spawned a later song in Mui's repertoire, with Cantonese lyrics by Terry Chan, and the title and chorus in English, called 'Big Bad Girl', recorded in 1995.[3]

Other notable examples of Cantopop songs being launched on the back of English language originals, although with a more guaranteed knowledge of the originals by Chinese audiences, include Taiwan-born and Canada-raised Sally Yeh's 1985 version of Madonna's 'Material Girl' (retitled 'Two Hundred Degrees'), Sarah Wong's 1988 version of Kylie Minogue's 'I Should Be So Lucky' (which became 'Please Don't Be So Clingy'), and Angela Pang's 1992 version of Abba's 'Dancing Queen' ('Make Me Shake My Body'). As Eric Chu (2003) has pointed out, many such cover versions remain very close, or even identical, to the originals in terms of their musical settings, and sometimes there are even affinities between the Cantonese lyrics and the sense of the original English lyrics. Chu also notes that up to ten Cantopop and Mandapop albums are released every week in Hong Kong, many incorporating a wide variety of different musical styles ranging from heavy metal to techno to pop ballads, and most spend no more than five weeks in the charts, so an extensive demand for available melodies leads to a widespread appropriation of western songs, including French, Spanish, German and Italian originals, along with songs from Japan, Korea, other Asian countries and the Middle East. Appropriations of musical phrases, and snippets from sources ranging from classical to film and television themes to pop songs, are also common (one of Faye Wong's music videos, for example, for the song 'Stop Halfway', directly cites Peter Gabriel's 'Sledgehammer' music video, with an aeroplane flying around Wong's head). But as Chu (2003: 6) notes: 'There has been no anxiety involved in Mandapop and Cantopop covers, the composers are always credited and the copyright fully paid for, although ... when it comes to sounds and instruments that are country-specific, it's a different matter'.

Cantonese and Mandarin lyrics virtually ensure that the songs become 'indigenized' to the extent that the original source is frequently forgotten, or becomes a distant echo, as in the case of 'Cold War' and 'Person in a Dream', Faye Wong's versions of Tori Amos's 'Silent All These Years', and the Cranberries' 'Dreams', both of which she first recorded in 1993 and which she sang in identical versions to the originals in her 2004 'Live@Hong Kong' concert, to rapturous applause. Recent concerts by Faye Wong have also included English-language cover versions of Sinead O'Connor's 'Thank You For Hearing Me' (an intriguing rendition in that it effectively removes the scathingly ironic overtones of the original), Burt Bacharach's Dusty Springfield evergreen 'The Look of Love' and Deborah Harry and Blondie's hit 'Heart of Glass'. But such examples of 'straight' cover versions of English-language songs are relatively rare in Wong's repertoire, have not been included in any of her studio recordings, and occupy a different role to her Mandarin and Cantonese resettings of English-language songs.

Raised on appropriation: the emergence of Cantopop and Mandapop

In her article 'Cantopop on emigration from Hong Kong', Joanna Ching-Yun Lee traces the origin of the English-language term 'Cantopop' (also used by Hong Kong writers, and sometimes referred to as 'Canto-pop') to a 1978 article in *Billboard* by Hans Ebert, revising the term 'Cantorock', which he had previously used in 1974 to describe Hong Kong's locally produced rock music (1992b: 14). The term 'Mandapop' (or Mando-pop) was later added to refer to Mandarin-language popular songs, which were often versions of Cantopop songs sung by the same singers with different lyrics 'to fit the different rhyme and tonal patterns of Cantonese and Mandarin' (Ching-Yun Lee and Witz-leben 2002: 355). Mandapop began to be marketed in Taiwan and the PRC in the 1990s, although both terms are confined to the English language.

The earliest Cantopop singing star was Sam Hui Koon-Kit (Xu Guanjie), who began his career in the English-language cover band Lotus, and who emerged as a solo artist singing in Cantonese in 1974, spearheading a Hong Kong native language song movement which led to the virtual extinction of the English language from Cantopop, a tendency which continues to the present. Hui sometimes combined topical Cantonese lyrics with western tunes, as in his version of Bill Haley and the Comets' 1955 hit 'Rock Around The Clock', which was transformed into a satirical song about inflation and rising prices in Hong Kong (see Oi-Kuen Man 1997 for an analysis). Ching-Yun Lee (1992b: 14) describes Cantopop as 'a new genre characterised by a distinctly British-American popular music style', emerging after Mandarin-language songs, which had evolved from Shanghai film songs, that lost their popularity in Hong Kong in the early 1970s. As elsewhere, the Beatles' visit to Hong Kong in 1964 was particularly influential on the local music scene, and Hong Kong pop music in the late 1960s and early 1970s frequently involved local artists 'performing English-language cover versions' (Ching-Yun Lee and Witzleben 2002: 354), with songs by the Beatles, the Rolling Stones, Simon and Garfunkel, Joe Cocker and the Andrew Lloyd Weber/Tim Rice musical *Jesus Christ Superstar* proving particularly popular (Witzleben 1998: 470). Witzleben notes that there is also an extensive repertoire in Cantopop drawn from Japanese pop songs, citing a boxed CD of 55 of the 'most important' songs by the singer Nakajima Miyuki which have been covered in Cantonese and Mandarin versions, including one of Faye Wong's signature songs, 'Fra-gile Woman' (1998: 472).

John Erni (1998: 62) has suggested that due to its predominantly surface orientation, Cantopop succeeds in capturing 'the permanent in-betweenness of our existence and our desire' through three prominent and prevalent fea-tures, all of which could be applied to the recontextualization of western pop songs: its lack of concern with differentiating the original from the copy; its commitment to 'endless repetition and recombinance' (p. 60); and its ready combination with karaoke as a means of representing 'the cultural condition of surface belongingness' (p. 61). Often derided as bland, middle of the road, shallow and consumerist by both western and eastern commentators (see Cheung 1997; Chan 1999; Tsang 1999; Western 2001), Cantopop nonetheless contains its musically and politically adventurous aspects, most notably in the 1980s output of the duo Tat Ming Pair (see Ching-Yun Lee 1992a), both of whom have worked with Faye Wong.

Faye Wong's *tian ci*

Fung and Curtin (2002) have provided a reasonably comprehensive overview of Faye Wong's career up to 2001, although they overstress her contribution to gender politics and make misleading comparisons to the 'Madonna phenomenon' and the Spice Girls, as well as reproducing a number of inaccuracies in song and album titles. Wong's first significant cover song occurs on her fourth album, *No Regrets*, released in 1993, with 'Starting From Tomorrow', a Cantonese version of British duo Everything But the Girl's hauntingly melancholic 'bedsit ballad' 'The Road', the rather overlooked final track on their 1990 album *The Language of Life*, which had been written and sung by Ben Watt. This stood out from the relatively mediocre roster of Cantopop tracks on *No Regrets* for Wong's strikingly pellucid rendition of its mournful melody, which on the EBTG original had Stan Getz playing a soaring tenor sax over subdued piano and orchestra. Lin Xi's lyrics are about a woman resolving to break up with her lover after recollecting her memories of him and 'playing the role of a weak woman for one more day', and although they fail to match the poetic qualities of Watt's lyrics, and the musical setting is a rather lacklustre copy of the original, Wong's lustrous, opera-trained soprano voice draws out qualities of emotion and *coloratura* from the melody in the vocal line which easily outdo Watt's rather low-key rendition. The song, a highly unusual, 'alternative' choice for the Cantopop canon, remained in Wong's repertoire for a few years, and was included on her 1995 *Live in Concert* album. A Mandarin version of the song entitled 'Weak', with lyrics by Pan Li Yu, also about a relationship break-up, was included on her 1994 album *Mystery*. It was a harbinger of change in Wong's repertoire.

Wong's *100 Thousand Whys?*, released in September 1993, marked a breakthrough in terms of her definition as a Cantopop artist, as she began to actively embody alternative western rock styles. The album included Cantonese versions of Sting and the Police's well-known song 'De Do Do Do, De Da Da Da', a Barry White song, 'Rainy Days Without You', and 'Seduce Me', a Miyuki Nakajima song, and two songs with English titles, Helen Hoffner's 'Summer of Love' (sung in Cantonese) and a ballad, 'Do We Really Care', sung in English. There were enough standard Cantopop songs, like the opening track, 'Lau Fei Fei', to placate her fans, and like its predecessor, the album sold more than 300,000 copies in Hong Kong, and was the best-selling album of 1993. But the undoubted *tour de force* of the album was 'Cold War', Wong's version of Tori Amos's song 'Silent All These Years', in an identical musical setting, with insistent piano backing, spare orchestral embellishments and double-tracked choruses, with Wong's vocal intonation and *coloratura* following Amos' quite closely. Lin Xi's lyrics, however, despite the political overtones of the song's title, maintain little of the implicit sense of Amos' rather surreal, poetic original, which since its appearance on the 1991 album

Little Earthquakes, and its connection with 'Me and a Gun', a song about being raped, has become an anthem of rape and child abuse, and was re-released as a single to raise funds for a charity organization which Amos co-founded, RAINN (the Rape, Abuse and Incest National Network). Wong's 'Cold War', in contrast, is a relatively conventional 'relationship song' about the lack of communication between a couple, and a conflict of understanding that is never expressed. The chorus runs:

> Facing each other not saying a word
> As if you and I have a rapport
> Never wanting any childish squabbles
> But our expressions silently hinting that this is a cold war
> How many years together without a word?[4]

A vague trace of the 'silence' and the 'years' from the Amos song is maintained, and the lyrics even mention a metaphorical mime artist who becomes symbolic of the pretence and simulation sustaining the relationship, but there is no hint of any sexual violence, which would of course be inadmissible in a Chinese context. The sense of the Cantonese lyrics of 'Cold War' is in fact closer to the Tori Amos song 'China', also on *Little Earthquakes*, which uses the image of the Great Wall of China to embody distance, separation and conflict in a relationship. This suggests an unwitting element of cultural exchange between the two artists, although they have reportedly never made contact. 'Cold War' remains one of Wong's most popular songs, and has remained in her repertoire for twelve years.[5] According to *Wang Fei: The Empress's Style* (1999: 33):

> 'Cold War' was the first appearance of 'Fayestream' music. This was the beginning of her unique vocalisation. Her use of a nasal tone, very rich in its features, was a formal invocation of Amos' original vocal. There has always been a tradition of re-wording songs in Chinese in Hong Kong, and Wong was acting within this. What was different was the song she had re-worded was a little different in nature from the popular vogue.

Wong's 1994 album *Random Thoughts*, her first album under the name Wang Fei, consolidated the radical new departure of 'Cold War'. Stefan Graman (1999) describes it as 'probably one of the most important albums in Hong Kong music history ... Even though it did not bring on a revolutionary change in the Hong Kong music scene, its contribution to the growth of the Hong Kong music industry is not to be underestimated'. At the time of this album Wong had begun to hang out on the Beijing rock scene with alternative, dissident punk-styled musicians such as Cui Jian, the Taiwanese rocker He Yong (famous for an angry punk anthem entitled 'Garbage Dump' before he attempted to burn his house down and become institutionalized) and Dou

Wei, who were part of the new Beijing alternative rock movement of the 1990s. Dou Wei was a singer, guitarist, flautist and drummer who had played in the well-known Beijing heavy rock group Heibao (Black Panther), and had begun to embody the musical influence of the Cocteau Twins in his band Zuomeng (Dream the Dream), before starting a solo career in 1994, and later renouncing rock music entirely in favour of spiritual development. Wong married Dou Wei in July 1996, and the couple had a daughter, but divorced in 1999. Nonetheless Dou had a lasting influence on the change in direction in Wong's music and played an active role as a producer in her work, as well as playing drums on some of her tracks and with her on tour. *Random Thoughts* was co-produced by Wong, Wei and Beijing rock artist Zhang Yatung, and was Faye's first completely 'alternative' album, which also brought her new audiences on the mainland. As Mabel Cheung's 2002 film *Beijing Rocks* (Mega Star/Media Asia) was to show almost a decade later, the Beijing rock scene of the 1990s was regarded by some Hong Kong musicians as an authentic source of vital, alternative, cutting-edge rock music which exposed the bland commercialism and artificiality of the Hong Kong music scene, despite the common perception in Hong Kong of mainlanders as 'country bumpkins', which Faye had suffered from with her first album *Shirley Wong* (1989).

The title track of *Random Thoughts* and a song entitled 'Know Oneself and Each Other' were Cantonese re-settings of two songs by the Cocteau Twins, 'Bluebeard' and 'Know Who You Are At Every Age', from their 1993 album *Four-Calendar Café*. The Cocteau Twins' *glossolalia* vocals and dreamy, jangly, ethereal guitars – a constant feature of the *Random Thoughts* album – were a strong influence on Wong's work for the next four years, and according to Max Woodworth (2004) in the *Taipei Times*: 'Wong shares the same distant-sounding, high pitched siren voice of the Cocteau Twins' Elizabeth Fraser, and the gauzy aesthetic of the Twins' album covers even made its way onto Wong's album cover art'. The cover of *Random Thoughts* was also something of a departure for Cantopop. Instead of a photo of Faye, it consisted of Chinese characters in various different sizes and shades of black and grey, while the photo of Wong on the back cover featured her with short hair and tank top, a tomboy image which she later cultivated in *Chungking Express* and which led to her celebration as a gay icon (see Chang 1998: 291). Simon Reynolds has characterized the Cocteau Twin's 'wordless siren-songs' appropriately as 'oceanic rock', comparing them to Hélène Cixoux's pre-Oedipal 'écriture feminine':

> The baby-talk nonsense of their song titles and Liz Fraser's vocals, which do without any hard consonants or fricatives, are all labial, take us back to the earliest love affair of all, that of mother and child. The Cocteaus are like mother's song, all succour and softness, closeness without having to say anything at all.
>
> (1990: 130)

With Wong herself giving birth to a daughter at the end of 1996 and appearing pregnant on the cover of her 1997 album *Toys*, the resonances with motherhood are appropriate, especially as she appeared to take these aspects of the Scottish duo to heart, and has been quoted as saying 'I like the Cocteau Twins' music because I feel that in their musical thinking I have something in common with them'. While the title track 'Random Thoughts' contained lyrics by Lin Xi which describe the intoxication, emotional conflict and turbulence of being in love, and 'Know Oneself and Each Other' also contained lyrics by Lin Xi, both songs were almost identical musical settings of the Cocteau Twins originals, and a number of the other songs on the album, including 'Pledge', also had a Cocteau Twins-like band sound. 'Person in a Dream', a faithful rendition of the musical setting of the Cranberries' 'Dreams' from their 1992 *Everyone Else Is Doing It, So Why Can't We?* album, remains the stand-out track on *Random Thoughts*, with its driving, jangling rhythm guitar and skittering drum patterns. Faye even managed to adapt the Cranberries' Dolores O'Riordan's distinctively Irish, high-pitched, lilting intonation, especially on the abruptly-ending long stresses of the 'la ah la's' in the song's chorus, which are rendered in the Chinese lyrics as 'Ah-la-ha, la-ya-ha, ya-ha-ah', and which Faye subsequently incorporated into other songs, suggesting that both O'Riordan's and Fraser's Celtic intonations may have had a lasting impact on her singing style, along with Sinead O'Connor's.[6]

In her 1994 album *Please Myself*, in many ways a less radical collection of songs, Wong experiments with a shorter lyrical form, clearly influenced by the Cocteau Twins, in both the title track, where she sings a wordless refrain, and the slow, sweet, melodic 'Float', which has lyrics by Lin Xi and a refrain of 'la la's'. The stand-out track is 'Being Criminal', a version of British independent group the Sundays' song 'Here's Where the Story Ends', from their 1990 album *Reading, Writing and Arithmetic*. This is somewhat in the vein of the Cranberries' 'Dreams', with a jangling guitar pulse, and Faye's vocals follow Harriet Wheeler's soaring, lilting choruses. *Di-Dar*, released in 1995, continues Wong's independent orientation, with the influence of the Cocteau Twins and Dou Wei apparent in some of the songs, and the title track, a self-composed piece with lyrics by Lin Xi, featuring a video strongly influenced by the 'goth' style of the Cure, with Faye wearing dark make-up. *The Decadent Sound of Faye* (1995) was a collection of cover songs in tribute to Taiwanese singer Teresa Tang, who had died tragically in 1995 of an asthma attack while on tour in Thailand. The word 'decadent' was an ironic echo of the epithet used by People's Republic of China *apparatchiks* to condemn Tang's music. Wong's association with Dou Wei and the Beijing rock scene, as well as her new-found penchant for trip-hop and independent rock, was clearly influencing her musical orientation as well as her rebellious attitude to the music industry, albeit in a subdued and subtle way.

Wong continued to absorb the vocal influence of Liz Fraser (with a touch of Dolores O'Riordan), to the point of recording two indecipherable, wordless songs, 'Where?' and 'Imagine', along with an instrumental by Dou Wei, on her 1996 album *Restless* (also known as *Impatience*). This album, arguably her most radically independent and experimental to date, also contained two Cocteau Twins songs, which they were specially invited to write for her, although they never met in person. 'Fracture' and 'Killjoy', both with lyrics by Lin Xi, were Cantonese versions of songs the Cocteau Twins later released as 'Tranquil Eye' and 'Touch Upon Touch'. Both songs have an abstract, opaquely poetic quality, with 'Fracture' dealing with the results of a 'fatigue of love' and a 'tragic embrace'. The lyrics of 'Killjoy' (also known as 'Repressing Happiness') are confusingly opaque, and not helped by the virtual indecipherability of the only available English translation on Graman's website. The rest of the album is suffused with the influence of the Cocteau Twins, and uniquely the music and lyrics of almost all the songs are composed by Faye, giving it an unusual coherence of style and content which contrasts with the standard stylistic 'scattergun' approach of most of her albums and Cantopop in general. The production and arrangements of Zhang Yatung and the inclusion of an instrumental track with input from Dou Wei give the album a much more rock-oriented focus than any of Faye's albums before or since. It is also noteworthy that despite its musical innovations and unconventional style, *Restless* maintained Faye's position as the most popular and successful female artist in Hong Kong. As recently as 2005, Faye stated in an interview: '*Impatience* is the album I am most satisfied with. That was the first time I completed an album I liked. I worked with great producers and I loved every song on it. I do things according to feelings and I do them when I think they feel right. For me, *Impatience* is an album that just feels right' (Tsui 2005: 21). Notoriously reticent in interviews, Faye here indicates that *Restless* was the culmination of her independent, western experimental rock inclinations, and implies that she had a degree of control over the album which she has not succeeded in achieving to the same extent in subsequent recordings. In 1995 Faye's continued association and identification with the Cocteau Twins extended to her contributing to the vocals of an 'Asian version' of 'Serpentskirt', a song on the Cocteau Twins' album *Milk and Kisses*. The song was, however, only included on the Hong Kong release of the album, and is otherwise only available on a very rare compilation of Cocteau Twins B Sides.[7] This gave rise to speculation that her admiration for the Cocteau Twins was rather one-sided, and her renditions of their songs have gained little or no recognition in the West outside their respective Cocteau Twins and Faye Wong fan groups.

The 1997 self-titled *Faye Wong* was predominantly more low-key and spare in its arrangements than *Restless*, and, as with future albums, all the tracks were in Mandarin, in keeping with a strong involvement by Zhang Yatung as arranger and guitarist, and Dou Wei on drums on two tracks. Lin Xi's lyrics are also present on seven of the ten tracks, and Faye's 'la la's' (or 'da da's' – the 'r' is actually sounded in Mandarin) are predominant in a number of the vocals. The album contained another two Cocteau Twins tracks, one of which, 'Amusement Park', is credited as being 'performed by Simon Raymonde and Robin Guthrie', who provide a typically ethereal, swirling guitar-based instrumental mix, recorded at the September Sound studio in London, for Faye's double-tracked, harmonizing vocals. 'Reminiscence' was a version of 'Rilkean Heart' from *Milk and Kisses* arranged by Zhang Yadong, a Hong Kong-based musician who has been an important influence on Wong as a producer, with lyrics supplied by Wynan Wong. It is a low-key song, with acoustic guitar backing provided by Yadong, and not recognizably a Cocteau Twins song at all, with none of the jangling guitars and ethereal vocals of their trademark sound. Indeed, almost all the tracks on the album, with the possible exception of the final two tracks, which seem aimed at a more mainstream Cantopop market, are in a minimalist folk-rock vein which highlights Faye's vocals, to the extent that the Cocteau Twins' contributions are barely noticeable. The simplicity and coherency of the album in terms of a blending of Cantopop and 'indie' rock styles suggested that Faye may have absorbed the Cocteau Twins' influence to the point of no longer needing their contributions. She has no longer had any recourse to English-language songs in any of her subsequent studio albums, relying almost exclusively on contributions from Hong Kong-, Beijing- and Singapore-based composers along with her own compositions on *Sing and Play* (1998), *Only Love Strangers* (1999), *Fable* (2000), *Faye Wong* (2001) and *To Love* (2003).

Copycat or re-interpreter?

The *Faye Wong In Comparison with* ... website (2003) contains text and illustrations assembled to provide evidence that throughout her career, Wong has imitated a number of US and European artists, both visually and sonically. Four Cocteau Twins tracks are listed, with reproductions of appropriate album covers, followed by references to the Cranberries' 'Dreams' and Tori Amos' 'Silent All These Years', complete with a visual comparison of the album covers for Amos' *Little Earthquakes* and Faye's 1993 album *10 Thousand Whys?*, both of which feature boxes and a shared use of squared images and white background designs. There are also visual comparisons of the album cover portraits on Bjork's 1996 *Post* and Wong's 1998 *Sing and Play*, and various other visual poses comparing Faye's costumes and hairstyles with Bjork (explained by the fact that both employed the same designer).[8] There is also photographic evidence to suggest (rather unconvincingly) that Wong copied Madonna's hands-in-the-air album cover pose from the 1998 album *Ray of Light* (which contains a song entitled 'Beautiful Strangers') on her album *Only Love Strangers*. 'Die-hard fans' of Faye Wong are addressed, and expressions such as 'desperate', 'weaker' (than the original) and 'nice try' are used to describe these alleged copycat gestures by Wong. Implications are made of plagiarism or at the least imitation, and Wong is portrayed as derivative of these supposed western models.

But to dismiss Wong's recordings and performances of songs by Tori Amos, the Cranberries, the Cocteau Twins and others as a mere copycat 'karaoke effect' is to misrepresent the enormous impact she has made on Cantopop and Mandapop throughout the Chinese diaspora. These songs represent only a tiny portion of her complete repertoire, and while they may have provided a considerable boost to her credibility as an alternative artist in Hong Kong, the PRC and elsewhere, they have arguably made little contribution to her success in the Chinese diaspora, where the alternative credibility of these US and European artists has little or no currency.

Indeed, Wong's almost perfect vocal imitation, appropriation and recontextualization of these songs into what is arguably a highly original, distinctive and idiosyncratic musical *oeuvre* could be said to have opened up new areas of experimentation and musical innovation in Cantopop and Mandapop. In the West, where due to the language barrier Wong has only ever appealed to the relatively separate world of Chinese migrants and small clusters of western 'Fayenatics', her recontextualization of these songs is not a recognizable issue for the first group, and arguably only provides further incentive to her appreciation by the second. Undoubtedly the musical direction of Wong's career has been strongly influenced by her (albeit vicarious) involvement in the mid-1990s with the alternative musical ethos and vocal and musical styles of the Cocteau Twins, the Cranberries, the Sundays, Everything But the Girl and Tori Amos, which she effectively absorbed into the musical styles of her later output (evident in the up-tempo, rock-oriented opening title track of her 2003 Sony album, *To Love*, where her presence as a composer is also particularly strong). But her reinterpretations of English-language songs in the much broader context of *tian ci* serve only to highlight the way in which western artists have generally been completely recontextualized in Cantopop and Mandapop as sources for new creative output based, like most forms of popular music, on recombinative cross-fertilization, adaptation, sampling and quotation.

They also demonstrate that far from being an 'unoriginal and repetitive' local phenomenon, Cantopop and Mandapop, complete with its tradition of *tian ci*, represent, in Witzeleben's expression, 'a border-crossing and dialect-crossing popular music culture, which is an explicitly Hong Kong adaptation of a primarily Western musical language, with a growing pan-Chinese component' (2001: 417). Most Anglophone listeners who hear Wong's versions of Tori Amos' 'Silent All These Years' or the Cranberries' 'Dreams' are struck by their almost complete resemblance to the originals in terms of vocal inflection, tonal emphasis and 'grain of the voice', as well as instrumental backing, yet are usually unaware that she is singing completely different lyrics from the originals. This suggests that *tian ci* can be deceptive; it can operate as a way of incorporating a perfect 'copy' into an original repertoire, of defamiliarizing or estranging what may be a well-known song in one language into an unknown quantity in another.

Notes

1   There are numerous Fayenatic websites in English, but *All About Ah Faye*, created by Stefan Graman, aka 'Mr Sweden', in October 1999, is the most detailed and comprehensive.

2   In *Wang Fei: The Empress's Style*, a Chinese language book collating material from various unacknowledged sources published in Taiwan in 1999. Thanks to Peter Lebaige for the translation.

3   On Anita Mui, *Anita*. The medley in track 26 of the DVD, *Anita Mui Fantasy Gig 2002* (Zhonghua Records) contains a version of 'Bad Girl'.

4   Translation by Diane Yeo.

5   'Silent All These Years' was the penultimate track on her 2004 DVD, *Live@ Hong Kong* (Sony Music 2004). Wong recorded a Mandarin version of the song on her 1994 album *Mystery*, with different lyrics.

6   In *Wang Fei: the Empress's Style*, it is stated that 'this sound has become her trademark and appears constantly in her later songs', but that 'Chinese does not have this tongue position in its pronunciation, where the vocal cavity is rounded and the tongue curled' (1999: 36). However, Peter Lebaige notes that, 'In fact the Beijing variation of standard Mandarin, the Beijing dialect, does have that tongue position, the sound often occurring as a suffix to words in spoken conversation. I find it hard to believe that Wang Fei wouldn't have noticed the similarity of the Irish sound to this sound in Beijing Mandarin, and hence would have had little trouble in vocalizing it' (email to the author, 2002). This suggests that O'Riordan's vocal style may have had a lasting impact on Faye's singing style and has been absorbed into her Mandarin inflections. Faye later recorded 'Break Free', a Mandarin version of 'Dreams' with lyrics by Li Yao on her 1994 Mandapop album *Sky* (Decca/Cinepoly).

7   In an interview with Bruce Stringer (2003) on a Faye Wong website Simon Raymonde states: 'We heard from Mercury that a big Asian rock star had covered some songs of ours, so we just asked them to try and get us copies. Then when we heard them we were actually quite impressed. Usually the Cocteau's covers bands don't quite get it, so it was a nice surprise, and instrumentally they even sounded like they had worked hard to get it right..On a whim we thought it might be cool to try and do something together, so we made a few polite enquiries. In the end ... we decided we would send her a couple of the forthcoming album tracks from *Milk and Kisses* and see if she fancied doing some more vocals for the Mercury Asian release. She did a great job and what she did we used! ... Faye certainly must have had some kind of fascination with Liz 'cause she got it so bang on, you know, it was kind of spooky ... We never met, never spoke, never exchanged emails. It was all done through [Hong Kong producer] Alvin Leong who was a great chap, but personally there was no interaction at all ... I had hoped the collaboration would develop further, but the people with the money thought otherwise'.

8   Another website, *Parallel* (2001), offers a more positive, extended comparison between Bjork and Faye Wong: both 'defy the trends', both have achieved 'international critical acclaim', both have been married to rock musicians, both are single mothers, both are 'hopeless romantics', both have worn clothes designed by Martin Margiela 'before he was well known', both 'have sparked off "copycats"', and both have been involved in internationally successful films.

References

Chan, J. (1999) Some aspects of Hong Kong pop songs, http://web.hku.hk/~jkbcan/HKPopSongs.htm (accessed 5 July 2001).

Chang, H. (1998) Taiwan queer valentines, in K.H. Chen (ed.) *Trajectories: Inter-Asia Cultural Studies*. London: Routledge.

Cheung, W. (1997) Pop stars can rock in any language, *South China Morning Post*, 1 July.

Ching-Yun Lee, J. (1992a) All for freedom: the rise of patriotic/pro-democratic popular music in Hong Kong in response to the Chinese student movement, in R. Garofalo (ed.) *Rockin' the Boat: Mass Music and Mass Movements*. Boston, MA: South End Press.

Ching-Yun Lee, J. (1992b) Cantopop on emigration from Hong Kong, *Yearbook for Traditional Music*, 24: 14–23.

Ching-Yun Lee, J. and Witzleben, J.L. (2002) Hong Kong, in R.C. Provine *et al.* (eds) *The Garland Encyclopedia of World Music: East Asia: China, Japan, and Korea*, vol. 7. London: Routledge.

Chu, E. (2003) Cantopop music and popular culture in Hong Kong. Tutorial Presentation for Music and Popular Culture, B.A. Communications, University of Technology, Sydney, October.

Erni, J. (1998) Like a culture: notes on pop music and popular sensibility in de-colonized Hong Kong, *Hong Kong Cultural Studies Bulletin*, 8–9: 55–63.

Fung, A. and Curtin, M. (2002) The anomalies of being Faye (Wong): gender politics in Chinese popular music, *International Journal of Cultural Studies*, 5(3): 263–90.

Graman, S. (1999) All about Ah Faye, www.graman.net/faye/htm (accessed 8 October 2001).

Oi-Kuen Man, I. (1997) Cantonese popular song: hybridization of the East and West in the 1970s, in T. Mitsui (ed.) *Popular Music: Intercultural Interpretations*. Kanazawa: Kanazawa University.

Reynolds, S. (1990) *Blissed Out: The Raptures of Rock*. London: Serpent's Tail.

Stringer, B. (2003) Faye Wong website, www.lajabour.com/article/simon.html (accessed 24 March 2004).

Tsang, A. (1999) The Cantopop drop, *Billboard*, 111(9), 27 February.

Tsui, C. (2005) Walking tall, *Post Magazine* (Hong Kong), 6 March.

Wang Fei: the Empress's Style (1999) Chinese publication. Taipei.

Western, N. (2001) Everywhere but Hong Kong, *South China Morning Post*, 11 May.

Witzelben, J.L. (1998) Localism, nationalism, and transnationalism in pre-post-colonial Hong Kong popular song, in T. Mitsui (ed.) *Popular Music: Intercultural Interpretations*. Kanazawa: Kanazawa University.

Witzelben, J.L. (1999) Cantopop and mandapop in pre-postcolonial Hong Kong: identity negotiation in the performances of Anita Mui Yim-Fong, *Popular Music*, 18(2): 241–57.

Witzelben, J.L. (2001) Film songs, film singers and intertextuality in Hong Kong popular song: some preliminary observations, in P. Doyle and T. Mitchell (eds) *Changing Sounds: New Directions and Configurations in Popular Music*. Sydney: University of Technology.

Wong, K. and Lan, S. (eds) (1998) *Brave to Be Myself: Faye Wong*. Guangzhou: Guangzhou Travel Publishing (Chinese version).

Woodworth, M. (2004) Faye Wong is all woman, *Taipei Times*, 26 November.

Discography

Everything But the Girl (1990) *The Language of Life*. WEA/Blanco Y Negro.

The Sundays (1990) *Reading, Writing and Arithmetic*. Rough Trade Records.

The Cranberries (1992) *Everyone Else Is Doing It, So Why Can't We?* Polygram.

Tori Amos (1992) *Little Earthquakes*. EastWest/WEA International.

Cocteau Twins (1993) *Four-Calendar Café*. Capitol Records.

Faye Wong (1993) *100,000 Whys?* Hong Kong: Cinepoly.

Faye Wong (1993) *No Regrets*. Hong Kong: Cinepoly.

Faye Wong (1994) *Mystery*. Hong Kong: Decca/Cinepoly.

Faye Wong (1994) *Random Thoughts*. Hong Kong: Cinepoly.

Faye Wong (1994) *Please Myself*. Hong Kong: Cinepoly.

Faye Wong (1994) *Sky*. Hong Kong: Decca/Cinepoly.

Anita Mui (1995) *Anita*. Capital Records.

Cocteau Twins (1995) *Milk and Kisses*. Mercury Records.

Faye Wong (1995) *The Decadent Sound of Faye*. Hong Kong: Cinepoly.

Faye Wong (1995) *Di-Dar*. Hong Kong: Cinepoly.

Faye Wong (1996) *Restless*. Hong Kong: Cinepoly.

Faye Wong (1997) *Faye Wong*. Hong Kong: EMI/A Production House.

Faye Wong (2003) *To Love*. Hong Kong: Sony.

14 Tribute without attribution: kopikat, covers and copyright in Papua New Guinea

Denis Crowdy

Introduction

As a country of some 5 million people in the Pacific region, from a western perspective, Papua New Guinea (PNG) remains on the margins of the international music industry.[1] While Australia, lying just to the south of PNG, is very much part of transnational Anglophone music networks, PNG is not, even though it is Australia's only ex-colony. Despite this industrial difference, overseas music has had a very important impact on the music scene in PNG, with clear rock, pop, reggae and hip hop influences evident throughout its history. This chapter examines the implications for covering and copying in a place that is not a central part of the popular music industries. The study of PNG use of overseas music provides a useful perspective on the assumptions that underlie popular music production and consumption in the transnational Anglophone and western markets. These include attitudes and approaches to creativity, intellectual/creative property and ownership, notions and practices of localization and artist–listener relationships.

Popular music studies has traditionally been focused on Anglophone markets. In contrast, this ethnomusicologically focused case study examines how particular western commercial styles circulate within a region with different ideas about authorship, and in different performance contexts. This is not merely the consequence of distance and (industrial) scale. The various subgenres and articulations of the music copy employed by PNG musicians reveal a complex interplay of local history, with selective interpretations of both the western canon and multinational copyright law. Drawing upon some examples of PNG cover styles, I argue that the more pragmatic forms of imitation and adaptation enjoyed by PNG fans and musicians are derived from a local industry uniquely placed outside of mainstream ideologies of creative agency that are found elsewhere in this collection.

The PNG popular music scene

Changes to musical practices related to western influence have occurred since the transitory and long-term residence of a range of visitors from various parts of the world. Few studies have explored the early influences of such visitors and settlers on PNG music scenes. Webb (1997) is a notable exception, exploring music in North Eastern New Britain (a long-time hub of musical activity in PNG) and early influences from settlers in the main town at the time, Rabaul. Guitars became more widespread after World War II and guitar and ukulele-based ensembles known as stringbands became increasingly common, reaching a peak of activity in the 1970s (see Crowdy 2001, 2005).[2] These groups performed in both village and urban settings[3] and strong regional associations linked to style became clearly evident by the 1980s. Bands using electric instruments began in the 1960s, performing rock covers, original compositions and electrified stringband styles. Radio has played an important role in communication with remote communities and recording local music has been part of this.[4] Field and studio recordings were made in the 1960s and 1970s for radio, featuring stringbands and other groups for regional and national broadcast. Radio programming also included overseas recordings, with a significant emphasis on country music.

A commercial recording industry started in the 1980s, originally centred in Rabaul, East New Britain. Activity shifted to Port Moresby after the 1994 volcanic eruption razed Rabaul (see Crowdy and Hayward 1999 for discussion of the effect of this on the music industry and Philpott 1995 for more detailed information on the development of the commercial music industry in PNG). Two large studios, Pacific Gold and Chin H Meen dominated the industry until the early 2000s, until Pacific Gold sold their archive to Chin H Meen, effectively leaving a monopoly. There have been, and continue to be, numerous small independent studios, but these have relied on the distribution networks of the larger outfits. The large studios have been strongly vertically integrated in dealing with all stages of the recording process, from artist and repertoire to recording, producing, duplication, marketing and distribution. Until the early 2000s, no national copyright legislation was in place. While that legislation has now been enacted, there is no collection agency (see Niles 1996a for an analysis on copyright and music in PNG). Artists do not pay to record, but receive royalties on sales, sometimes only once a sales threshold target (sales measured by the completely vertically integrated company itself) has been reached (see Mabi 2002).

Table 14.1   Stringband and powerband subgenres

Term	Meaning	Definition
Hapkas	Half-caste	An imitation of melody with translation of the lyrics
Miksim	To mix	Music that is heavily derivative of western pop and rock (although usually original) utilizing a heavily anglicized *Tok Pisin*
Ovasis	Overseas	A faithful reproduction of western song with a rough translation into 'foreigner talk', an even more heavily anglicized pidgin
Brukim bus	To 'break the bush', meaning to take a short cut	An imitation of melody with completely new lyrics
Kopikat	'Copy cat' – to copy directly	A cover that incorporates the copy of music and lyrics in the original language

The influence and use of overseas music

The most thorough study to date on PNG popular music is Michael Webb's *Lokal Musik*, which explores *Tok Pisin* (PNG's main lingua franca – sometimes referred to as 'pidgin') songs from both the stringband and power band genres. Songs that draw on overseas influences form a complicated set of subgenres which are categorized following commonly voiced terms. Webb (1993: 103–4) has summarized the subgenres evident in stringband and power band *Tok Pisin* songs (see Table 14.1).[5]

Immediately evident from the number of subgenres here is subtlety in language use. This is to be expected in such a linguistically complex society. There are between 700 and 800 vernacular languages, and three official lingua franca: *Tok Pisin*, *Hiri Motu* and English. English is the official language of formal education; *Hiri Motu* is mainly confined to parts of the Papuan coast (and appears to be declining in use); and *Tok Pisin* is the most widely and commonly used language in the country. Artists will often ensure that their album contains a range of different languages to appeal to many local markets.

In only one of the subgenres shown in Table 14.1 – *kopikat* – is the original text unmodified. Translation is therefore important. Language itself represents a different set of meanings surrounding status, origin, education, location and notions of 'Otherness'. Clearly, language choice has some political and social import; it makes a statement about who one is talking to, from what position, and who might be listening. The act of changing language in so many of the subgenres immediately localizes the material. The politics of English, as the language of colonialism and formal education, is of particular importance here.

The practices of *hapkas*, *brukim bus* and *miksim* may all feature modifications to the musical style, borrowing broader musical features such as the melody and overall form of a song. This, of course, is commonly carried out in the process of covering a song by applying one's own creative stamp to an existing work. What is important here is that the style histories, resultant listener expectations and musical aesthetics are quite different, and I will return to the significance of this after exploration of some relevant examples.

The subgenre *brukim bus* is named after a series of three albums recorded in 1985–6 at Pacific Gold Studios. The first and second albums were based on the music of 1970s outfits Creedence Clearwater Revival (US) and Daddy Cool (Australia), and the third on North American middle-of-the-road singer, Lobo. Greg Seeto, studio owner and manager at the time, describes the project on the cassette insert:

> 'Brukim Bus' is a Band of PNG Musicians who record for Pacific Gold Studios in Rabaul with such groups as 'Painim Wok', 'Barike' and 'Junior Unbelievers'. They all got together to have some fun and decided to record these songs as a tribute to one of their favourite groups – 'Creedence Clearwater Revival'. The new lyrics to these songs were written by Telek and Tom Lulungan and the stories behind these new lyrics are all about life in PNG today – some funny, some sad, but all of them true. If you've ever been a fan of 'C.C.R', then you'll really like these new Pidgin versions of the old hits!
> (Cassette insert, *Brukim Bus*, PAC–76 1985)

Webb (1993: 201) quotes Greg Seeto as stating that *Brukim Bus* was a project he instigated to improve the writing skills of musicians starting out as engineers in the studio. Modification, rather than accurate reproduction, was an integral characteristic. Webb describes this aspect of tribute, pointing out that the bands used as 'inspiration' were already a decade or so old:

> The choice of bands on which to base the series is curious and seemingly inconsistent with Pacific Gold's 'contemporary' image, considering that these bands were no longer in existence when the *brukim bus* versions were made and the songs were all at least a decade old. An explanation includes the fact that many of Rabaul's early electric bands were formed around the time these songs and

their performers were current, and there may have been nostalgic significance associated with the choice.

(1993: 202)

Changes to location as well as language, while maintaining the overall tenor of a song, occur also. This is clearly evident on the band Memehusa's song 'Asua Medley', which starts with an original song sung in *Tok Pisin* with a bouncy ukulele part accenting beats two and four overlaid with characteristic keyboard sounds of PNG pop. After a modulation and keyboard solo, it shifts into a rendition of John Denver's 'Take Me Home Country Roads', with *Tok Pisin* lyrics:

> *Hailans rot karim mi go*
> *draivim mi mi laik go*
> *lon West Goroka*
> *we wanpela meri, switpela meri i wetim mi*
> (Highlands road, take me along
> drive me, I want to go
> to West Goroka
> where a woman, a sweet woman waits for me)

The second verse in particular contains references to several well-known locations to travellers along the Highlands Highway. This is an obvious song for localization, of course, due to both its popularity around the world and the theme of returning home. This version is interesting, however, in the extent to which it modifies the original story, drawing on similar memory associations with a country road, but removing the obvious travelling home theme. Compare this to another localized version – the Jamaican version by Toots and the Maytals, for example, which is sung in English with 'West Jamaica' replacing 'West Virginia' along with other minor variations relevant to the regional variation of English used. Interpretation of Memehusa's song is complicated by the fact that the band are from Central Province, where *Motu* and English are traditionally more commonly spoken (as well as another lingua franca, *Hiri Motu*) than *Tok Pisin*. There can be some degree of regional animosity, or at least cultural distance between Central Province and Highlands people, suggesting Memehusa is deliberately appealing to a wider audience or even attempting to placate such tension.

While many examples exist where imitation is clearly obvious, there are more fragmentary moments that form important parts of songwriting in PNG. Recently, a visiting musician from PNG, in Sydney to play at a celebration for the thirtieth anniversary of PNG independence, sang a song I had heard before. There was something particularly familiar about it; I recognized an extended melodic section, but could not ascertain at the time exactly what it was. Singing it to myself later, it appeared to use an extended phrase from Abba's 'Fernando', before taking a different melodic and rhythmic direction more tightly linked to the long lyrics. Local relevance is all the more powerful here as the connection with the original becomes more tenuous, and much harder to track. Collecting examples for this chapter, I have a number of songs that I have yet to trace – a track with a very familiar refrain in the chorus in the style of US gangsta DJ Shaggy, for example. Despite playing it to a number of music teaching and research colleagues, we still cannot place it – a further example of the intriguing use of unexpected sources and adaptation.

Although not representative of a separate genre, the variety of style selection is demonstrated by a song titled '*Kamkumu Medley*' by Catch In Reefs. Starting with the well-known refrain from Grandmaster Flash's 'The Message' – 'Don't push me, cause I'm close to the edge/ I'm trying not to lose my head', a spoken narrative intersperses a medley consisting of various PNG songs (including the national anthem) with phrases from Queen's 'I Want To Break Free', Stevie Wonder's 'You Are The Sunshine Of My Life' and 'I Just Called To Say I Love You', and the phrase 'I wanna go home, lord I wanna go home' from the country classic 'Detroit City' by Bobby Bare. The song has a strong humorous thread running through it, hence perhaps the variety of styles used, but nevertheless the selection provides an interesting insight into the overseas repertoire readily engaged with.

Local ownership issues

Because PNG is not part of the transnational network of music distribution, music shops in PNG carry a very different (and very local) range of music. It is easier to buy, and one is more likely to hear, local songs adapting overseas material than the originals themselves (beyond those being played in the current radio playlists that favour the 'classic' rock canon). This is perhaps a similar situation to covers in the West, where the song being covered is particularly obscure, or is from a generation or style not familiar to most listeners.

Local response to such use of overseas material is by no means one of immediate acceptance. Criticism periodically surfaces about the lack of creativity involved (in letters to the editor of the local press, for example) or comments about local music styles being derivative. Consider the following comments about an African gospel musician featured in one of PNG's daily newspapers in a column usually devoted to gossip:

> There's no doubt that Nathalie Makoma has had an extraordinary impact on PNG. It seems like a case of the right person singing fresh-sounding music at the right time. We wish the Makoma group all the best for their tour later in the year ... The sensational coverage of Makoma and of Nathalie reminds us of a similar tour a good few years ago now, when [Australian pop star] Marcia Hines flew in to Port Moresby, and 'laid 'em in the aisles'.

There's no doubt that quality performers singing something that is a departure from the endless and unvaried 'musical' diet we're force-fed by most PNG radio stations can really grip the public.

Which, we hasten to add, is not to say that we don't have talent in PNG. We've got loads of it – but many PNG musicians with skills outside imitative reggae or rap are lucky indeed to ever get themselves onto a CD, and even luckier if it gets played regularly on radio. As for well-promoted live concerts – dream on.

('Column 1' 2004)

These comments are widely known to come from a theatre and film critic (not an indigenous Papua New Guinean) who regularly proffers strong views on arts issues. There is no obvious reason why reggae or rap should be any more imitative than local theatre, and certainly no attempt here to subject the local features clearly evident in PNG reggae and rap to deeper analysis. Countering this, I suspect, is a less frequently voiced but strongly felt indigenous listener satisfaction at the modifications to an outside style, making it more immediately relevant and accessible and, in some sense, Papua New Guinean.

Although some features of western practice are present, the PNG bands' use of covers remains distinct, particularly in the reasoning behind the selection of a particular 'canon' of overseas songs. I spent some years playing in a band with ex-members of 1980s band Sanguma, known for their original songs that blend traditional and jazz/rock elements, and was amused, and later annoyed, when we were constantly asked by drunk patrons to play 'Black Magic Woman' (composed by blues guitarist Peter Green and made famous by Santana), a song that was often performed by the band members in the 1970s and 1980s.[6]

The critical issue that such anecdotes raise is the nature of selection. Why are some songs, bands and genres featured more than others in the selection of covers? Possible reasons might well include their exposure on radio and other media; or particular aspects of style that resonate, such as vocal timbre, subject matter and musical style. Further study is needed to be able to say much more about this, but it is clear that early country performers (such as Jim Reeves) have had an important impact.[7]

Localization

The most prominent process where PNG composers use overseas material is the act of localization: bringing the musical result closer to home and making it more socially and stylistically relevant to a local audience. Part of the reason for this lies in differences in relationships and distances between artists/listeners and song subjects. Papua New Guineans are quite likely to bump into well-known artists at a local market or in the street, and will even strike up a conversation if they are related or even from the same area. Extended family relationships and a reasonably small population mean that people might even be directly related to one or more well-known artist. Song lyrics frequently discuss known people, places and events. Most people will be able to describe at least one such close connection. This is quite a different situation to artist–listener relationships in the West. This integral feature of experiencing music goes a long way to explaining the imperative behind the localization of overseas music. To some extent, this parallels artists in a tribute band adopting at least part of the persona of those they pay tribute to and represent. In one sense they are closing the personal gap (albeit more indirectly than the PNG case) between artist and fan.

The recording of the song 'Tiny Bubbles', with modified lyrics in English and Motu by the band Clockwork Orange, illustrates this. In 1995 Jack Clunn, the lead singer of Clockwork Orange, was taken to court for defamation (*Gabe* v. *Jack Clunn* 1995). An elder from the village of Clunn's maternal grandmother accused Clunn of referring to him in the song's lyrics as being involved in sexual offences with minors, and that despite the indirectness of the expression used, it could only be traced to him. The court found against Clunn and ruled that damages be paid to the elder. The lyrics were sung as a modified part of the song 'Tiny Bubbles' (although Clunn refers to 'Pearly Shells', the same song with different lyrics). In an interview with Don Niles in 1996, Clunn relates his perspective on the claims:

> I will go down on record in telling you that even though I accept the court's decision, it was ruled against us, I do not necessarily agree with the judge's decision and as I categorically said under oath that when I wrote the lyrics to that original song of Pearly Shells I did not know the gentleman concerned that took us to court, I did not know him from a bar of soap until he was pointed out to me way after the cassette had been recorded and was selling.
>
> (Niles 1996b)

Clunn points out the dynamism of songs composed for particular events, and this is also clearly demonstrated with the modification of well-known covers in PNG. Clunn was renowned for making up lyrics in different languages. I witnessed this at a gig at a Port Moresby hotel in the mid-1990s, with Clunn modifying lyrics and inserting bawdy phrases in the Hula language, much to the amusement of Hula women in the crowd (and bypassing all those who didn't speak Hula). This was clearly a case of communicating to a specific group of people, as he was singing to a group of people known to him to be related or from the same area as one of his wives.

Although PNG bands cover PNG songs, lyrics changes are not made to nearly the same extent, thus reinforcing the point about localization just discussed. The lack of direct links between original artist and audience evident in overseas music suggests that within PNG it is much less problematic to modify overseas songs. They are sufficiently culturally removed to act as a sort of public domain from which to draw and modify. Distance from the transnational music industry means that copyright breaches were essentially ignored, if noticed at all. Lack of internal copyright law assisted here too, clearly. Of course, much evidence exists of a mirror process at work where the distance from the centre is reversed – the use of non-western material by western musicians and multinational recording companies without concern for the origins. It is crucial to focus on differences in power in such cases, and how hierarchies of control translate into a lack of recognition for musicians in PNG.

Intellectual property

Tribute and cover acts in the western music industry are particularly structured in relation to copyright laws and notions of intellectual property. There is considerable infrastructure devoted to ensuring remuneration to those considered owners of the original compositions. To some extent this seems to be an unquestioned 'right' in the context of the long tradition of copyright legislation. As governments increase the periods of copyright protection well beyond the death of the composer, evident in US and Australian laws, and matched by international agreements, it appears that the maximization of revenue dominates over the broader advantages of a larger public domain of works. Where such laws are absent, or are simply ignored, a more effective public domain body of works may exist that is appropriate to specific concepts of tributes, covers or versions.

The complications of sampling, remixing, digital copying, file sharing and the emergence of 'creative commons' licences might well be seen as a reaction against such tightening of creative property rights. No doubt these issues will become increasingly central, and it is worth considering situations where the industry and rights are dealt with in very different ways for critique, analysis and suggestions for the future.[8]

These issues are particularly relevant in PNG at the moment, since copyright law has recently been introduced. Although there is still no collection agency, it is possible that the relatively free use of overseas material could decline as the possibility of legal action is more likely. Although copyright is almost always touted as being something that provides more rights to individuals, reinforced through monetary compensation, it may also reduce the variety of influences and styles from which local performers draw.

In various discussions with PNG musicians over the years, copyright law has been generally regarded as a good thing for musicians, due to its protective aspects and the potential for increased earnings for local composers. Copyright tends to benefit those who sell large numbers of recordings, and those with the capital to exercise their legal rights in the courts. Given that most PNG artists sell a relatively small number of recordings, and that the companies to date have been dismissive of copyright, there is certainly a space in PNG for an argument about copyright as ultimately reducing the effective pool of material regarded as being within the public domain (as overseas music has been, to some extent). That companies such as Chin H Meen have been producing and selling pirated material for most of their existence tends to suggest that whatever the case, a loose group of artists without institutional support have little chance of exercising their rights, one way or another.

Conclusion

Copying is a term used to describe part of the process of paying tribute or covering an existing song. This apparently simple term also carries the baggage of a particular approach to creativity, one perhaps steeped in the Romantic notion of the artist as a lone figure at times struggling, at times pouring forth something completely original and inspired from on high. The reality is, and has been, of course, quite different, yet it is remarkable the extent to which this notion is enshrined in law. In many of the cases discussed here, overseas music has been a resource towards creating and adding to local styles. The value of the copy lies in the process of localizing, and adjusting and claiming partial ownership through modification. The obvious counter to this is that artists should create something entirely new and completely Papua New Guinean, whatever that may be, and that copying is an easier process and artists are too easily tempted to 'slip' (a moral judgement there) into copying. I would argue that not only is this derogatory in that it questions the agency and decision-making ability of the artist, but that it fails to see that copying and modification may coexist with other forms of creativity. The terms tribute and cover are thus useful in that they accent the more complex processes involved in different concepts of copying. This is useful in a world where music is increasingly shared in digital formats, and 'copy' is increasingly consistent with 'clone'.

In PNG, overseas material is more culturally distant, meaning that it is much easier to modify and draw on – almost as though part of a public domain of creative material. This distance (and lack of fear of use due to marginalization) has led to a variety of creative techniques, and has broadened the repertoire of PNG local music. Whether the absence of this approach would have forced composers to create more local songs, and hence a more identifiable PNG style, is difficult to ascertain. Tribute and modification of overseas music has played an important role, one that would almost certainly have been diminished had stricter rules of intellectual property been adhered to.

Attribution is not an integral part of the use of overseas music in PNG because of the cultural and industrial distance – the public domain effect of overseas music in relation to local material produces very different forms of subcultural behaviour and generational memory linked to particular bands and genres. This is not to say that PNG fans do not take on aspects of the dress code or traits of favourite bands, it is just that such acts of affiliation are mediated through a different social and musical context. Finally, why something is selected, how it is changed and what of it is kept are key elements to the use of overseas music in PNG, and are in themselves linked to tribute. Observing those processes in places that exist outside the industrial frameworks of the West offers an essential perspective on cultural flow and modification, indeed one that may serve to illuminate analyses of music closer to home.

Notes

1   This marginalization is perhaps illustrated by the entry on PNG in Peter Manuel's book on popular music in the non-western world as a couple of pages at the very end of the book following Hawaii (Manuel 1988: 241–3).
2   See Webb and Niles (1987) for a general overview of historical periods in relation to PNG music.
3   About 85 per cent of people in PNG live in villages rather than towns or cities.
4   Formidable geography and poor road infrastructure mean that many places are only accessible by air or foot.
5   Note that stringband is only listed as exhibiting *brukim bus*; the remaining subgenres are more common in power band music.
6   This is perhaps equivalent to the Australian rock group Cold Chisel's song 'Khe Sanh' – a notorious request from drunken patrons.
7   Slide guitarist Mike Cooper has pointed out a similar phenomenon in relation to Reeves with African musicians stating his significance as an influence – King Sunny Ade, for example (personal communication, 29 September 2005).
8   I have found discussions with colleagues about land use to be insightful here. Goddard (2001), for example, points towards possible conflicts as a more flexible system based on oral history, memory and discussion in relation to land rights. This tends to give way to the more emphatically recorded process of common law in PNG.

References

'Column 1' (2004) *The National*, 14 September, www.thenational.com.pg/0914/column1.htm (accessed 3 March 2005).
Crowdy, D. (2001) The guitar cultures of Papua New Guinea: regional, social and stylistic diversity, in A. Bennett and K. Dawe (eds) *Guitar Cultures*. Oxford: Berg.

Crowdy, D. (2005) *Guitar Style, Open Tunings, and Stringband Music in Papua New Guinea*. Boroko (Port Moresby): Institute of Papua New Guinea Studies.

Crowdy, D. and Hayward, P. (1999) From the ashes: a case study of the re-development of local music recording in Rabaul (Papua New Guinea) following the 1994 volcanic eruptions, *Convergence*, 5(3): 67–82.

Gabe v. *Jack Clunn and Pacific Gold Studios Pty Ltd* (1995) PNGLR 153, www.paclii.org/cgipaclii/disp.pl/pg/cases/PNGLR/1995/153.html?query=%7e+gabe+v+jack+clunn+and+pacific+gold+studio+pty+ltd (accessed 14 September 2004).

Goddard, M. (2001) Rethinking western Motu descent groups, *Oceania*, 71(4): 313–33.

Mabi, T. (2002) Artists know what it's all about, *Post-Courier*, 5–7 April, www.postcourier.com.pg/20020405/view05.htm (accessed 7 April 2002).

Manuel, P. (1988) *Popular Musics of the Non-Western World*. New York: Oxford University Press.

Niles, D. (1996a) Questions of music copyright in Papua New Guinea, *Perfect Beat*, 2(4): 58–62.

Niles, D. (1996b) Unpublished interview with Jack Clunn, from the collection of the Institute of Papua New Guinea Studies.

Philpott, M. (1995) Developments in Papua New Guinea's popular music industry, *Perfect Beat*, 2(3): 98–114.

Webb, M. (1993) *Lokal Musik: Lingua Franca Song and Identity in Papua New Guinea*. Boroko (Port Moresby): National Research Institute, Cultural Studies Division.

Webb, M. (1997) A long way from Tipperary: performance culture in early colonial Rabaul, New Guinea, and the genesis of a Melanesian popular music scene, *Perfect Beat*, 3(2): 32–59.

Webb, M. and Niles, D. (1987) Periods in Papua New Guinea music history, *Bikmaus*, 7(1): 50–62.

Index